Running the Palestine Blockade

11/96

To Irene

This is the true account of "my ship" rescuing the rescued. Love Sydney

CAPT. RUDOLPH W. PATZERT

Running the Palestine Blockade

The Last Voyage of the Paducah

NAVAL INSTITUTE PRESS
Annapolis, Maryland

Library of Congress Cataloging-in-Publication Data

Patzert, Rudolph W., 1911–
    Running the Palestine blockade : the last voyage of the Paducah / Rudolph W. Patzert.
        p.   cm.
    Includes index.
    ISBN 1-55750-679-5
    1. Palestine—Politics and government—1929–1948. 2. Holocaust survivors—Cyprus. 3. Haganah (Organization) 4. Palestine—Emigration and immigration. 5. Patzert, Rudolph W., 1911–
I. Title.
DS126.4.P355   1994
956.94′04—dc20   93-28122
                                                                                          CIP

Printed in the United States of America on acid-free paper ∞

9   8   7   6   5   4   3   2

First printing

Frontispiece: The gunboat USS *Paducah* in service on the Great Lakes in the 1920s. (Dossin Great Lakes Museum, Detroit)

FOR THE AMERICAN AND CANADIAN VOLUNTEERS WHOSE COMMITMENT MADE THIS TRIP POSSIBLE

Contents

Acknowledgments

My thanks to Eli Bergman for his research into the British Archives, for his knowledge of the history of the period and of the events in which we took part, and above all for his encouragement. To Dave Gutmann for his tapes and photos about the voyage.

To Joseph Almog of the Clandestine Immigration and Naval Museum in Haifa, Israel, and Eddie Kaplansky for their joint efforts in securing rare photographic materials from the Hagana Archives.

To Leonard and Jeanette Rotter for their continuous support and their information about places and people in Romania. To Phil Bock for his memory of the voyage, and to the members of our crew for sharing their experiences; they have maintained their unity as if the voyage of the *Paducah* had never ended.

To my son Bill for his technical assistance, enthusiasm, and confidence. To my son Andy for his support in the difficult period when the book was in its beginning. And most of all to my wife Terry, who braved the war years when I was at sea and then, when I disappeared into the world of the Aliyah, maintained her courage while raising our two young sons. She helped with the final touches of this book.

Running the Palestine Blockade

Prologue

Three harbor tugboats, two to the bow, one to the stern, plus the ship's engines, worked against the swift current of the Elbe River. The SS *Washington*, her two smokestacks giving off wisps of white smoke, stretched out into the Elbe, 24,289 tons of superbly designed passenger ship now in the grip of the tugboats.

Aboard the 668-foot-long ship, halfway up the saloon deck, a man stood quietly staring through a window towards the Hamburg side of the river.

His face was somber as he contemplated the busy waterfront. A church tower spiraling into the sky was covered with copper, green with age. It gave a medieval appearance to the old waterfront. Below it was the Landungsbrucken, the floating landing, where ferry boats discharged their passengers.

The man was U.S. Ambassador William E. Dodd, and he was returning to his mission in Berlin. The year was 1934; the month, July.

The ship, on which I served as a seaman, had spent five days in New York, five to six days crossing the Atlantic, and five days in Hamburg. This meant that news reports were interrupted. But from the ship's newspaper —four typewritten sheets compiled daily by the radio operators—crew and passengers were aware that something of great importance to the world was happening in Germany.

On June 30, three weeks previous, the "Night of the Long Knives" had occurred. Adolf Hitler, having achieved the title of chancellor, had set his sights on the remaining position that would give him absolute power over Germany—the presidency. Determined to remove all obstacles, Hitler had flown secretly to Munich, where, accompanied by his personal bodyguards, he had arrested at gunpoint his main rival and former friend, Ernst Röhm, chief of the Brownshirts, the terrorist paramilitary unit of the Nazi party.

1

Fear was growing in Europe and in Germany as to what Hitler's next step might be.

While the ship lay at its berth in Hamburg, German workers who had come aboard to paint the ship lunched with the crew in our mess rooms. From them we heard of the anti-Semitism of the Nazis, of the gutting of the trade unions, of the disappearance of church leaders who had spoken against the Nazis.

When I went ashore to buy a sailor's knife, I found a small shop recommended by several seamen. Inside an old man sat in a chair in the corner while a middle-aged woman bustled about, taking care of the shop. The man's eyes were dim, and he was trembling. Suddenly I saw the patch on his arm, a Star of David in yellow. On his coat was a World War I medal, the Iron Cross.

I saw for myself the emerging face of Hitlerism. A young and inexperienced sailor, I was shocked by what I witnessed but did not yet understand its significance.

I had considered myself fortunate to get work on the *Washington* the previous year: jobs were hard to find. Two months earlier I had stood in line with other hopeful seamen on the great passenger pier on the Hudson River in New York City waiting to get into the employment office of the United States Line. The *Washington* and its sister ship, the *Manhattan*, were the pride of the U.S. merchant marine. Fast, new, luxurious, they were the way to travel to Europe in the thirties.

All told, I served on the *Washington* for seventeen trips and, when it was in Hamburg, I made some German friends who were opposed to Hitler. When they asked me to bring them news of what was happening in the world and inside Germany, I managed to bring ashore copies of the "Brown Book." This small book, three inches by four inches, printed on onionskin paper, carried news of imprisonment, executions, and acts of resistance against Hitler. To get the books past the customs police, I picked a rainy, unpleasant day—the worse the weather, the better—so that I could wear my sea boots without drawing suspicion. Little did they know the big boots were stuffed with Brown Books. In my innocence, I gave little thought to the consequences of being caught, but I was lucky.

After the outbreak of World War II, I served five more years in the U.S. merchant marine, mainly in the stormy and sub-infested waters of the North Atlantic. At the end of the war, I sailed as executive officer on an army transport bringing occupation troops to Germany. The ship went to

Bremerhaven. The city was a shell—half-standing ruins, great debris, and few humans.

After the signing of the peace in 1945, merchant shipping almost stopped. With the exception of a few ships carrying relief to various parts of the world, the great wartime fleet was tied up in a few weeks' time. Thousands of Liberty and Victory ships, which had made such an enormous contribution to our victory, were towed empty and crewless to various "Bone Yards" on the East and West Coasts of the United States. There they were sealed in paint and plastic and anchored or tied to decrepit docks. Their work, their encounter with the seas of the world, was over.

Sailors, including captains, were also on the beach.

So, the phone call to my home in May 1947 was a great surprise. "Captain, are you free to take a ship?" a man asked. "Tomorrow?"

Stunned, I answered, "Yes." Where and what kind of a ship were secondary questions.

The caller gave me the address of a small, unfamiliar shipping firm, the Weston Company. It was in an old downtown New York building, covered with the grime of the city. There was no name on the door of the one-room office. There I was briefly interviewed by Paul Shulman. He obviously knew my wartime shipping record. Where had he gotten it? From the Masters, Mates & Pilots Association?

"Yes, from Captain Ash, the secretary," he said as he pushed a one-sheet contract toward me.

Not asking too many questions, I signed the contract for a two-week delivery job. He had literally meant "tomorrow." The next day I flew to Miami to join the ship and commence a voyage longer and more challenging than I could have imagined. This book is the story of that experience.

1 ✳ An Old Boat and a Fresh Crew

The subway train came into the station with a rush of wind and a squeal of steel brakes. The doors slid open, and I pushed my way into a car jammed with people heading home to Brooklyn, their day's work done. I barely got a grip on a cool white stanchion before the train, jolting forward, threw us all swaying backward. The train clacked down the dark tunnel under the river. The air smelled damp and musty. I kept the heavy briefcase in my right hand close to my body and looked carefully around the car.

At the first station in Brooklyn people flowed through the open doors. I wedged myself into the stream and was carried along with it. Up on the street the warm early summer night smelled heavily of factories, of people living close together, and of the Lower New York Bay. The shabby street was lined with old apartment houses and small shops, but bright neon lights spelling "Barney's Bar and Grill" splashed red and amber over the pools of water in the street.

At the pier, the watchman, an old man sitting in a rickety wooden chair, looked up at me and asked, "What ship?"

"The *Paducah*," I shouted back over my shoulder.

The *Paducah*, my ship. Though forty-five years old, she was sturdy and solid. Built as a gunboat for the U.S. Navy, she was small, only 190 feet long, with a 36-foot beam, 900 gross tons. But she had twin screws with two reciprocating triple-expansion engines. Her bow was sharp and had a nice flare, and two smokestacks raked back at a jaunty angle. She looked her age—experienced, tough—but she appeared damaged where the old gun emplacements remained, now bereft of armament. She showed the integrity of her builders. I was already acquiring an affection for the old SS *Paducah*. She had been through two wars. During the latest she was first on coast patrol and then convoy duty and finally served as a training ship for gunnery practice. And this voyage would very likely end her career. But she

4

was bound on an honorable mission, and wherever she might end up, her old iron plates could rust in glory. I didn't feel at all guilty about heading her into her last trip.

In the beginning, I didn't have to have any feeling about the trip at all. I was hired as her captain to take her to Europe, and I would take her to Europe. That's all I had contracted to do. What the *Paducah* did and where she went after that was technically none of my business. However, it was known, if not yet broadcast, that she would take refugees from Europe to Palestine. Inside myself, I was ready to continue one of the unresolved tasks of the war.

The crew and I were becoming familiar with the *Paducah*. We had boarded her at a Miami, Florida, dock. She was fresh from repairs after having been discharged from World War II. A raw crew, an old ship, we had shoved out into the Gulf Stream, opened her to full speed, and made a remarkably fast trip to New York. A shakedown voyage for ship and crew.

Now, she lay darkened alongside the dock, a guarded cluster light illuminating the gangway. The fall of water from the overboard discharge splashed into the river in a low murmur. The gangway rose sharply to the cargo port with the heavy steel door swung back. Alongside the cluster lamp sat a heavyset, clean-shaven young man reading a book. He looked up when he heard my feet thump on the gangway cleats. "Captain?" he inquired.

"Yes. Everybody on board?"

"Yes, sir. Watches are set. The mates and engineers are all aboard. We're ready, sir."

His name was Sholom Solowitz, and later I found out he had been in the Navy and had a Chief Boatswain's Mate rating. A formidable position.

I went to my cabin, a small, neat room on the next deck up, the lifeboat deck, forward and on the starboard side.

In my cabin the first thing I did was to take the ship's papers, including the Certificate of Registry—the citizenship papers of the ship—from my briefcase and put them into the ship's safe. For this trip the *Paducah* would sail under the flag of Panama. I closed the safe and whirled the dial to lock the door.

I took off my shore clothes and hung them in my small closet. I didn't know when I would wear them again. Then I climbed into my bunk and went to sleep.

I didn't know how long I had slept before shouting woke me. I switched on my bunk light and hurried into some clothes. Out on deck I ran barefoot toward the shouting. A slight young man was bent over the rail, looking down. I looked over the rail and in the dark could make out a small boat moving away from the ship.

"What is it?" I asked.

"I don't know," the young crewman answered. "I was making a round of the deck, and I saw this boat without lights coming alongside. I yelled at them, but they didn't answer."

The boat had pulled away, but I could still hear the oarlocks creak over the quiet water and could just make out its outline.

"Break out all hands," I ordered.

The boat disappeared into the black night, but the dip and splash of its oars could still be heard, faintly. I returned to my cabin to put on shoes and more clothes.

Out on deck the crew was assembled. They looked sleepy, but I could feel their excitement. A few of them had taken the time to put on shirts, but most were bare-chested above their dungarees. In the dim light, with their uncombed hair, they looked like a rough-and-tumble gang of cutthroats. But I knew better. I had been given a sketchy description of my crew. All officers, deck and engine room, were professionals with marine licenses endorsed by the U.S. Coast Guard. The crew, including the radio operator and chief steward, were volunteers serving without pay. A few of the volunteers had sea experience, either in the merchant marine or the Navy. Most of them, however, had never been to sea; they were green and untried. They couldn't tell a capstan from a marlinspike. It was foolhardy to take an old ship to sea with such a collection. I hoped that they believed in our mission firmly enough to get us through.

"Where's the chief officer?"

A tall, handsome man stepped forward—Evan Morgan, the chief mate.

"Very glad to see you again, Mr. Mate," I greeted him. "Everybody here?"

Morgan nodded.

"I called you out here," I told them, "because for the rest of the night you'll have to guard the ship. I don't know just what's going on, but something strange is threatening."

I turned to Morgan. "Break the men up, half and half, two watches, for the rest of the night, half on deck, the other half in their bunks. Assign each man an area. Have them carry anything that can be used as a club. If anything happens, call me immediately."

Morgan took over.

2 * Cleared and Ready

The breakfast bell woke me. So the night had gone by without further trouble. That day we would sail: I rapped my knuckles on the nearest wood to appease the hostile fates and court good luck.

At breakfast Morgan looked tired, his handsome face drawn under the stubble of a black beard. He was six feet at least, with the body of an athlete.

"How did it go?" I asked.

"Quiet. No more alarms. I guess they got discouraged."

"Well," I said, "all we need now is our water and we can shove off."

"When's the water barge due?" Morgan asked.

"Nine o'clock."

But nine o'clock came, and there was no water barge. Without four hundred tons of water for the boilers we could not sail. I worried for an hour, and then the ship's agent, a harassed-looking individual, came aboard. He was a lawyer who was hired to look after the shoreside technicalities, and his muddled handling of details did not endear him to me or to the crew.

"You'll have to go out in the river and anchor," he told me. "Our contract for the pier expires at eleven o'clock."

"Where's the water?" I asked, making no effort to take the angry edge off my voice.

He looked at me wearily and sighed. "The water barge will come alongside as soon as you're anchored."

After a moment he put out his hand. There was something apologetic about the gesture, as though he were confessing that he had been the cause of all our difficulties.

"Well," he said, "I won't be coming aboard again. Good-bye . . . and good luck." He said it with warmth. I shook hands with him and thought

7

suddenly that maybe I had misjudged him. And as he gathered up his briefcase and left, I began to like him.

Pierre Baird, the chief engineer, looked up as I knocked on his open door. "We have to anchor out in the stream, Chief. How soon can you get your engines ready?"

He grabbed his cap and headed for the engine room, not even pausing as he said, "Forty-five minutes to warm her." Chief Baird was a very short-spoken engineer.

I found Sholom, the bosun, out on deck leaning over the rail. He was smoking a big black cigar. The bigger and blacker they were, the better he liked them. It was a Navy holdover, a chief bosun's mate who considered cigarettes effeminate. He snapped to when I spoke to him. "Tell the mate to be ready to leave the dock in forty-five minutes."

"Yes, sir," Sholom said.

When we let go, the green crew didn't do too badly. They handled the six-inch yellow lines clumsily, but they got them in. Sholom was everywhere at once, shouting orders mixed with curses. He viewed incompetence with disgust—which meant he was going to have a rough trip. I noticed for the first time that we had another competent seaman aboard; he was "Heavy," a two-hundred-and-fifty-pound Irishman from Boston. He aided Sholom and did the work of handling lines around winches, making fast to the cleats and iron bitts of the ship, the things a knowledgeable sailor does. Heavy's name was Walter Greaves.

With Dave Greer, the second mate, at the wheel, I handled the engine room telegraph. Dave and I knew each other from the New York waterfront. The telegraph, the means of communication between wheelhouse and engine room, had a broad dial marked with the various speeds— "Ahead," "Astern," "Full," "Slow." With both engines slow astern, we eased out into the East River. The old *Paducah* handled well with her two propellers. She, apparently, was a sweet little ship. We found a clear space off Brooklyn Heights and let go the anchor; the heavy chain ran through the hawsepipe with a jarring rattle. Within ten minutes a huffing little tugboat brought the water barge alongside, and we got it tied up and the hose connected. Charlie Fariello, the first assistant engineer, leaned over the rail and called, "How long to pump your tanks empty?"

A man in overalls on the barge yelled, "Five hours!"

Five hours. That would make it five-thirty in the afternoon. I began to worry. Where was the immigration inspector? Had that lawyer of an agent instructed the immigration office to have one come aboard?

With the barge pumping water into our tanks, and with Heavy and Sholom directing the deck gang in a general cleanup, lashing the oil drums on the boat deck and getting the *Paducah* shipshape, I turned in and took a nap. There are times when a captain hasn't much else to do but bear the title. And it is best then to bear it lightly.

The sun was slanting its setting rays through my porthole when Elihu Bergman, an able-bodied seaman, knocked on my door, thrust in his taut young face, and announced excitedly, "Here comes the immigration inspector." I swept the miscellaneous papers into a corner of my desk and found the crew list just in time to look up and greet a lean-faced old man in the dark green uniform of the immigration service.

This was the last hurdle to clearing the ship.

"Come in, Inspector. Have a cup of coffee?"

He shook hands and said, "No, thanks. I want to get this done and get home." He sank heavily into my big chair beside the desk, fussed with his glasses, picked up the crew list, and studied it solemnly. I watched him. After a time he looked up at me through his thick lenses. "Quite a few Jewish names here, Captain." It was neither precisely a question nor a statement, but a little of both. I lifted my eyebrows and shrugged my shoulders.

He went back to checking the list. He looked up again and eyed me closely. "Are you Jewish, too, Captain?"

"No, I'm not, Inspector."

When he was finished, he stood up and put his glasses away. He cleared his throat and started to speak, but he didn't. He muttered under his breath and gathered up his papers. Then, with a close look into my face, he stuck out his hand. "Good luck!" he said. "I'm not the one to stop this ship." And he left hurriedly.

It was the closest thing to an official endorsement of the voyage from a member of the U.S. government that we would receive. But then, it was not official.

Sholom was standing outside my door. I was glad to see him there. He came from the rough streets of Brownsville, Brooklyn, and he was worrying about the ship. I thought, "Well, Sholom, let's see how this voyage goes; I'm going to need you." I grinned at him and asked him to send the mate and the chief engineer to my cabin. He took off on the double.

I paced my little cabin while waiting. It looked as if we would sail on schedule, but I kept my fingers crossed. Anything could happen before we were past the lightship and into the open sea. For that matter, anything could happen in the open sea.

Baird came in wiping his hands on an old sweat rag. His face was beaded with perspiration. Must be hot in the engine room, I thought.

"Everything ready, Chief?"

"Ready. Full up with oil and water. We can sail any time."

It was ten minutes past five by the clock on the bulkhead. "The pilot is ordered for five-thirty," I told Baird. "We'll shove off as soon as he comes aboard. I'll have the mate test the steering gear right away."

"Right," Baird said, and he turned to leave.

Morgan came in as Baird went out. I relayed the information to him and instructed him to have the third mate test the steering gear.

When Morgan left, I went to the galley and drew a cup of strong, hot coffee from the shiny urn, threw some sugar into it, splashed in the milk, and sat down to sip it and light a cigarette. As skipper, this would be my last peaceful moment, the moment before we put to sea. A pump in the engine room throbbed like a beating heart. Beyond the galley I could see the sailors sitting and talking in the crew's mess room. There were thirty-six men aboard, and thirty of them were volunteers who had offered themselves for this voyage.

The ship's still unstated mission was to transport Jewish refugees, survivors of concentration camps and others who had been persecuted by the Nazis in Europe, to a new home in Palestine. All were now in displaced persons camps. The voyages of the *Paducah* and other ships carrying refugees were conceived and planned by the Hagana—the army of the Jews of Palestine. My knowledge of the Hagana was limited, but I knew that it wasn't terrorist, though it was classified as an illegal organization by the British who governed Palestine under the League of Nations Mandate. At a time when the refugees' need was desperate, the British, more concerned about other interests, the Suez Canal, and their oil sources in the Middle East, had restricted Jewish immigration to a small monthly quota.

As yet I didn't know exactly where I was going, only that it was to a port in Europe. I wouldn't know more until a stop in the Azores to pick up water and sailing orders.

And now the sun was gone. The porthole above my head was a circle of graying light. I rinsed the cup and set it in its rack. It was time to start this voyage.

3 * Under Way—and Under Surveillance

The pilot puffed up the ladder to the bridge, crossed the bridge's wing, and stepped into the wheelhouse. "All ready, Captain?"

"All ready. Should we start heaving?"

"Yes. Pull it up."

I turned to the third mate. "All right, Mr. Christie. Tell the mate to stand by. He can start heaving up the anchor when he's ready."

Paul Christie said, "Yes, sir," and disappeared around the corner of the bridge.

There was a light southwesterly breeze, and from the feel of it the weather this night would be good. Venus, low in the west, was shining with a gay light. And the bright beads of city lights were blinking on around us. Abaft the bridge the lifeboats were nestled securely in their davits. Up forward, Sholom drained the water from the anchor windlass, and a sailor stood by the hawsepipe with a water hose. Morgan stood at the rail waiting for the bosun to finish. A ferryboat, lit up like a birthday cake, glided past. A few passengers on her deck looked at us curiously in the dusk. The bosun put the big gears of the windlass in position, stood up, and called, "All ready!" The words floated nicely up to the bridge. Morgan raised his hand with the thumb and forefinger forming a circle.

"Put the engines on standby," I ordered the third mate. He rang the engine room telegraph and set the big pointer to "Standby" on the dial. The engine room rang back, and the little arrow settled on "Standby." Up forward the old windlass grumbled and creaked as it slowly snaked the big six-inch links of chain up through the hawsepipe and sent them tumbling down into the chain locker. The water hose hissed as the sailor washed the mud off the rising chain. Link by link it came up, the ship trembling a little with the effort of the windlass. Then it was all up, the windlass was secured, and the bell on the fo'c'sle clanged rapidly to tell us on the bridge that the ship was free of the harbor mud. The pilot, studying an approaching tug, estimated its direction and speed.

"Slow ahead starboard engine, slow astern port engine," the pilot ordered, and the engine room telegraph jingled. "Wheel hard left," he ordered, and from the man at the wheel came the echo, "Wheel hard left, sir." The *Paducah* came around in a nice, tight turn. She was alive now, taking on a gentle rolling motion as she turned, and we could feel her propellers chopping the water. "Full ahead, both engines," the pilot ordered, and the telegraph jingled. We headed down the bay, and the little waves kicked up by the southwest wind slapped against our bow.

On our right were the green blinking buoys, and on our left the red ones, marking the channel to the sea. They swam past as we gathered speed. Along the shore roads of the city, tiny cars with their headlights blazing scuttled back and forth like purposeful fireflies. The great mass of the city itself looked like one huge building shining its lights through embrasures in a vast wall, the dark river circling it like a deep moat. Night swooped in fast from the east as we sailed down our blinking path to open water.

I left the pilot on the bridge and went into the chart room, closed the door before snapping on the light, and checked our course from the lightship to the Azores. Spread out on the big desk was the great North Atlantic Sailing Chart, containing all the details of distances, depths, currents, and winds, all the lore accumulated in five hundred years of crossing and recrossing of the ancient Western Ocean. The *Paducah* might be going the other way—not to the new West, but back to the old East—but she bore the full freight of the old hope and the old dream of a renewed land filled with idealistic people.

With parallel rules I laid out our first course: ninety-two degrees, almost due east. Just as I snapped off the light, the third mate stuck his head in the door.

"Funny-acting launch out here," he said. "Will you take a look?"

I took a pair of night glasses and went out to the wing of the bridge. The launch was directly abeam of us, about fifty yards off, her speed matching ours. She was obviously pacing us. She was long and black and sleek. In the darkness her red port light looked like a baleful eye staring back at us. Through the night glasses I could see a man at the wheel, his face etched dimly in the binnacle light. Near him, facing us, was another man. An object in his hand reflected the light from the binnacle. Then a bright flash lit up the darkness.

The sleek launch continued to ride along with us. There was another flash. I heard the pilot swear. And then it was clear to me: they were taking pictures of us. A third flashbulb blinded us.

"Mr. Christie," I yelled to the third mate. "Muster some men. Get 'em up on deck and arm them with anything you have. If that launch gets within throwing distance, throw everything you can at it."

Christie took off. The pilot looked at me curiously. But he asked no questions, made no comment.

It was lucky the *Paducah* was unarmed, I thought, because I was mad enough to sink that long, sleek, black launch with its popping flashbulbs. It was very clear to me now: within a few days there would be in London a complete description of the SS *Paducah*, together with a fairly accurate estimate of her speed and a set of detailed photographs. Months before we got there, if we ever got there, every British warship in Mediterranean waters would have our picture. They would be waiting for us.

The launch tailed us, its red port light unblinking, all the way to the lightship. Then she wheeled around and headed back to the city, her tiny white stern light gleaming on the frothy wake she churned up. She took our curses with her.

The engine room telegraph jingled as we slowed down to drop the pilot. His launch slid up to us and eased alongside. As he went over the rail and down the rope ladder, he waved goodbye. When his launch pulled away, we were alone, heading into the Atlantic. The telegraph jingled again for full speed ahead.

"Course ninety-two degrees," I told Christie.

"Course ninety-two degrees," Christie called to the wheelsman.

"Course ninety-two degrees," the wheelsman repeated.

4 * Struggling Seamen

We seemed to smell the fog before we saw it. We could sense something charged with a vague and shadowy excitement in the air of the night around us. Visibility decreased so gradually that we scarcely noticed it. First the stars just above the horizon grew dim and then were gone, but those directly above shone brightly on. Off to the southwest we thought we saw a creeping cloud on the water, but were not sure, because the horizon was black all around us. Then a few wisps of gray moisture came floating in. And before we knew it, the fog was upon us, blotting out all the stars. From the bridge we couldn't see the fo'c'sle head.

"Slow, both engines!" I yelled to Christie, and the third mate jumped to jingle the order down to the engine room on the telegraph. The engine room jingled back. The *Paducah*'s speed slackened, and she became sluggish in answering the wheel. Now every two minutes the fog whistle screeched out a warning to all other sightless craft that we were here.

I sent Christie below to get his oilskins and to post an extra lookout. When he came back, I went to my cabin and put on my own wet weather gear, and we settled down to the routine of a ship in fog. Down below, the engineers were alert for a possible swift and frantic order to reverse engines; the men on the bridge and the lookout forward stared into the blank, gray misty wall until their eyes teared, and their ears strained until they heard sounds that weren't there. The ship edged carefully and quietly forward at her slowest speed; every two minutes the raucous whistle ripped the stillness apart; and men trying to sleep stirred restlessly in their bunks.

All around us in these congested waters were small fishing boats, muscular little tugs with barges, cargo ships, and huge passenger liners, some outward bound like us, others coming in and groping feebly toward a glimpse of the lightship that would tell them where they were. The heavy traffic was blind but not deaf. We heard their whistles from far off. The night seemed to be filled with the plaintive cries of lost and wandering souls.

I stood on the starboard wing of the bridge, leaning forward, peering into the thickness, half fearing to see something monstrous loom up in our path, too late to turn aside, too late to stop, too late to do anything but crash.

I shook myself and paced back and forth. Our running lights gleamed hugely. On the starboard side a wide circle of fog was painted green, on the port side red.

At midnight the watch changed. The wheelsman gave the course to the man relieving him. Dave Greer, the second mate, took over from Christie. I stayed on. We didn't talk; we listened. A sailor in oilskins brought a pot of steaming coffee up from the galley.

A whistle I had been hearing behind us seemed to be drawing nearer. I went to the extreme edge of the bridge and listened intently. It *was* drawing nearer! Another ship on an offshore course similar to our own. "Half speed, both engines," I called to Greer, and I heard the telegraph jingle. We picked up speed and gradually pulled away from the other ship. Her whistle fell far behind, and we went back to slow speed. The night dripped wearily away.

At four o'clock in the morning, Morgan's watch came on. Another sailor in wet oilskins brought up another pot of steaming coffee. There was no break in the fog.

At five o'clock a grayness seeped into the night. By five-thirty it became a dull white. The sun was up. The wind freshened and slowly veered into the northwest. I looked at Morgan; he felt it too. By seven o'clock the wind was strong, and the fog was beginning to break up; it blew past us in patches. Occasionally we caught a glimpse of our own fo'c'sle. Sometimes we could see fifty yards of sea, dirty-gray. A hole opened up, and we saw the gray line of the horizon. And in ten more minutes the fog was gone. The sun shone weakly, but there was some warmth in it, and it was cheerful. We went back to full speed. The *Paducah* rolled gracefully in the waves coming up in the strong wind. It was our first morning at sea.

After breakfast I went back to my cabin. It felt good to be on the water again. The old ship yielded easily to the heaving swells as she plowed up froth-topped green furrows that spread out and away from us and dwindled down again.

I was tired, but I took time to stow my gear away before I turned in to catch some sleep. My cabin was small, about seven feet square. Against one bulkhead was the bunk, and built in under it were two big drawers. The desk and the big chair were against the second bulkhead, there was a porthole in the third, and against the fourth was a built-in closet from deck to overhead. I slung my two suitcases onto the bunk. From one I unpacked my clothes, putting them in the drawers and the closet. From the second I unpacked some personal effects and the books I had brought along. These I lined up on my desk. There weren't many: a few battered old volumes I had never finished, some texts on navigation. I put my empty suitcases out of sight, and my cabin was furnished. I was dog-weary, but I set out to make a cursory round of the ship.

She was deserted: every man not on duty was asleep. She was also dirty. Shore rubbish littered the decks fore and aft, but that would be taken care of today. The first thing a sailor wants when he clears the land and gets to sea is to rid the ship of the shore-side dust and dirt. I looked into the machine shop, where everything was in apple-pie order. The shop had an old engine lathe, and evidently generations of Navy machinists had been trained on it and loved it: every free inch was decorated with little gadgets turned on it as examples of skills. In the forward hold, deep down, was our "cargo": food in cans and sacks, a load of aluminum army mess kits, and lumber, planks and two-by-fours. All of this was for the "passengers" the *Paducah* would carry. The lumber would be used to construct bunks in every available space.

Everything was in order. I went to my cabin and turned in. As I fell asleep, I wondered if we would have trouble getting water in the Azores.

It was late in the afternoon when the sound of water sloshing on the deck wakened me. By the shadow my cabin door threw, the sun was near setting. The shadows crept back and forth with the rolling of the ship. Through the porthole I heard the bosun shouting angrily, "Clean out that scupper, damn it! Can't you see it's jammed?" After a pause the voice rose again, its tone one of profound impatience: "No, no, not that. The *scupper*. Look, this hole that the water drains through is a scupper. The scupper is jammed with dirt. Now clean out the scupper!"

I slipped on my shoes and stepped out on the deck. Sholom, his close-cropped, curly hair seeming to bristle with indignation, directed the stream from his hose over the side while a bewildered young man in bare feet bent over awkwardly to clear the scupper.

"Trouble, bosun?"

"No, sir," Sholom said. "He just doesn't know anything. But I'll teach him."

In the chart room I found the ship's position at noon neatly marked off. Measuring with dividers and estimating the time elapsed, I calculated that we had averaged five knots since we dropped the pilot. Not bad, running at slow speed all night. I looked at the weather report that Martin Gooen, the radio operator, had tacked to the little board over the chart room desk. There was a high pressure area extending from Maine well out over the Atlantic; it should be good for three or four fine days, at least.

On the bridge Dave, the second mate, was leaning over the rail, looking at the sea. "Can your wheelsman steer?" I asked.

"This one can," he said, indicating George Goldman, who was going down the deck. Although his given name was Eugene, Goldman would answer only to George. "I just sent him down to call the watch. We've worked it out so that there's one good man to each watch."

"Everything going all right?"

"Fine. She hits a hundred and fifty revolutions a minute on each engine steady. Gives us about ten knots."

"Seen any ships?"

"Not a ship. We're all alone."

I leaned over the rail and noticed that the chain pipes were filled with concrete. The mate was on the ball; in a blow we'd ship a lot of water through those pipes if they weren't filled. Morgan probably did the job himself. I looked around: the ship was bright from the bosun's wash down. All traces of the grime that accumulate alongside a dock were gone.

Dave Kellner came into the wheelhouse. He was five foot six, thin, with a sensitive face that seemed always to wear a worried look. George, whose six-foot bulk made Dave seem wispy, gave the wheel to him and stood back to watch. Dave gripped it as though he were about to rip the spokes out, and he bent far forward to watch the compass card. He spun the wheel jerkily to the right, quickly jerked it all the way left, and I was sure I could hear the steering-engine clank and clatter on the stern as it followed Dave's erratic moves.

"Easy, Dave, easy," George said. "Just give her enough wheel to bring her back. The more wheel you give her one way, the more you have to give her the other way. And then you're swinging all over the Western Ocean. A gentle touch is all she needs."

Dave nodded tensely, his eyes boring into the compass card.

On my way to my cabin the chief engineer stopped me. "I've got a lad below who says he can't stand the heat in the fireroom. Do you want to talk to him?"

"Have you?"

"Yes," Baird replied. "But he insists it's too hot. Can't stand it."

I looked at Baird. The boy couldn't stand the heat. So send him to the captain. It was the skipper's worry.

"I'll talk to him," I told Baird.

I had read the sketchy records of the crew. They didn't tell much. Nearly all of the men aboard had been in the Army or the Navy or served in the merchant marine during the war. Most of them had seen service overseas. But there were some youngsters who were discovering for the first time that glowing principles didn't always square neatly with the facts of life.

The boy came into my cabin almost shyly. He was pale and looked quite young.

"It's too hot in the fireroom?" I asked.

"I just can't stand it," he said. "I feel weak and dizzy down there."

"What do you propose to do?" I asked. "Just leave the engine room?"

"But I could work on deck where it isn't so hot."

"And somebody else could go down to do what you can't do? No," I told him, "we won't do it that way. Everybody aboard has one job. That's the job he's got now. And that's the job he'll work at.

"As captain, I have the authority to order you to stay below. I won't give you that order, but I'll tell you what I will do. I'll call a meeting of all hands, and you can explain to them why you can't work in the engine room. Want it that way?"

He studied the question for a moment, then looked at me. "No," he said. "I wouldn't want that. I'll try it again, Captain." And he turned and walked out.

Darkness crept over the ocean and the ship.

Morgan, the chief mate, on the four to eight watch, had switched on the running lights. The check showed their individual qualities. Port side-light red, starboard green. The mast head forward light was hidden by the thickness of the mast, but the yellow halo shone into the blackness. And the after mast's yellow globe was an identifying beacon to other ships.

5 ✳ Prayers in the Mess Room

In all my twenty years at sea I had
never tasted ship's food that could compare with the meals served by
David Shass, our steward and cook. On the third or fourth day out we got
an ordinary ship's supper of pork chops, mashed potatoes, string beans,
and bread pudding. Nothing special about it, but I couldn't remember
eating anything that tasted so good. As I thought about it, Dave stuck his
big-jowled, reddish face through the galley door. He wore a formless
brown felt hat with ancient sweat stains around the band. I never saw him
without it. He blinked at us through thick lenses and inquired, "How's the
chow, Cap'n?"

"The best afloat," I told him, and he smiled. "How do you do it?"

"That's the secret," he boasted, "that's the secret, Cap'n. Been prac-
ticin' for thirty years on all the seven seas. It takes time, Cap'n, time and the
proper touch." And he popped back into his little galley.

"That guy's a prize," Al Henderson, the second assistant engineer, said.
"Where'd you get him?"

"I didn't get him. He came aboard as a volunteer."

"Is he a Jew?" the third assistant asked.

"I don't know," I replied. It hadn't occurred to me to wonder about it.

"He claims he's half-Jewish," Henderson informed us.

"You'd never know it to look at him," the chief engineer said. "What's
he want to go to Palestine for?"

Dave Greer, the second mate, had been eating hurriedly so he could go
to the bridge and relieve Christie for supper. But now he put down his
knife and fork before speaking.

"I don't know how you can tell by looking at a man if he's half-Jewish
or not," he said. "And he might be going to Palestine for a number of
reasons, all of them good, and any one of them better than the simple one
of drawing wages. As a matter of fact, however, he's trying to get to Egypt.
He's got a girl in Cairo, a French girl with some sort of little business. She's

19

promised to marry him if he becomes a Catholic. If you've noticed, he carries *The Penny Catechism* around with him. He's studying it to prepare for his conversion. I don't know if he'll make it or not," Dave laughed. "In thirty years as a ship's cook, a man can pick up an awful burden of sin."

Dave went back to eating, and the second and third assistants resumed an argument about the capacity of the ship's evaporator. As far as I knew, they were good engineers. I had noticed that they both got quite dirty on their watches in the engine room, which was a mark in their favor. Like all the ship's officers, they were not volunteers, but drew full wages, and they had contracted only to take the ship to a European port. Dave Greer was the only Jew among the licensed officers. He was a good second mate and a good all-around man.

I first met Dave on the New York waterfront in the early thirties. Later I heard about his life. He had been a boxer, professional for a short time, ballet dancer, and who knows what else in his early years. He was a short man with an almost bald head. Although always animated and smiling, he did not swap confidences and intimacies with anybody, not even during those quiet hours on the bridge under the bright stars when men feel impelled to reveal their secret selves and talk their hearts out.

However, he told a story of being on one of the convoys to Russia, reaching Murmansk after terrible damage to the ships of his convoy. And there, despite the suspicions of the Russians, he met a lovely young woman at the Seamen's Center, a ballerina from Leningrad who had gotten into disfavor for some reason or other. I didn't know what their relationship was, but she remained vivid in his memory. Despite his non-Hollywood appearance, Dave always seemed to attract interesting and beautiful women.

I went back to the stern to smoke, leaned over the rail, and watched the wake boiling up from our twin propellers and the sun gliding down to set almost directly behind us. The weather was holding good: calm seas, clear days, fair nights.

Walking to my cabin, I saw Dave Kellner dashing along the deck. He did everything with intensity and was in such a hurry now that I stopped him. "You're racing your motor, Dave. What's the rush?"

"It's Friday night," he said in a tone implying that I should know without asking. Dave and Moshe Kallner, one of the messmen, were, so far as I knew, the only two aboard who were Orthodox Jews. Dave prayed every morning and evening. He had served three years in the Pacific as an infantryman in the American army. Every morning he had prayed, standing erect and facing east toward Eretz Israel. And now, on the *Paducah*, he was actually going there at the steady rate of ten knots.

"I'm getting a *minyan* for the Sabbath," he told me breathlessly. "A *minyan* is ten men. We need ten men for the prayers."

As he hurried away, I called after him, "Dave, may I attend?" He shouted back, "Yes. But I must hurry. The first star will soon be out."

In the crew's mess room the electric lights were switched off, and on the long table were two candles. They were from an emergency stock kept against the possible failure of our lighting system, but I said nothing. There were more than ten men present. Some wore yarmulkes, the little black skullcaps, but others did not. Dave sat beside me. "Everyone should wear a hat," he whispered, "because according to the Law, 'Thou shalt not enter the presence of the Lord with thy head uncovered.' "

There were four bottles of red wine on the table, and plates of sandwiches.

From the galley side of the mess room Dave Shass, the steward, came in and took a seat. He wore his dirty old brown felt hat. I wondered if he had his catechism with him. Was he really half Jewish? The word was starting to lose meaning in this mélange of a crew.

6 ✳ The Price of Water

Morgan and I worked over the chart together. We expected to raise the coast of Fayal by three o'clock in the afternoon. It was a little after breakfast, and I went and stood at the bridge rail. Forward, Eli Bergman was chipping at the concrete in the chain pipes with a light sledge and a chisel, Sholom watching him.

"Dammit," Sholom roared, "*hit* the stuff! Lemme show you!" He grabbed the hammer, threw the chisel aside, and walloped the concrete with a full two-handed stroke that sent chips and chunks of it flying like bullets as Eli backed out of range.

I liked to watch Sholom work. He attacked a job with hot impatience and made a personal contest out of it. He got his hands into a job right up to the elbows. He was excited by work, and nothing was more offensive to him than to see someone dawdling at it.

Sholom was making sailors of Syd Abrams and Eli. Syd's only "sea experience" had been on a fourteen-foot boat on a lake in Washington; Eli had recently been demobilized from the Army. Though they had no experience on ships, they were idealistic young men and had committed themselves to this voyage.

I asked Sholom about them once.

"Those guys are OK, Captain. I figure it this way; they didn't have to make this trip, did they? I mean, it's in their favor that they volunteered. They've got guts.

"There's another guy in the fo'c'sle," he snorted. "He wants to open a Hungarian restaurant when he gets home. With Gypsy music! You know the kind of place—it's so dark you can't see to eat and some guy strolls around cryin' on a fiddle. With a college education, he has to go and open a Gypsy chophouse with fortune tellers?"

After lunch I went to my cabin and stretched out, hoping to get a couple of hours' sleep. If I could get the ship's water that night, I intended to sail in the morning, so I probably would be up all night.

But I didn't sleep. I worried about getting water in Horta. I had a radiogram naming our agents there: Henderson & Coathe, Ltd. Why a British firm? The New York people must have known what they were doing, but I did not understand why a firm from the nation that was determined to limit immigration to Palestine was chosen as our agents.

Even if I had not been worrying, I would not have been able to sleep with the tremendous traffic in the passageway outside my door. Sailors, mates, engineers, firemen, oilers, and wipers went clumping past in bathclogs to the washrooms in a burst of cleanliness. I recognized all the symptoms of what old seamen know as "channel fever"—the nervous anticipation that grips a ship's crew when a strange port is approached. It was an epidemic. Shore clothes were brought out and brushed, shoes were shined, and there was a great splashing of after-shave lotions and gaudysmelling hair preparations. We had been at sea for a little more than a week, but all hands, green men and old-timers alike, behaved as though we hadn't sighted dry land for ten months. They were giddy to the point where ordinarily reserved and sedate men goosed each other and giggled.

Everybody had the fever except Dave Blake, our mystery man. We knew nothing about him except the little that he allowed us to know. He was not a Jew, but he intended to settle on a kibbutz in Palestine and work as a farmer. He was under six feet tall, slim, and good-looking, with soft brown hair and eyes. He was well educated, with more than one degree, and studied Hebrew in his spare time. The crew had such respect for his knowledge that fo'c'sle arguments were appealed to him for settlement. He was from Schenectady, New York, and was a trained chemist. He worked hard and never grumbled. Dave did not invite questions and seldom answered those that were asked. The crew speculated endlessly about what caused him to renounce what must have been a promising life in favor of settlement in a land strange to him among a people not his own. Most of the men aboard had guessed to their own satisfaction that it must have been a tragic love affair. Blake didn't care what they thought. And he was the only man aboard who was not preparing to go ashore.

At three o'clock I went to the bridge. At four o'clock there was a thickening of gray clouds at the place where, by our calculations, there should have been a mountain. An hour and a half later the black, grim coast bulged up out of the sea; the mountain itself was hidden in mist. Through our glasses we made out a tiny white speck to be a lighthouse. Slowly the land bulked up. High on the mountainside, we could see a small village, a group of tiny white houses clustered together like a flock of tethered goats. Ahead of us a shoulder of land reached out in a black hump and dropped precipitously into the ocean, and at its base we could see the sea swells breaking against the rocks in bursts of high-flung spray.

We rounded the point and the port was before us, its small harbor nestling behind the protecting arm of a long, gray concrete breakwater. The small city began at the water's edge and wandered irregularly up the side of the mountain to the very top. Scattered about were windmills turning lazily in the soft breeze, their blades shining in the evening light.

We stopped our engines, and Morgan blew two long and two short blasts on the ship's whistle, the signal for the local pilot. While we waited for him, a long blue shadow edged over the town and reached out into the harbor and finally engulfed us as the sun sank behind the mountain.

A small launch bustled out, and the pilot climbed up the rope ladder. He was a little man with a face as wrinkled as a dried apple. With the kind of skill that could be mistaken for careless unconcern he guided us past the breakwater to a safe anchorage inside the harbor near shore.

Customs and immigration officials came aboard and crowded my cabin for a flourish of document-signing, and a port medical man lined up the crew to investigate the general state of their health. A swarm of small boats, known everywhere to seamen as "bumboats," crowded around the *Paducah* offering bargains on a variety of cheap wares, mostly of an alcoholic nature. But I did not see the agent's launch.

Morgan joined me on deck. "Going to give shore leave tonight?"

"I don't know yet," I replied. "If we can get water tonight, we'll sail as soon as it's aboard. In any case, have a watch at the ladder all night. I don't expect any trouble here, but it's better to have someone awake on deck."

Lining the rails, the crew haggled with the bumboat men and shouted questions about the attractions ashore. I saw Dave, the cook-steward, hauling a bottle aboard at the end of a line. Then I saw a trim, clean, respectable-looking launch head out to us. It eased politely through the crush of bumboats, headed rapidly straight toward our side, and then, with a quick reversal of the engine and skillful twist of the wheel, came to a crisp stop at the foot of our rope ladder. A tall, thin man climbed stiffly aboard, and I walked to meet him.

"Captain?" he asked. When I nodded, he offered his hand and said, "My name is Carley. I represent Henderson & Coathe." He clipped his words with a British accent.

"Glad to know you," I said, shaking the hand held out to me. "You've been in touch with our agents in the States?"

"Yes. We've made all arrangements for your water."

"Good. Then we can take it on tonight and sail in the morning."

"Ah," Mr. Carley said, "I'm afraid you'll have to lay over. It's only a small irregularity, but your credit hasn't been verified yet by Lloyd's in London."

I had a sinking sensation.

"We'll get our water as soon as you receive verification?" I asked.

"But of course," he said with a tight smile that had no friendliness in it.

"I'll cable my agents in the States tonight."

"Ah," Mr. Carley said, "I fear that will have to wait till morning. Your radio's sealed in port, you know, and the shore cable office is closed for the day."

"Then nothing can be done tonight?"

"I fear not," he said with his tight smile. "But I'll see you in the morning? Our office is only one street up from the boat landing. You can't miss it."

"I'll be there," I told him. "Early."

He shook hands again and stalked stiffly to the ladder. As his head bobbed down the side, he smiled tightly at me. I didn't like Mr. Carley.

I watched his launch putt-putt toward the city, where lights were coming on in the gathering dusk. I smelled the heavy mixture of the hundred odors of a busy port in a warm climate, and I could feel again the presence of an old enemy.

I decide to play my hunch. My hunch was that Mr. Carley didn't want us to get water.

Baird invited me to come in when I knocked at his door.

"Have you ever been ashore here, Chief?"

"No, why?"

"Thought you might know an angle for getting water without the agent. I think they know about us here."

"Already? Well, we can't go far without water."

"You're right, Chief," I agreed as I walked out.

Supper was noisy in the crew's mess room, with loud threats to the safety of the female population of Horta. In the galley Dave was happy in his old hat with a jug of cognac in handy reach, and as he rattled his pots and pans, he sang the refrain of an old cowboy ballad: "If I don't get rye whiskey, I surely will die. . . ."

After supper I called Morgan, Heavy Greaves, and Sholom to my cabin and told them my suspicions. "I want you three to go ashore with me. We'll bust around the bars like tourists and see if we can't latch on to somebody who'll sell us four hundred tons of water."

"If we can't buy it, we'll get it by hook or crook," Sholom said.

"Well, we'll try to be as legal as we can," I told him. "Now, I want five or six good men to stay aboard. Let's pick them out."

We agreed on George Goldman. He was big, an old sailor, reliable. Heavy suggested Martin Gooen, the radio operator, Sholom suggested Blake, and I named Dave Gutmann and Lewis Brettschneider.

"I'll tell the second mate to take charge. Morgan, round up the rest of the crew and tell them the score. Tell them they can go ashore, but to watch themselves and stay as sober as they can. They'll have to be back aboard by midnight."

The four of us walked into the first cantina we saw. It was not far from the boat landing. The bartender was very fat, and his shirt-sleeves were rolled up. Morgan and I ordered cognac. Sholom asked for a beer. "Beer," said Heavy. Pointing a fat finger at us in turn, the bartender checked the order, "*Cognac! Cognac! Cerveza! Cerveza!*"

"Speak English?" I asked. He shrugged, smiled, and said, "No."

"Try him in Spanish," I told Heavy, who spoke a little of a lot of languages . . . the fruit of years at sea. "Ask him where the nightlife is, the cabarets."

"He says he will call a friend of his who will show us around," Heavy translated. "He says there are some very nice cabarets, with nice girls, very cheap."

The fat bartender went to the door and called to someone in Portuguese. A short, paunchy man came in. There was a stiff dignity about his head, in curious contrast to the slack roundness of his body. The brim of his hat was turned well down over his eyes. "You wish to see the town, gentlemen?" We followed him out.

He led us down the street and into a narrow, dark, evil-smelling alley. The four of us looked at each other, and instinctively we slowed our pace. "It is not far, gentlemen," our guide said. "Do not be afraid."

"You speak good English," I remarked.

"Yes," he said. "I sailed in British and American ships when I was a young man."

We twisted around a turn in the alley, and at the far end of it we saw a large red bulb gleaming dully over a doorway. It looked like a Hollywood setting for a sink of sin. Our guide led us through the door, and we climbed a long flight of stairs. The cabaret was a long, poorly lighted room. At the far end five musicians sat on a raised platform; in a corner was a small bar. The bartender wore a green shirt, and behind him were rows of bottles on shelves. Except for a small square in the center, the floor was crowded with tables. Our guide led us to one, and we sat down and ordered drinks from a waitress who blessed us all with a smile that had no innocence in it.

Scattered about the room were some of our crew. At the moment Syd was self-consciously balancing on his knees a girl who was not exactly a featherweight, and Eli was bent toward another girl who looked at him solemnly. The musicians broke into a slow tango, the dim lights were dimmed further, and a pink spotlight glowed over the square dance floor.

The waitress brought our drinks. Morgan sipped his, coughed, and exploded: "Good Christ! Taste that!"

I tried mine. It was like trying to swallow live steam. "Hell. Let's get out of here."

"Do you know another place, something a little quieter?" I asked our guide.

"Sure," he said. "I thought maybe you wanted plenty of music and girls."

We took a taxi this time and went over a hill and down into a more respectable quarter of the city. Our guide led us into a cafe and through it to a small, cozy room at the back. He spoke to a waiter in Portuguese, and the waiter brought us a bottle of good French cognac.

"Let's introduce ourselves," I said to our guide. "I'm the skipper of that little ship that anchored just after sunset."

"I know," he answered. The four of us stared at him, surprised.

"My name is Basta, and I'm the owner of that cantina you stopped in first. I had it arranged that if you stopped there, I was to be called. I also had it arranged that if you stopped at any other cantina, I was to be called."

"What's the idea?"

Basta shrugged. "You need water."

"All right," I said. "We need water. How do you know so much?"

"It's simple," Basta continued. "My cousin works in the offices of Henderson & Coathe."

"A wise guy," Sholom said, and he started up out of his chair.

I motioned him to sit still. The guy was putting on such an act that I would have liked to take a poke at him myself. But we did need water.

"What else do you know?"

"Mr. Carley had a wire from London telling him to delay you as long as possible."

We sipped our drinks and thought that over.

"Where do you fit in, Mr. Basta?" I asked.

"I don't like the English," he replied, smiling.

"So?"

"I'm also a businessman. For a fee," Mr. Basta finally said, "I can get you your water."

"Can you get me four hundred tons tomorrow night?"

"Yes."

"For how much?"

"For the price of the water plus a fee of three hundred dollars."

It was a holdup. I would have liked to be able to sit back and give Sholom the signal to dump Mr. Basta. But we couldn't afford it. We needed water more than we needed the luxury of avenging our outraged sensibilities. But I wouldn't haggle with the man; that, I felt, would have degraded us too much.

"How will you arrange the loading?" I asked.

"I will have a water barge alongside you a little after nine o'clock," Basta said. "By nine o'clock it will be quite dark, and there will be little harbor traffic. The barge will come out to you on the offshore side. You will have your engineers ready to take the hose aboard. It will take about six hours for the pumping."

"Do you want American money or Portuguese?"

"Dollars would cause me difficulties. I will take escudos."

"I'll pay you tomorrow night after the water barge is alongside. Will you come aboard?"

"I'll be there."

"Good. It's a deal." We shook hands on it, and Basta raised his glass: "To a prosperous voyage," he said, and he smiled his actor's smile. Sholom was still bridling at the holdup. But we touched our glasses and drank the toast.

"And now I must go," Basta said, and with a hammy little bow that strained his paunch he strutted out of the room.

Heavy reached for the cognac bottle and filled his glass. He gulped all of it down, shook his head, and said, "Just to take the taste out of my mouth."

7 * Stealing Away

The little town straggling up the hillside looked old and tired in the early morning sunlight. There was not enough breeze to turn the windmills, and they stood motionless, as though too lazy to work. There was not much activity to be seen anywhere; the whole town appeared languid and drowsy. I hailed a bumboat and climbed down our ladder and went ashore.

The narrow street leading up from the landing was quiet. A few doors beyond the entrance to the offices of Henderson & Coathe, Ltd., there was a doorway with a small sign: Cable Office.

It was dark and cool inside, and a thin young man handed me a blank when I told him I wanted to send a cable to the States.

I wrote: "*Agent says credit not verified. Something fishy, watch your end.*"

I watched the thin young man as he counted the words. He showed no interest in the message, but I was reasonably sure that Mr. Carley would know its contents soon enough.

"Ten escudos," the young man said, and I was reminded that I had no Portuguese money. He directed me to the nearest bank, and I changed enough dollars to pay the cable costs and to take care of Mr. Basta. When I was finished in the cable office, I strolled next door and went upstairs to the offices of Henderson & Coathe, which were neat and undecorated except for a large photograph of King George and the Queen and the two princesses framed over a desk.

Mr. Carley came in, and his dry austerity seemed out of place in this warm, moist climate.

"Good morning, Captain," he said. Although he showed all the formal signs of politeness, he was very distant.

"Good morning. Has my credit been verified yet?"

"Not yet. But quite likely it will come through today." He didn't even smile when he said it.

"I've just sent a cable to the States."

"Ah. That should certainly help matters."

"Well, will you notify me on the ship when it comes through?"

"Very well," he said. "Good-bye." And he put out his hand. It felt like an ice cube when I shook it.

The warmth of the street was welcome after that cold encounter. On the boat landing I looked at the *Paducah* at anchor. Her appearance was a bit unusual, with her sharp bow and her rakish stacks. And apparently the young man on the boat landing near me thought she was unusual, too. For I noticed that he was busily photographing the ship with a little camera slung around his neck on a strap. And he was hatless. He ignored my presence. He wouldn't have if he knew what I was thinking: how simple it would be to walk over behind him and with a slight tap send him splashing into the Bay of Horta. Of course, he *might* have been a tourist. Anyway, I decided his little endeavor hardly mattered. His were not the first photographs taken of the *Paducah*.

I hailed a bumboat. On the short ride out to the ship I mulled over the situation. I was now certain that the efforts of the British to stop us would be considerable.

At nine o'clock that night I was standing with Sholom at the rail on our offshore side with my ears tuned for any sound. I heard nothing. A light blinked at the end of the breakwater.

"If that Basta double-crosses us," Sholom said slowly, "I'll take Heavy and George, and we'll go ashore and take that cantina of his apart. How do we know he's not working for that agent?"

"We don't know anything. But he'll be here. Even if he was working for Carley, I think he would still want that three hundred dollars."

"We ought to go ashore and take his cantina apart anyhow."

We stood and listened. A half-hour passed. Then we heard it. Something was coming toward us. It was a water barge, towed by a tiny tug, both of them without lights. Sholom called some men, and we dropped rope fenders over the side and tied up the barge. A hose was snaked up to us. Charlie, the first assistant engineer, made the coupling, and the barge started her pump with a sound like a low, muffled sob.

An hour later Basta came aboard, and I took him to my cabin. He handed me a bottle of the best French cognac and sat in my big chair. Silently I counted out his money. He folded the bills carefully and tucked them into a pocket. I got two water tumblers and opened the cognac and poured two drinks. "Success," he toasted, I nodded, and we drank.

He fumbled in a pocket and brought out a folded yellow paper, well-worn. "I have brought you a poem," he said, handing it to me. "Read it when you have time. And now I must go. The barge will finish pumping before daylight." At the door he paused and looked back. "Also," he declared, almost as though he were delivering a challenge, "I have to make a living." And with that he hurried down the passageway and was gone.

I unfolded the yellow papers. The poem was entitled "Naval Battle Between the American Privateer *General Armstrong* and Three British Ships of War, in the Azores, September 26–27, 1814." It was signed "By a Portuguese Sailor." In three pages of doggerel, it recounted with glee how a small Yankee brigantine defeated three British frigates in the War of 1812. I would have to tell Sholom that Mr. Basta had some virtues.

Immediately after breakfast next morning I hurried ashore and was at the customhouse when it opened. I signed the necessary documents and paid the fee to clear the ship. On my way back to the boat landing I debated whether to call again on Mr. Carley. I would get a lot of satisfaction out of thumbing my nose at him. But I decided that it would be both petty and a waste of time, and I was in a hurry to get out of Horta. I did not like the place. I didn't take the time to say good-bye to Mr. Basta, or even to pick up a pilot; I could take her out without one.

Aboard, I hurried to the bridge and gave the signal to Morgan and Sholom, who were standing on the fo'c'sle. Everything was ready. We heaved up the anchor with a groaning chain and headed out past the breakwater for the open sea. I looked back at the town through the glasses. There, framed in an open window in the building near the landing dock, staring, was Mr. Carley. I waved gaily at him and then, fearing he could not see the gesture, ran to the whistle cord and blew a short blast. Even if he couldn't hear that, he could surely see the woolly blob of steam that floated up from the whistle and hung a moment in the air, a visible Bronx cheer.

I stayed on the bridge because it was a bright, warm day, and I was not tired, even after being up most of the night. I was wondering what we would run into next. At this moment I did not even know where we were going; we would be informed of our next port of call by a radiogram from the States, and I hoped they would not keep us waiting too long. After clearing the Azores, all we could do was to set a course a little north of east and wait.

"You want me, Captain?" Heavy asked as he stood at my open door.

"Yes. Come in. I want to talk to you."

Heavy wedged himself into my big chair. He must have weighed over two hundred and fifty pounds. He was fat, but it was a hard, muscular fat. And any man who would make the mistake of thinking that Heavy's bulk would slow him up in a fight would be a sad fool.

I brought out Basta's bottle of cognac. "Have a drink?"

"Well, Captain, I wouldn't spit it out."

"I heard you made this trip on the *Ben Hecht*."

"I was on the *Ben Hecht*," Heavy chuckled. "Another rust bucket."

"What about the blockade? Do you think we can get through it?"

"Well," Heavy said, "I guess it's possible. Some ships get through. But look at the odds against it: the British have got radar; they can see you in the dark, through fog or anything else. They got planes and destroyers on patrol all over the Mediterranean. They got Gibraltar; it's hard to get through there without being seen. And on top of it all, they got an intelligence system tied together in every port in Europe. But some ships get through."

"How was it on the *Hecht*?"

"We had six hundred people aboard. Great crew. The British kept me a month in Acre Prison, then they deported me. 'We're letting you off light this time, Yank,' " Heavy said in a passable imitation of an English accent. " 'But if we should capture you again, it'll go hard on you. You can't say you haven't been fairly warned.' Aye, I've been fairly warned, so I have."

"How'd you get aboard the *Hecht*?"

"Easy. I'd heard around the waterfront that volunteer seamen were wanted for the run to Palestine. So when I see an ad in a paper asking for money for Palestine, I go up to the office to see if they know how I can get a ship. They put me aboard the *Hecht* the same day."

"What made you interested in the run to Palestine?"

Heavy looked at me with his eyebrows lifted. "What makes you interested in the run to Palestine, Captain?"

I poured two more drinks of Basta's good cognac. It was one of those questions a man finds hard to answer, even though the answer is plain and clear and simple in his own mind. We men talk easily and readily about everything until we come to a subject that touches us deeply, and then we become halting and tongue-tied, and we can find no words to say what we feel. The question stopped me. What were we afraid of? Why couldn't we stand up proudly and say it to each other: we believe in democracy; we believe in people and in brotherhood and in freedom and liberty and justice. But the words have been so often debased in the mouths of so many that we find it hard to say them.

I lifted my glass. "To a successful run." Heavy touched his glass to mine. Despite what we couldn't say, we understood each other.

By early evening the last of the blue mountains of the Azores had dipped out of sight and the *Paducah* again was in the exact center of the vast encircling horizon. As the night came down, the wind came up strong out of the northeast, and we ran into our first blow.

Out on the lifeboat deck Heavy and two of the men were checking the lashings on the oil drums, taking up the slack and making them secure as the ship began to pitch and roll in the rising seas. The wind approached gale force, 35 to 40 miles per hour. Spray sent up by the dipping bow rattled over the decks with a velocity that stung. The wind was off our port bow, and we were heading into the waves; I noted that the old ship rode them easily and well.

Then suddenly she seemed to veer and fell off until she was broadside to the wind, and as she took a long, deep roll, I heard a crash from the galley as pots and pans and crockery tumbled to the deck. The man at the wheel must be asleep, I thought, as I ran to the bridge.

"Steering gear," Morgan said as I entered the wheelhouse. "I have the first assistant checking it. The wheel just went dead."

"Stop the engines," I ordered, and the telegraph jingled. The wind became very loud as the ship went silent. We quickly lost our headway and lay wallowing in the troughs between waves. There are few moments in a lifetime when a man feels as totally helpless as a captain aboard a vessel he cannot command. We wallowed for a long time before Fariello came into the wheelhouse wiping his hands on a piece of cotton waste.

"She's OK now," he said, and Morgan rang for full speed ahead. We gradually picked up speed, and the man at the wheel brought her around to her course again. My mastery had been restored.

"What was wrong?" I asked Charlie.

"Just a worn-out contact. I replaced it."

"What caused that?"

"Too much handling of the wheel, I guess," Charlie said.

"Will she be all right now?"

"I think so. It could burn out again any time. But don't worry. I've got plenty of spare contacts." Still wiping his hands, he walked out.

"How do you like that?" I exclaimed to Morgan. "It might burn out again any time, and I shouldn't worry. He's got plenty of spare parts! We've got to sail through minefields and I shouldn't worry. That steering gear will haunt me in my sleep now!"

Toward midnight the wind slacked off. By morning the sea was almost calm, and the sky was clear. Shortly after breakfast we got a radiogram: "*Your destination is Lisbon. Agents are Malieros Frères.*" Up on the bridge we laid out a course for the capital of Portugal and estimated it to be a five-day run from the time we had left Horta.

The following afternoon I was sitting at my desk in my cabin when one of the men stopped at my door. "Excuse me," he said. He stepped into the cabin and offered me a black-bound book. He was shy and embarrassed. "I thought you might like to look through this." He was out of the cabin and away before I could reply.

I leafed through the book, *A Book of Jewish Thoughts*, selected and compiled by Joseph Herman Hertz, Chief Rabbi of the British Commonwealth. It was a collection of inspirational writings, with quotations from the Talmud and the Torah (the first five books of the Old Testament) and from the works of famous men. The following quotation caught my eye:

If I am not for myself, who will be for me?
And being for myself only, what am I?
And, if not now, when?

That had been said nearly two thousand years ago by a man named Hillel, whom the book described as one of "the most renowned of the rabbis," who had been born in Babylon thirty years before Christ. "And being for myself only, what am I?"

Our engines had stopped, and we drifted in the blackest night we had seen. The sky was overcast, blotting out the stars. A mile off on our port side was the coast of Portugal, but the sea and the sky were so dark that we could not distinguish the mass of the land except during the fitful flash of a lighthouse. A half hour earlier we had contacted a pilot boat and had spelled out our name to it with a flashlight, but since then we had not heard a sound. We stood on the bridge staring into the darkness, nervous and uneasy.

"Why the hell don't they put a boat over?" Morgan yelled, his voice booming over the quiet water. Then we waited and listened, and in the deathly stillness the water lapped gently against our side.

Finally, from a long way off, we heard the faint rattle of wooden blocks and the sound of wood scraping on wood as a boat was lowered into the water. Then came the rhythmic dip and splash of oars, and a single weak light, no stronger than a candle, bobbing in the swells as it slowly approached us. At last our flashlights picked up a small boat, one man rowing, another sitting in the stern.

When he got to the bridge, the pilot did not offer to shake hands. Instead, he looked at us a little fearfully.

"No berths," he said. "The harbor's all full." He seemed to gain confidence as he looked at us. He was a squarely built, stocky man with a heavy black mustache slashing across his dark face.

"We'll anchor in the river," I said. "Have a cigarette, pilot." He accepted one gingerly and glanced quickly at me when he noticed the American brand. I gave him a light. "How about a cup of coffee?"

"American coffee?" he asked.

"Sure."

"You're from America?"

"Out of New York," I told him.

He sipped the coffee and smacked his lips. "Your crew are Americans?"

"Every one of them."

He seemed to relax a bit. "The harbor's really full," he said. "You want to go in anyway?"

"Yes."

And with a suddenness that startled all of us, he snapped out, "Full speed ahead!" The telegraph jingled, and the ship came alive as the engines began to roll. He was all nautical splash and dash then, rapping out his orders crisply, and he put on a beautiful show of perfect seamanship as he guided the *Paducah* into the tricky channel of the Tagus River in the ink-black night. I had studied the chart, and I knew that there was treacherous going there, with a constantly shifting sandbar on one side of us and the dark shore on the other. I was nervous: if this pilot should know who we were and didn't like us, he could ram us aground here so hard that we would never get off. But he whipped us through the bad spot, and the channel widened again into one of the finest river harbors in Europe. There were so many lights gleaming in the city that they blinded us.

"Where'll you put us?" I asked.

"At the quarantine anchorage."

"Much current in the river?"

"This time of year, no. In the spring, when the snow melts in the mountains, then it runs here six or seven knots. Now"—he shrugged his shoulders—"only four, five knots."

"That's still a lot of current," I remarked, but the pilot ignored the comment.

He maneuvered us into place, and at his orders we stopped our engines and let the anchor go, the chain ripping out in a thunderous rattle.

I took the pilot to the mess room, and we had some more coffee and a night lunch. But he didn't talk. After a while I asked, "Isn't your boat taking a long time to come for you?"

"It will not come for me tonight," he said.

"Oh?" I exclaimed in surprise. "Well, I can have a spare bunk made up for you."

"It's not necessary," he said. "This will do." And he stretched out on the bench and closed his eyes. I left him there.

Outside, the city of Lisbon sparkled and glittered in the night. I stopped at the door of Morgan's cabin. "Have the men on watch keep a sharp lookout. Tell 'em to keep an eye on the pilot. He's sleeping in the mess room."

I went to my own cabin and turned in. As I was falling asleep, I thought that I had to get hold of Heavy and show him the answer I had found in that book.

8 * The "Inspection"

In the morning the police came scrambling aboard while we were still dawdling over our coffee at breakfast. I went out on deck to greet them. The city shone in the clear morning. Like Horta, it nestled at the bottom of a hill. All the way up, the hill was cut back in terrace upon terrace, and the city rose over the harbor in layers. At the very top, dominating it all, was an ancient fort. From the fishermen's piers below came the smell of rotting fish.

Sholom stood at the ladder looking at the three policemen, and they didn't have to be smart to tell from his face that he didn't like cops. He nodded toward me as I approached, and one of the policemen came to meet me. "Captain?" he said, and I nodded. "We have come to arrange passes for shore leave for your crew."

"You mean my men can't go ashore without passes from you?"

"That is right, Captain. If you will give me the personal identification papers of all your crew, I will take them ashore and make out the permits."

"And if I don't give them to you?"

He spread his hands. "Then the men cannot leave the ship."

"Well," I told him, "you wait right here, and I'll ask the crew what they think about it."

"You, the captain?" he started but broke off short. He looked embarrassed. "That is, ah. . . . "

"Yes." I told him. "On this ship, the crew makes such decisions for themselves." And I turned and walked away.

I sent Leonard Rotter, a fireman, to assemble everybody on the boat deck. When they were all together, I reported my conversation with the policeman. "You can do as you please about this, but you should think about this possibility: if the police take your personal records ashore, it could be that photostats of them will find their way into the hands of the British. This is just a guess on my part, but it's worth thinking about."

36

The men talked it over among themselves. One of the wipers, a tough, quiet young man, still wore the marks of his shore leave in Horta, where some of the guys had gotten into a scrap: one eye was discolored, and a cut on his face was not healed. Another man bore different reminders. His left forearm was covered with nasty scabs; beneath the scabs was the freshly tattooed form of a young lady, the details of her anatomy etched in brilliant red and blue ink. I could imagine Heavy arguing with him on their night together ashore: "Hell, man, if you can't *be* a sailor, you might just as well try to look like one." Heavy, who had been going to sea the larger part of his life, had a few lurid tattoos of his own. He could show wandering young sailors much of what there was to see down the winding alleys in ports around the world.

Unanimously, the men decided to forgo shore leave in Lisbon.

The policeman was clearly disappointed when I informed him: "The crew has voted not to give you their papers."

"I am sorry, Captain," he said with formal politeness. "There will be two of my men posted at your gangway during your stay. You will be free to leave the ship at any time, as well as any other person you appoint to conduct ship's business ashore." He stopped a moment at the ladder to speak to his two men, and then he climbed down into his launch and putt-putted importantly toward the city. Most of the crew lined the rail and stared after him.

In the mess room the pilot was still drinking coffee; he must have been fond of the American brand. I asked him, "Can you tell me how to get to Malieros Frères?"

"Ah," he said, "they are your agents? You can come ashore with me, and I'll point it out to you; it's on my way. I expect my launch at nine o'clock."

On the dock the smell of decaying fish was so powerful it was almost dizzying. The odor clung to us as we walked up a drab street toward the city.

The offices of Malieros Frères were large and well lighted and filled with the bright chatter of typewriters. I was directed to a small man with a carefully trimmed, tiny mustache, something of a dandy, who smiled and invited me into his private office. I followed him in a small cloud of perfume.

"You have been notified that we were coming?"

"Yes," he said with a smile that showed all his teeth. "Your Paris agents have directed us to arrange fuel and water for you. But I'm afraid we can't get you any oil. There is a great shortage of fuel oil here now, you know."

This was the first I had heard of my Paris agents. But I was afraid to ask him who they were; I did not want to stir up any unnecessary suspicions or questions. I was not surprised that he could not get oil for us; there was indeed a great shortage of fuel oil in Europe. But I couldn't help thinking of the big Shell Oil docks and the huge storage tanks just across the river.

"Do you have any information about our next port?"

"No. Your agents merely ordered oil and water for you."

"When can we get the water?"

"This afternoon, if you like."

"Good. Send it out as soon as you can."

"If you have your documents with you," he said, "I will enter your ship at the customhouse."

I handed him a large envelope containing the ship's papers.

"I'll be aboard the ship. You'll notify me as soon as you hear from Paris?"

"Of course. Immediately."

The steward was waiting for me at the top of the ladder when I reached the deck.

"Can I talk to you for a minute, Cap'n?"

"Sure. Come on to my cabin."

He was pretty high, but the only thing that revealed it was the misty quality of his eyes behind the thick lenses of his glasses. Sweat stood out on his red face. He was a great cook, drunk or sober, and with all his drinking he hadn't missed a meal yet.

"Will we be here long, Cap?"

"I don't know yet, Steward."

"I got a special reason, Cap. It's a . . . well . . . I got a girl, Cap!" He poured it out in a rush now. "In Cairo. We're going to get married, see? Met her during the war. She's been waitin' for me, Cap, waitin' all these years, just as faithful as a, as a . . . oh, she's faithful, Cap. Writes regularly. And I thought if we were going to be here for a while, I could get a plane and just jump over there and sort of cement things. You know what I mean, Cap?" And he smiled a smile that looked more like a leer.

"I think I know what you mean, Steward. But if everything goes right, we'll be out of here tomorrow or the next day. Maybe there'll be more time at the next port. I'll do what I can."

"I'd sure appreciate it, Cap. That girl's been faithful for a long time." He walked uncertainly out of my room.

At one o'clock a water barge came alongside and tied up.

At two o'clock a launch came out from Malieros Frères. I was to come ashore at once. I took Sholom with me.

The foppish little man of the morning was not in, but a tall, lean-faced, alert-looking old man greeted me.

"Your Paris agents have phoned," he informed me. "We're ordered to clear your ship for sailing as soon as possible. We expect a phone call from them at four o'clock."

"Have you cleared the ship yet?"

"There seems to be some difficulty at the customhouse. You'll have to appear there yourself, it seems. It's not far, just four blocks up on this same street."

At the information desk at the customhouse a young man with glossy black hair and large black eyes muttered, "*Paducah, Paducah,*" as he looked through his records. "Ah, yes," he said, "here it is." He examined the paper for a moment. "The reason your ship hasn't been cleared, Captain, is because it hasn't been looked over yet by the port inspector."

"Since when does the port inspector have to look over a ship before clearing it? Is this something new?"

"Why, no, Captain," the young man said, his big eyes opened wide. "It is always required when we think a vessel is unseaworthy."

"Unseaworthy?" I shouted, and Sholom stepped up to the desk and planted his big, doubled fists on it. He showed all the signs of being about to declare war.

The young man with the glossy hair went cold. "Sorry, Captain," he said in a tone that proved he was not sorry at all. "We have a notation here concerning the seaworthiness of your ship. The port inspector is in Room Three." The young man dismissed us, but Sholom stood there glaring at him with his fists doubled up. I pulled him away. "Come on, let's go see the inspector."

Sholom glared at the young man over his shoulder as we headed for Room Three. "That guy got to me," he muttered.

We walked into Room Three without knocking, and a surly-looking individual behind a big desk glowered at us. He was a short, heavy man, very dark, his black hair cropped close to his head. He spoke to us in Portuguese. We didn't understand a word, but it sounded unfriendly.

"Do you speak English?" I asked.

"A little," he replied, still gruff. "What you want?"

"I'm the captain of the *Paducah*. You have to inspect her?"

"But surely!" he said. "She is not seaworthy."

I was getting angry. "Who says so?" I shouted.

"I say so!" he yelled and banged his fist on the desk.

Wrong tack. I couldn't afford to antagonize this character. I held out a package of cigarettes. "Smoke, Inspector?" He hesitated a moment, then took one. "May we sit down?" I asked. He grunted, and we sat down. Sholom looked at me curiously.

"OK," I said, trying to sound calm and friendly. "She's unseaworthy. Now, what do we have to do to clear her?"

"I must board her. I must see where she is not according to our standards."

"Good. Would you like to come aboard now?"

"Now is impossible!" He was shouting again. "Two days, three days, maybe four days before I can board her."

"But I must sail today," I said as gently as I could.

"You do not sail till I say so!" and he banged the desk again. Sholom looked at me appealingly: with his eyes, he said, "Please, Captain, let me at this guy." I was mightily tempted to give him the signal; if ever I wanted to see a man get his lumps, this was the man.

The door to an inner office opened, and a young girl entered with a stack of correspondence. Instinctively and unconsciously, Sholom let his breath out with a low whistling sound. The girl smiled as she put the stack of letters on the inspector's desk. She was stunning, positively, gorgeously, breathtakingly stunning. As she stood beside the desk of the inspector, that hard character looked softer in the glow of her beauty. She examined us coolly and thoroughly, and then she walked slowly to the window and stood there, looking out. An idea hit me between the eyes.

"Well, Inspector," I said, careful not to make my voice sound too drippy, "since we'll be here for a time, we'd consider it an honor if you would be our guest for dinner this evening."

He remained silent for so long I began to think he hadn't heard the question. Then the girl spoke softly, "We are free tonight."

"But, of course," he said cheerfully. "We accept your invitation, Señor."

"Fine. I'd appreciate it if you would recommend the restaurant. We're strangers to the city."

The inspector looked at the girl. "The Bilbaina is a nice place," she said.

"Good," I said. "The Bilbaina. Eight o'clock?"

"Eight o'clock."

As we went out, the girl smiled at us, and I thought that I had never seen anything as perfectly beautiful as her face.

"What happened in there?" Sholom asked when we got outside.

"Beats me," I said. "I don't know what it is, but there's an angle there."

"I was just about to blow up when you shifted your course."

"Well, now we have to feed the bastard. But we'll see what happens."

"God, isn't she terrific?" Sholom said.

At eight o'clock Sholom and I climbed out of the taxi, and I paid the driver. Then we both stood there for a moment looking at the outside of the Bilbaina. The girl certainly picked the best. We were both wearing the best clothes we owned, and we were freshly shaved, clean and neat, our hair nicely combed. But standing in front of the ornate entrance to the Bilbaina, we looked shabby. We shrugged and went in.

The headwaiter bore himself like an ambassador, and he looked at us as through our flies were open. We were shunted to a table in a corner, and we were on our second cocktail when the inspector and his girl entered. She was wearing a dreamy-green dress. Sholom and I looked at her, and then we looked at each other and sighed. The inspector wore a tuxedo; back home, he could easily have been mistaken for a bouncer in a clip joint. The prospect of entertaining him for an entire evening decreased my appetite. He grunted into his chair and didn't even say hello. I was beginning to feel the strain when the girl said brightly, "My name is Coletta."

I responded with my own name, and I introduced Sholom as one of my officers—I didn't want the inspector to feel offended by dining with a bosun. Then I looked expectantly at him. "Servas," he said. "I am Servas." Now we knew this much about each other.

I figured Servas for just a bureaucrat who had probably brawled his way into his job with his muscle and a little pull and was heady with authority. His threat to delay the *Paducah* could have been the result of British intrigue, but it might be nothing more than a private little shakedown he was trying to bluster through. I figured he was absolutely gone on Coletta, and I figured her as a bright young girl who was just beginning to understand the possible value of her extraordinary beauty. Obviously Mr. Servas would do anything Coletta suggested, and I thought she was not interested at the moment in anything more than doing the town at the expense of an American ship captain. I might be wrong, but I decided to play it this way.

So we ate, and I kept running the Manhattans to Servas, who drank them, and Sholom and I were flatteringly attentive to Coletta. So was every other male in the Bilbaina, and Coletta loved it. When she proposed a nightclub, we eagerly dashed off to a nightclub, where we ordered champagne and Servas danced every dance with Coletta. Then we went to another nightclub, with more champagne, and a third one, with still more champagne.

By four or five o'clock in the morning Mr. Servas was really feeling the booze. We had little trouble getting him into a taxicab. We were brothers, and he loved us, and he proved it by inviting us, including Coletta, up to sleep over in his apartment. I almost had to kick all the skin off Sholom's shin to keep him from jumping at the chance. I wanted no complications: Mr. Servas loved us, and I wanted to keep it that way. He embraced us both, and I embraced him and refused to part until he promised to have lunch with me aboard the ship at noon. Coletta insisted that she would get him there. So we assisted Mr. Servas to his door, and Coletta kissed us both goodnight. For a moment I thought Sholom would faint, but I got him back into the cab, and we headed for the docks and the *Paducah*. And then I realized how near I'd come to swooning myself.

I was pretty groggy at breakfast time, but I drank a coffee and settled down to worrying. We had water, but only enough oil for another thousand miles at most. Would a Paris call come through? Would Servas clear the ship?

When I finished breakfast, I went into the galley. Dave grinned at me, his face sweaty and his old hat cocked back on his head. His eyes were glassy. "Good morning, Cap," he shouted, and then he sidled up to me and whispered confidentially, "Cap, would you have a little drink with me just for the sake of friendship?"

"Well, just a nip, Dave, just a nip."

He produced a bottle of cognac. I tilted it up and took a fair-sized swallow, hoping it would cut the edge off the morning-after feeling. Dave tilted the bottle up and knocked about an inch off the contents. I shuddered just watching him.

"Now, look, Dave," I told him. "I've got two very important guests coming aboard for lunch. I want to treat them good, see? Do you think you could whip up something nice for them?"

"Cap," Dave said, "you're talkin' to a *cook*! I'll give 'em a meal they'll tell their grandchildren about."

At ten o'clock a launch came out with a message from Malieros Frères: "Please be at our office at eleven o'clock to accept a phone call from Paris."

Hurriedly, I went to Morgan's room and told him about Mr. Servas and his girlfriend.

"I don't know what time they'll come aboard, or even if they'll come aboard. But if they do get here before I come back, I want you to look after them. Take them to my cabin and entertain them, and if Mr. Servas will drink, give him all he'll drink. The girl loves attention, so give it to her, but don't make Servas jealous. As a matter of fact, maybe you'd better round up the chief and all the officers and tell them about it and have them there. Tell them to dress up and shave. And have Sholom there, too; she knows him. He's one of the officers, see?"

"OK," Morgan said.

"This guy Servas is holding us up. I hate to mess around with him, but we have to get the ship out."

"OK," Morgan said again, with a smile.

"But, oh, brother, wait till you see Coletta," I told him on my way out.

I sat in front of the telephone for twenty minutes before it finally rang.

"Hello, hello." The voice came through clearly. "Captain, do you have enough oil to take the ship to Bayonne, France?"

"How far is Bayonne from here?"

"About one thousand miles."

"I'll just barely be able to make it."

"Good. Then clear the ship and sail as quickly as possible. We'll meet you in Bayonne." And he hung up.

When the launch taking me back to the *Paducah* came within sight of her, I could see a great deal of activity at the bottom of the accommodation ladder. Both the cops were there and several of the crew. Others lined the rail and looked down. I urged the man at the launch's wheel to put on more speed, but he smiled and in sign language said she was going as fast as she could. We seemed to creep.

Now the men at the bottom of the ladder were pulling something out of the river. It was a man. They carried him dripping up to the deck and disappeared, the men lining the rail following them. It seemed to take the rest of the day for the launch to bring me alongside. I scrambled up the ladder two steps at a time, and at the top I met Heavy.

"What happened?"

Heavy grinned. "The steward jumped over the side."

"What! Is he all right?"

"Sure. We undressed him and put him in his bunk. He's drunk."

"Why did he jump?"

"He said he was tired of ships and was going to fly to Cairo. Lucky he grabbed the ladder. This current would have washed him out to sea."

"Did anybody come aboard?"

Heavy grinned again. "They're in your cabin."

The place was jammed. Coletta was sitting on my desk with her legs crossed. She had a glass in one hand, a cigarette in the other. The inspector was sitting on my bunk, leaning back against the bulkhead. "Ah, my friend!" he shouted when I entered; he started up to greet me but didn't quite make it and leaned back again. The chief engineer, his three assistants, the three mates, and Sholom were hovering about the exquisite Coletta, and all of them looked a little moonstruck. With a smile and a wink she could have struck any one of them witless. I motioned Morgan into a corner.

"How's the steward?"

"He'll be OK. I locked him in his room."

"How's the inspector?"

"Happy. We've been pouring liquor into him. He loves it."

"Well, don't give him too much. I want him sober enough to sign a clearance. Keep Coletta amused. I'll be back in a minute."

In the galley I found a mess boy slicing big sausages.

"Make me up a tray with something fancier than sausage," I told him. "Make it *look* good. You know, cut the crust off the bread and throw some pickles and olives and stuff around. Ritz it up. And a couple of pots of strong coffee. Bring it to my cabin as soon as you can."

When the food arrived, we managed to separate Mr. Servas from the water glass he had been using for cognac and sit him down in front of some hot coffee. He didn't want any food, but Coletta ruffled his hair and said, "Eat." He ate. I boasted about the coffee being the best that can be bought in America, and that impressed him so much that he drank four cups of it, black. When he had perked up a little, I asked him the question and then held my breath waiting for the answer.

"How was the inspection?" was the question.

"Inspection?" he said vaguely. "A-a-ah! The inspection." He slapped his big thigh loosely and laughed. "Ha. The inspection. Very good. My friend," he said, looking up at me, "you have a fine ship. She is everything perfect, everywhere according to standards. Let us drink to it." He retrieved the water glass, and we had a drink all around.

I whispered to the chief that we would sail as soon as I could get the inspector ashore to sign a clearance. He motioned to his assistants, and they left to get the engines ready, Coletta blowing kisses to them. Morgan and the other two mates took off, too.

Sholom and I managed to get the inspector down the accommodation ladder and into the launch, and the inspector heaved himself into a seat and pulled Sholom down beside him with a heavy arm around his shoulder, all warm and buddy-like. I went back up and escorted the lovely Coletta down the ladder. Sometimes it was fun to be a captain.

An hour later we were back aboard with a pilot. We heaved our anchor and rang for full speed ahead. With the river current boosting us, we raced toward the open sea at a clean fifteen knots, the smell of rotting fish following us most of the way.

9 * Blown into Bayonne

After dropping the pilot we headed west until we cleared Cape da Roca, and then we brought the *Paducah* around and pointed her north for the run up the coast of Portugal and Spain. The weather was all warm and gentle June. Sholom and his men washed down the ship. She dried rapidly in the sun, coming up bright and clean, and tiny crystals of salt from the sea water sparkled like spangles on a pretty girl's party dress.

When we were well clear and the coast was only a thin line on our starboard side, I went to the steward's room and found him sitting on the edge of his bunk with his head in his hands. He looked up at me and managed a sheepish grin.

"How do you feel?"

"Oh, don't ask, Cap'n," he said. "Don't ask. It's too painful to discuss."

"Think you can manage supper?"

"Cap'n, I'll give you a supper you'll remember. Don't know what happened to me. This is the first time I've ever missed a meal. Must have been somethin' I drank."

I walked down the passageway and stopped at Baird's room. "How do you figure the oil, Chief?"

"I'm worried," he told me. "It's going to be awfully close."

"Do you think we'll make it?"

"Can't tell," he said. "Let's just hope we don't run into any head winds."

I stepped next door to the first assistant's room. "Hi, Skipper," he said.

"Listen, Charlie, tell me the truth: how's the oil situation?"

"Nothing to worry about," he said. "We won't have any left over, but we'll make it. I'm getting those firemen broken in; they're beginning to know their jobs."

"The chief is worried."

"Aw," Fariello waved his hand, "he worries about everything. Forget it. Go sleep easy. If I have to stand every fireman's watch myself, we'll make it."

"I haven't been towed into port yet," I remarked. "I don't want to break that record this trip."

"Forget it," Fariello assured me.

It was late in the evening when we rounded Cape de Finisterre, the End of the Land, a wild and rocky mass almost two thousand feet high that dove steeply into the sea here after shouldering out to form a crossroads where many ships passed. There were big passenger liners up from South Africa and the Mediterranean coming close together at this spot to locate themselves for the run to the English Channel. There were heavily loaded cargo ships rounding the cape going south. And there was a large number of smaller craft coming out of the Bay of Biscay or, like us, edging eastward around Cape Ortegal into the bay proper. And I was glad it was the month of June and the season of clear skies and gentle winds, for the Bay of Biscay is feared by all sailors for its wild and savage winter storms, when gales rip and smash and there is no lee anywhere for safety.

We were fairly close in to the coast when we passed the entrance to the port of La Coruña. Two Spanish destroyers charged out to look us over. They were painted battle gray and were as fast as whippets. I watched them through glasses. But they kept a fair distance and, after circling us once, poured on speed and raced back toward the harbor, leaving snarling wakes behind. And I remembered an old history lesson: "In 1588 the Invincible Armada set sail from La Coruña. . . . " Set sail with nearly one hundred and fifty ships, if I remembered correctly, and thirty or forty thousand men, and only half the number came limping back to take refuge, not in La Coruña, but in Gijón, farther along the coast, as though in the bitter shame of defeat the fleet could not again enter the port whence it had set out for conquest. Watching the destroyers, I wondered if their skippers ever thought of the Invincible Armada.

Walking down the passageway, I caught a glimpse through an open door into the room of Brettschneider and young Gutmann and Heavy and George Goldman. "Sailors!" Brettschneider was scoffing contemptuously. "I don't suppose any of you ever read Boswell, did you? If you had, you'd know that old Dr. Sam Johnson summed up seamen in one short sentence. He said, 'No man will be a sailor who has contrivance enough to get himself into jail.' "

"Don't be throwing your damned college education around," George said furiously, "and quoting from books you've read. I say— "

I passed beyond hearing before I knew what George said. Brettschneider had made the voyage on the *Ben Hecht*. He, Dave Gutmann, and Heavy had been imprisoned in Acre Prison, an ancient Crusader fortress; Dave still told of the infestation of lice they all endured in Acre. Brettschneider was indefatigable in his independence. I had heard him several times in arguments and discussions with other members of the crew aboard the *Paducah*. On this, their second voyage to Palestine, these men contributed a great deal to the work and the morale of the ship.

The weather held good as we nibbled away at the sea-miles, keeping well in toward the northern coast of Spain. It was midnight when we picked up and passed the light at Santander, and shortly after we dropped it astern, we would pick up the light at San Sebastián, the summer resort town of Spain. Also between the two, a few miles in from the coast, was the little town of Guernica, or the spot where there once was a little town called Guernica, before the Nazi planes flew over it and bombed it out of existence. It was the first mass bombing of a civilian population. I fell asleep thinking of Spanish kings and holes in the ground where towns once stood and of the run down Suicide Alley on the west coast of England with the Stukas screaming down on us.

Morgan woke me. "Come on out on deck," he said, grinning. I put on some clothes and followed him. It was just past dawn. Morgan pointed silently, and there, dead ahead of us, rearing up into the clear sky above the misty horizon, were masses of snowy mountains so wild-looking even from this distance that they seemed to be rioting in the morning light. "Picos de Europa," Morgan said. "About seventy miles away." I stood at the bridge rail staring at them until breakfast time.

Early in the afternoon we passed clusters of small Basque fishing boats out for sardines. Their seine nets looked as delicate as lace. We waved at them as we passed, and the fishermen waved back. The weather was perfect. The flag atop our signal mast hung lifelessly; there was not a breath of breeze except for the stir of air we created ourselves with our ten-knot speed. As we neared the mouth of the Adour River, we came closer to the Spanish coast, and through the glasses I could see the brown cliffs and small yellow houses.

But astern of us, far off, stretching from the Spanish mountains far out over the sea until it disappeared into the north, was a long, thin, dirty-colored cloud. I did not like the look of it; it spoiled the serenity of the perfect sky. We were about thirty miles from Bayonne.

When I looked back again, the cloud was bigger, closer, and blacker. I watched it. It was racing toward us at an incredible speed. It looked like a squall, except that it was bigger than any squall I had ever seen. The whole western sky was blotted out now.

The flag atop our signal mast began to flutter uneasily. And then it was standing straight out as the wind and the rain hit us and the sky overhead turned greasy-looking. The Spanish coast, twenty miles away and bright in the afternoon a moment ago, was obscured by a yellowish haze. The sun itself was gone, and the day went suddenly dark. South of us the lightning ripped, and then the long thunder came booming over the water. This was going to be a real blow.

At the big desk in the room behind the wheelhouse I checked the chart again for the minefields off Bayonne. A clear channel half a mile wide was shown. Plenty of room for safe passage. But outside, the rain was hissing and the sea was rising, dirty-gray and angry-looking, and the *Paducah* was beginning to roll and pitch as we ran before the wind toward the coast.

It was early evening but already growing dark when we crept up to the edge of the minefields six miles from our port. We searched and searched, but we could see no buoys marking the clear channel. We stopped our engines and blew our whistle for the local pilot. We waited for a restless hour, maintaining just enough steerageway to keep the *Paducah*'s bow pointing toward the Bayonne breakwater, and our bow leaped up under the waves and then dove down again with a long, dizzying swing. The lightning crackled continually.

Shore lights had not come on yet, but we could still make out the end of the breakwater and the white structure of the lighthouse at Biarritz. We took cross bearings on them and fixed our position in relation to the mine-free channel, and then we crept slowly toward the river's mouth. We blew and blew our signal for the pilot, but we got no response. We were all nervous. If our cross bearings were off, it meant we were wandering among the mines. When we got so close that we could see the waves breaking over the sandbar where the Adour emptied into the bay, we stopped again, going slow ahead and slow astern just enough to keep our bow toward the break-water. We realized now that no pilot could reach us in these heavy seas.

Suddenly I thought of the oil. "Call up the engine room and ask the chief how long we can cruise!" I yelled to Christie.

In a moment he came out of the wheelhouse. "Four hours at the most," he reported.

My best move would have been to head out to deep water again and just prowl till morning. But I couldn't do that with only four hours of oil. I couldn't even maintain steerageway where I was. There was no choice: we had to anchor there and shut the ship down and hope we would hold till daylight.

The lighthouse on the high rock at Biarritz came on, its long yellow beam fingering through the rain as it slowly revolved. Then the smaller light on the end of the Bayonne breakwater snapped on. "Take another bearing!" I yelled to Christie, the wind tearing the words out of my mouth. I crossed through the wheelhouse to the other wing of the bridge, where Morgan was standing. "Get Sholom, and stand by to let the anchor go!" In the yellow beam of the lighthouse he looked at me anxiously before scampering down the ladder.

Christie and I checked his bearing on the chart. If he had made no error, we were still in the channel.

We went out on the bridge again and waited there until Morgan's voice was heard faintly through the tumult of wind and rain: "All ready to let go."

"Full ahead port engine. Full astern starboard engine," I ordered Christie, and he jumped to the telegraph.

"Wheel, hard right," I told the wheelsman.

The old *Paducah* came around slowly, as though with difficulty. In a few moments she was broadside to the heavy seas and lay well over, wallowing ungracefully in the deep troughs. Then a big one hit her full with a shuddering shock and exploded into a spreading mass of spray that was turned into whips by the wind. With a heaving effort she pulled herself around. Slowly the bow came up into the weather; she pitched badly, but she kept her decks dry. "Slow ahead both engines," I ordered. "Wheel amidships, steady as she goes."

I waited until she was steady and facing the wind. "Stop both engines. Keep her heading into it."

She lost all headway almost immediately. I shouted forward to Morgan, in the dark. "Let go!"

The chain went spilling out with a roar that seemed to dull the thunder. And standing there where no one could see me, I closed my eyes and held my breath, tensely hoping that the anchor didn't strike a mine as it went crashing to the bottom. It didn't.

Cupping my hands, I shouted toward the fo'c'sle head: "Four shackles in the water!" Morgan's voice came back repeating the order, and I could hear the men letting out more chain slowly. Four shackles would be enough length in this water.

"Keep a sharp check on your anchor bearings," I told Christie. "If she starts dragging, call me at once." As the yellow finger of the lighthouse beam came around, it revealed a sheen of sweat on his forehead.

All night we pitched and tugged at the end of our anchor chain. The seas hissed along our sides as they charged toward the beach, and the wind keened as it flailed us with lashes of spray. Our anchor held. Toward morning the storm began to slacken off.

10 * The Hagana's Wise Old Youngsters

When the sun came up, the wind was gone and the seas were rounded off into great running swells. The cloud was broken and scattered into small ragged tufts that took on a purplish tint in the light of the dawn. A small pilot boat came out and sidled up to us cautiously like a crab. The men in it fended themselves off with their hands, and the pilot, standing with one foot on the gunwale, waited until the *Paducah* started an upswing and then leaped for our rope ladder and clambered aboard while the men in his boat pushed off quickly. The pilot had light blue eyes and a heavily suntanned face. He knew little English, but he managed to explain, by way of apology, that during the night it had been impossible to cross Le Barre.

We heaved up anchor, turned the *Paducah* around, and headed toward the river mouth. The swells were smooth-topped now, but they still had enough force to burst into spray and flying spume as they crashed upon the breakwater and threw themselves over it. Le Barre still looked very rough to me. But there is an old sailor's saying that stormy coasts make good pilots. It was true in the case of this one. Without hesitation he took us around the breakwater, making sharp little gestures with his hands to reinforce his orders to the wheelsman. One instant we were in the middle of the angry turbulence at the bar where the river mingled violently with the sea, the *Paducah* heaving and pitching, and the next we were across it and on the flat, smooth river itself.

The pilot skimmed us within a foot of the stack of a sunken ship. "German?" I asked him, and he nodded brightly, "Oui." I thought he liked to go as close to it as he dared. Like dancing on the grave of an enemy.

The Adour River, about a half-mile wide, flowed here in big sweeping curves, and on both sides were green woods, the trees growing almost up to the edge of the water. The thrashing storm of the night was like something that happened to us long ago. The pilot maneuvered us to a dock. Just ahead of our bow, part of the hull of a bombed ship could be seen above water. When the lines were made fast, we jingled the telegraph and set the pointer on "Finished with Engines." The answering jingle from below was like an exclamation of relief.

The chief came up from the engine room. "We'll have to shut her down tonight if we don't get oil. We just made it."

It was twenty-six days since we had left New York.

In the crush of officials in my cabin—customs men, police officers, and immigration inspectors—someone asked, "How long is your stay here, Captain?"

"I don't know yet. I'm waiting for my agent."

A little man with a spade beard pushed his way through and shook my hand. "I am your agent," he announced. "Have you all your documents?"

"Can you identify yourself?" I countered.

Another voice spoke up, "He's your agent. I represent the owners of the ship." After he presented proof of this, I gave Spadebeard the envelope containing the ship's papers, and he took off.

Now I looked at the man I had been waiting to meet. He was younger than I thought he would be, not more than twenty-five or twenty-six. He was slim and well built and had red hair and looked no more important than a clerk in a small office. He had an accent, but of a kind I'd never heard before and couldn't place. I was surprised at his appearance. I sup-posed I had expected to find a tall, imposing old man with a flowing beard, carrying a gnarled staff and bearing himself with the authority of Moses and the wisdom of Solomon, an Old Testament prophet leading his people out of the wilderness. The person before me was just an ordinary-looking youngster. Except when he smiled. When he smiled, he looked like a man who had been everywhere and had seen everything and could never again be shocked or frightened or fooled. When he smiled, he was not a youngster anymore. And when we shook hands, he had a warm and solid grip.

"What's your name?" I asked.

"Well," he said, "you can call me 'Gingi.' Congratulations on getting here."

"Thanks. It was a nice trip. But what do I do now?"

"Now," he said, "you can relax a bit, after your 'nice' trip. We will refit the ship here for our passengers. That will take about six weeks. One of our men will be in charge of that work. You need oil; I have arranged for one hundred tons to be delivered this afternoon. And I suspect you need sleep, too, after last night's storm. So I will leave you now. But I'd like you to have dinner with me and two of my friends this evening. Shall I pick you up at six o'clock?"

"I'll be ready at six," I told him. He smiled his wise smile, and when he left, I concluded that he was a very competent young man.

At six o'clock a hearse-like French taxi pulled up on the dock, and Gingi thrust his head out. I climbed in, and we drove up a road that paral-leled the river. I judged the center of the city to be about three miles from our dock. We passed a small lighted square. Behind the square a few peo-ple sat at tables on the sidewalk before a cafe sipping drinks and quietly reading newspapers. Nearby was a movie theater. Behind the square, standing on the highest point and dominating the entire city, was the an-cient cathedral, built in the thirteenth century. We crossed a massive stone bridge to an island in the river, and the taxi hurtled into a narrow, winding street at a speed that I considered reckless, but Gingi showed no concern. The people walking on the street and the groups of kids at play paid no attention to our cab. We stopped with a jolt in front of a small establish-ment with a rough board sign over the doorway, Basque Cafe.

Gingi introduced me to two men at a table. One was Haim Weinshel-baum, a short, middle-aged man with a round face and eyes that seemed extraordinarily keen. The other was Moka Limon, who was even younger than Gingi. Moka was extremely tall, well built, and as he rose to shake hands, I noticed that he bore himself like a soldier—not stiff, but straight, and with nothing slack about him anywhere. His hair was dark, straight. When he said, "I am very glad to know you, Captain," I noted that his accent was like Gingi's.

None of us talked much while we ate. Once during the meal Haim leaned back in his chair with an odd, almost frightening expression on his face. His round cheeks were flushed, and his keen eyes went into a dead stare. The other two glanced at him but kept on eating as though they had noticed nothing. He looked like a man who had drunk too much wine. After a time he sat up again, and he noticed my curiosity. "Excuse me," he said. "It's nothing. The British interrogated me once. I get occasional severe pains where they hit me around the head. They will go away in a moment."

His explanation was so casual and matter-of-fact that it startled me. I had begun to feel rather proud of myself and the manner in which we had detoured around a couple of obstacles on the way over. It struck me now that this was high school stuff. And I began to feel humble when I looked at the three quiet men at the table with me. Haim continued to eat as though nothing had happened. These guys, I told myself, weren't playing games. These guys were serious.

When the coffees were served, Gingi asked me point-blank: "Are you staying with the ship?"

I had felt for some time now that I would stay with the ship. I did not make a conscious decision about it, but the certainty grew upon me that I would not be able to leave the *Paducah* till her trip was done. "And being for myself only, what am I?" That was part of it. There was more. There was Gutmann, and the solid but quiet determination of the men in the crew, in all their personal differences and diversity. There was Dave Wurm, with his fierce industry, and the amiable surfaces of Eli and Syd, camouflaging their strict self-discipline and dedication. I was apparently taking sides. But until three minutes before, I had not been prepared to commit myself.

"You have time to think about it," Gingi said. "But you will try to find out as soon as you can which of the officers are leaving. We will have to get replacements for them. Moka here will be in charge of the ship for us. You, of course, will have complete control of navigation and of the crew. Moka will be responsible for the installation of bunks and all the refitting work, and the passengers will be his worry. He will live aboard the ship from tonight on. He'll show you the town tonight. Haim and I have to go."

It struck me that they were leaving rather abruptly. They didn't talk much during the meal; there was hardly any conversation at all. They didn't ask me any questions, or probe into my background, or show any interest in why I, a Gentile, should be concerned with the run to Palestine. Yet they had asked me to stay with the ship, and they were not the kind of men to trust just anybody who came along. The dinner was probably arranged so that they could get a close look at me and size me up.

"Before you go— " I halted them. "You didn't give me a chance to answer before, but I'd like to tell you now that I want to stay with the ship. But don't you, ah, aren't you interested in knowing more about me, who I am, where I come from? How do you know who I am?"

Gingi smiled his wise smile. "My friend," he said, "I don't want to sound immodest, but after seeing all that we have seen with our own eyes, we are able to estimate a man during the time it takes to eat a dinner. Besides, we have asked questions of others. We know enough about you to trust you. Otherwise we should have asked you to leave the ship at once. We're glad you've decided to stay. Thank you. Incidentally, we were fairly certain that you would. That's why I didn't press you for an immediate answer."

They shook hands and left. I felt like a young boy who has just had a friendly pat on the back from a wise old uncle. I didn't know why I should have felt like that. I was older than Gingi.

Moka was smiling, but he changed the subject. "What would you like to do tonight?" he asked.

"What is there to do?"

"In Bayonne, not much. It's a quiet town. It goes to bed early. Biarritz stays awake longer. Would you like to drive over there? It is only five miles."

"What nationality is Gingi?" I asked.

"Palestinian."

"And you?"

"Palestinian."

"You were both born there?" I exclaimed, and Moka laughed. I knew it was a stupid question as soon as I uttered it, but I couldn't help it. The notion of people being born in Palestine struck me as a brand-new idea. I had always regarded Palestine as a place where people went, not as a place where they were born.

"No, I wasn't," Moka replied. "I was born in Russia in 1924. My parents left in 1934. Haim was born in Poland, but he has lived in Palestine for twenty years. It is something like your country: some are born there; some come from outside. But for us, Palestine is still a young country: we still want to share what we have. We encourage people to come to us."

Now it was my turn to change the subject.

"How old are you?" I asked him.

"Twenty-four."

"Have you been doing this work long?"

"You mean the ships?" He thought for a moment. "This will be my second ship. Want to go to Biarritz?"

On the bus I tried to make conversation. "When will you be able to start refitting?"

"Tomorrow."

"So soon?"

"We have a full set of the blueprints and plans of the ship. The workmen know exactly what to do."

"Will we load the passengers here?"

"No."

"Where will we pick them up?"

"We will know when it is time to know."

He said it quite firmly. In the future, I decided, I would not try to learn anything before it was time to know it.

The bus made the run to Biarritz in about twenty minutes. I could not see much of the place in the dark. There were huge hotels built in a semicircle near the edge of a high bluff over the Gulf of Gascony, small expensive shops filling up the spaces between them. On a lower level, halfway down to the sandy beaches, was the casino. And on a rocky point at one end of the cove was the lighthouse with its revolving yellow beam.

"This is the playground of European royalty," Moka said. "It was chosen as a resort by Napoleon III. Napoleon the Little."

The Caravel was a small place that seemed pretentious by its very simplicity. An outer room was fitted with a bar of richly glowing mahogany and was furnished with three small tables. On one wall, illuminated delicately by hidden lights, was a large painting of Columbus' *Santa Maria*. It was a very quiet room, and everything in it was in a low key, but the place seemed to scream, "This is quality."

"Try one of the house specials," Moka advised me. "Brandy and milk and egg and I don't know what else. They're very good. Tell me, what is the meaning of the word *Paducah*? Does it have a meaning, or is it just a name?"

"Paducah," I told him, "is the name of a town in the state of Kentucky.

About all I know about it is that it was the hometown of Irvin S. Cobb. He was a humorous writer. But my grandfather fought in the First Kentucky Cavalry for the Union in the Civil War. He was captured and spent a year in Libby Prison. He had six children."

"You are from Kentucky?"

"No, I was born in Astoria; that's a part of New York City. But when I was twelve years old, my family moved to a small town in Florida. I lived there for four years. Then I left home."

"Ran away to sea. A classic pattern."

"No. I didn't run away to sea. I ran away from poverty. I had never seen a ship before I hitchhiked back to New York from Central Florida. I got a ride on a truck that let me off at the docks in New Jersey. I took a ferry across the Hudson to 42nd Street. That's when I first saw the ships."

"And you were in the ships during the war?"

"Yes."

"I, too," he said. "The Palmach wouldn't let me enlist—the Palmach is the striking force of the Hagana, sort of like commandos. I started training for it when I was quite young. I broke discipline—the only time in my life—and went as a seaman on a Norwegian freighter. I had to be in the war, you know. I suppose you could say that I'm still in it. Not a bad life, at sea. Only I found it lonely. What did your father do in Florida?"

"He bought an orange grove. But it was a failure, and he lost his savings."

"I, too, grew up around orange groves. Well, we have two things in common in our backgrounds: oranges and the sea." He lifted his glass, and we drank to the things we had in common.

Lew Brettschneider and Dave Gutmann came from the ship into the Caravel. They looked at us hesitantly; there was still restraint between crew members and captain. I invited them to sit at our table, and I introduced them to Moka. "Try the house special," he told them.

"Will the British bother you here in Bayonne?" I asked.

"Yes," he said promptly. "As soon as they learn that the ship is here, they will start their operations."

"Operations?"

Moka nodded. "Sometime tomorrow I want to have a meeting with the entire crew. There I will explain how they work. I'll describe some of the experiences we've had with them."

Brettschneider finished his drink quickly and ordered another. "Be respectful of that concoction," Moka said with a smile. "It doesn't taste like it, but it's quite powerful."

"It's all right," Brettschneider said. "I can take it."

He took them in rapid succession, and after each one he hunched lower in his chair. From time to time he glanced at Moka with an expression of curiosity. Brettschneider was always active, looking and inquiring. He was bold and respected by the crew and was an asset aside from his regular hard, dirty work in the ship's engine room. Officially he was a "Fireman." Actually, he cleaned floor plates, carried stores, watched the fires in the boilers as a relief water-tender.

Now Sholom came in; the Caravel was like a crossroads. We pulled up a chair for him, and he stood up again to shake hands with Moka. "I'm sure glad to know you," he said with genuine respect.

We ordered him a house special. He took a sip of it, set it down, and exclaimed, "Damn it! I'm glad to be here!" He took another sip and said, "I don't mean here in this bar: I mean being here. And to think I almost didn't make it."

"How's that?" I asked him.

"The guy who screened us for this trip. . . . I drove down to his office in a new car. Paid for with cash—I had some money saved from the Navy and was doing some odd jobs. But I didn't intend to tell this guy my business. And the first thing he asked me: 'How do you make your living?' I looked him straight in the eye and said, 'My mother supports me.' He gave me a funny look, and I guess he put my name at the bottom of the list. How do you like that! I was one of the last men called."

"Well, I'm sure glad you're here, Sholom," I said.

Moka laughed.

On the way back to the ship in a taxi, he said, "We'll find a hotel for you ashore. It's going to be hard to sleep on the ship with all the noise created by the work."

11 * Departures

Morning was as fresh as dew, and the bright green trees crowded close to the banks of the easy-flowing river. We could hear the sound of birds, and the smell of wood smoke was in the air.

I was the last one in the mess room after breakfast, dawdling over a third cup of coffee. Dave Shass came in from the galley, and he was all smiles. "Just want you to know, Cap'n," he said. "I'm off the stuff. Not entirely, you understand. I'll take a drink for the sake of sociability, but nothin' to excess. Tell you the truth, Cap'n, that header into the river scared me. When the stuff makes you jump over the side, it's time to ease up on it, I figure. And about that trip to Cairo, Cap'n. Forget it. I'll wait till we get to where we're going. Because I think when I get to Cairo I won't be comin' back. I'll be settlin' down for good and forever."

"I'm glad to hear that, Dave," I told him. "We'd hate to lose you before the trip is done. None of us has eaten like this since we left home and mother's cooking."

After breakfast the French shipwrights came clumping up the gangway, all of them dressed in faded dungarees and blue denim jackets, most of them wearing berets. They carried their light tools with them and hauled the heavier stuff aboard at the end of a line. Moka conferred with the foreman briefly, and the men went to work with great efficiency, apparently knowing exactly what to do. They broke out the load of lumber in our forward hold, and a young man set up a portable electric saw. In a moment the whole ship echoed its high whine as the long two-by-fours were cut into lengths for the upright supports of the bunks that would be built.

"It didn't take very long for these men to get under way," I remarked to Moka.

"Remember," he said with a smile, "we've done all this before."

A tall, heavy man with a dark, handsome face walked up to us. "I want you to meet a friend of mine," Moka said. "This is Gedda Shochat. He also is a native Palestinian. He'll be in charge of installing a loudspeaker system throughout the ship."

"Glad to meet you, Captain," he said, and then he conferred for a moment with Moka in Hebrew.

"He's quite a man," Moka said after Gedda left. "At thirty-four he volunteered for the Royal Air Force. Told them he was twenty-six and made them believe it. He passed the physical and served for the duration of the war as a pilot in India."

I wandered about the ship, finding Frenchmen everywhere. I felt the old resentment that a sailor feels every time his ship is tied up to a dock and shore workers come aboard. In the long days at sea the ship became our home, and these men were intruders. Alongside a dock a ship is not really our own, and we have neither privacy nor possession. The ship reverts to what she really is, just a big piece of machinery built to carry things, and we don't like it. There is no romance about a ship that is tied to the land— she has life and meaning to us only when she's at sea with none aboard but the men who belong to her.

Wandering about, I passed two workmen, and I thought I heard English spoken. I walked up to them and asked, "Do you speak English?"

A man with red hair sticking out under his beret turned and looked at me and said, "Aye, and what did ye think we were speakin', Hindoostani?" He was a little cocklebur of a man. "Ye're the skipper, ain't ye?" he said. "I'm Henry Tabor, from the Clydeside, and I'm a Scot and a Jew and a bit of an electrician, too. And ye'll curse the day I came aboard, for the fearful system of sound we're installin' will blast the ears off your head day and night once it gets to workin'. But ye couldn't do without it, and ye'll find that out before ye're through. I'm glad to meet ye, Captain." He grinned as he shook hands.

Wherever I went, there were men cutting and hammering and measuring off distances with tape measures and putting figures into small notebooks and studying blueprints and digging into the wiring of the ship. There was no quiet anywhere, not even in my own room with the door closed.

After lunch the entire crew, officers and men, were assembled in the mess room. The place was crowded and blue with smoke as Moka stood up solemnly to speak.

"I want to thank all of you," he started, "for getting the ship here against certain obstacles you met on the way. There will be more and bigger obstacles from here on, but I am not going to give you an inspirational speech, because I don't think you need it. But I want to caution you.

"Most of you, I'm told, have been through the war in one of the services. So you know the meaning of security. The British, unfortunately, are aware of the ship's mission. They will do what they can to prevent her from completing it. You'll be here for six weeks at least, and you'll meet a lot of people ashore. Do not discuss the ship or her business with them. Tell no one anything. You'll meet people who will be very curious. They'll ask a lot of questions. Do not answer them. Tell them you don't know. Stay away from people who ask questions.

"Be careful even in talking among yourselves; you may be overheard. Don't talk about the Hagana or the men you know who belong to it. Call them 'Shou-shous.' And if you must mention the ship's destination, call it 'Oklahoma.'

"All of you must be alert at all times. The safety of the ship and the success of its mission will depend to a great extent upon the conduct and behavior of each of you. The British haven't arrived in Bayonne yet. But they'll find us when they can, and they'll harass us when they do. Don't help them by carelessness. That is all."

The men filed out of the mess room silently. Each looked serious.

When they were all gone, I asked Moka, "Do you think we can get through the blockade?"

"We will try," he said.

"Is it possible?"

"Of course it's possible. We have done it before. But it's difficult."

"What happens to the crew?"

"If we get through, it is simple. Those who wish to settle in the country will remain. Those who want to go home will be furnished transportation. If we don't make it, if we are captured by the British, it will mean detention on Cyprus. We'll get you out as soon as we can. But we can't offer any guarantees. You'll be prisoners of the British."

I felt quite serious myself when I left the mess room.

In the afternoon I went to the second assistant engineer's room. The third assistant was with him. I intended to talk to each of the officers alone, but these two were so friendly I decided to deal with them together. "You can quit here," I told them, "or you can stay with the ship. Have you made up your minds yet?"

"We were just talking about it, Captain. We're both getting off here."

"OK. I'll pay you off tomorrow."

"We wish you a lot of luck the rest of the way, Captain," the second assistant said.

"Sure, I'm staying," Charlie Fariello said without hesitation when I asked him. "I don't like what they're doing to the Jews. I've never liked it. And if I can help a little bit, I'm willing to help."

It was Baird who surprised me. "I'd like to stay with the ship," he said. I would have bet my sextant that he would quit here.

He noticed my surprise. "Don't ask me why," he said. "I don't think I could tell you. I'm not sure myself. I came aboard for the job, but I've been thinking about it all the way over. By rights I should draw my wages here and go on home and keep out of trouble that doesn't concern me. But I don't know. I'll stay." We shook hands on that.

I didn't have to ask Morgan if he was going through or not. Having a job on a ship was necessary for Morgan to be alive.

I didn't have to ask Paul Christie, the third mate, either. He told me first. "I've been looking for you, Captain," he said. "I'd like to pay off here as soon as I can."

"I'll have your money for you tomorrow."

"Right," he said, and he seemed very cheerful about it.

Walking down the deck looking for Moka, I passed the chief and Charlie Fariello together at the rail. They called me over.

"Charlie has an idea," the chief said. "He thinks we can promote two of the men below to stand the engineers' watches. That way you won't have to get replacements."

"We don't need three wipers down there," Charlie said. "I can make Gutmann and Lewis Brettschneider engineers. I'll make Kohlberg an assistant engineer. He can be an all-around man. The chief and I are willing to help them. And for the general work around the engine room, cleaning, minor repairs, I can make one of the men a wiper."

"Have Gutmann and Brettschneider learned that much on this trip?"

"They're not licensed ships' engineers," Charlie said, "but they know their way around the engine room, and I'll give them a hand. Gutmann and Kohlberg sailed in engine rooms of Liberty ships during the war. Brettschneider had engine room experience on tankers and has a good grasp of the problems. He has an engineering degree from City College. I think they'll make out."

"What do you think about it, Chief?"

"I'm willing to take a chance with them. Charlie has practically convinced me."

"Well, if it's all right to you two, it's all right with me. Have you told them about it yet?"

"No."

"Well, tell them, and see what they say. Warn them that if they take it, they'll have to stay on the ball."

I found Moka on one of the lower decks on his hands and knees with one end of a steel tape measure in his hand. The other end was held by Henry Tabor, the Scots-Jew, physicist, and electrical engineer. He was mastering the intricate science of ship design and stability the rough way. It was his job to crawl throughout the *Paducah* to make careful measurements of all of her dimensions. Later he would compute to an inch the exact center of gravity, and from that he would tell us how and where to distribute our passengers for a safe load.

When Moka was finished, I took him to one side.

"Two of the engineers are quitting," I told him, "but we won't have to get replacements for them. The chief engineer is willing to promote two of the men to take their places. The third mate is quitting. So all you have to get for me now is a mate."

"You'll need two mates," Moka said quietly.

"Two?"

"Yes," he said. "We're taking Morgan to be captain of another ship."

I didn't say anything. But I couldn't think of anyone I would rather not lose than Morgan. I realized with a rush how much I had grown to like this tall, quiet, dependable man.

Life on the *Paducah* settled into an easy and quiet routine. There had been a sense of tightening up since the two engineers and the third mate left. Those of us on the ship now were bound a little closer, all of us with a common aim. Friendships between the men were cementing. Living and working together was rubbing off the rough corners. Eli and Syd had become outstanding in their deck skills. When I asked Dave, the chief steward, about his mess crew, he praised them all. "Wurm, Kallner, and Ball are first-class." Charlie had commented that the men in the engine room—Bock, Nieder, Kite, Lipshutz, Gilbert, Lombard, and Rotter—were standing up to the heat very well.

The woods that grew right down to the dock were honeycombed with paths, and many of the men had taken to strolling quietly through the trees in the early evening after supper, wandering and exploring and listening to the calls of the birds they had never seen before. One path followed the winding and curving Adour River all the way to Le Barre, where there was a settlement of fishermen. Some of the men had made friends with them and spent evening hours there, drinking wine. Henry, the Scot, had become a great favorite of the crew. His words were thick with the burr of his brogue, but with his sharp wits he could outtalk Sholom and Rotter together. But Henry was somehow a lonely figure. He crept through the ship with his tape measure, and he spent hours in the chart room poring over technical volumes in three languages. When his day's work was finished, he went back to the town alone, peddling a battered old French bicycle into the dusk.

Since the pounding and sawing made sleep on the ship impossible, the crew and officers had been distributed around the town. I had a room at the Grand Hotel, an ancient hotel in Bayonne, away from the expensive tourist traffic of Biarritz. Most of the men had found their own lodging; the word was that Eli and Syd had the upper apartment of a house of ill repute. When asked directly if they had an inside route in the hotel, they smiled.

Lew Brettschneider, Dave Gutmann, and Larry Kohlberg had made some sort of an agreement among themselves. They had leveled their three new titles of second engineer, third engineer, and day engineer to "The Three Deuces," so that the honor as well as the responsibility would be shared equally.

On their days off, most of the men headed for the beaches at Biarritz and lay in the warm sand and fell in love collectively with all the lovely French girls in their minimal bathing suits, which were nothing but a pair of small bandanas. Or less—many of the women were topless. And the hopes of the men were kept perpetually high by statistics quoted by somebody to the effect that there were eight French women for every man. They kept forgetting that a lot of American soldiers were stationed in and around Biarritz during and after the war and that Americans were not an irresistible novelty, but the local inhabitants reminded them of it by quoting their own statistics on misbehavior.

Dave Gutmann said he and Brettschneider were having little success with the local girls. Apparently Lew with his flaming red hair and Dave with the red tinge in his reminded the French girls of the German submariners who were based here during the war.

For a quiet evening, most of us went ashore before supper, riding the streetcar into Bayonne and getting off at the square, where the people sipped their drinks and read their newspapers in the waning light at the sidewalk cafes. We walked through the square and into a narrow little street where there was a small restaurant in the shadow of the soaring spires of the cathedral. It was a cozy restaurant with white tablecloths, and the waitress was a beautiful young Spanish girl who had been asked for a date by almost all of the men on the *Paducah* and had smilingly declined them all. We loved Dave's cooking, but on most nights we preferred a long and leisurely French meal with a bottle of Bordeaux wine. We never finished eating before nine o'clock, but as the movie never started before nine, we didn't hurry. French dialogue had been dubbed in, and we were fascinated by the perfect accents of our Hollywood stars.

We were sleeping on board the *Paducah* again now. If the night was warm and clear, we usually passed up the streetcar, which stopped running at midnight, and walked the three miles back to the ship along the path that wound through the trees and twisted with the river, which flowed silently along in the night. Aboard the ship we stopped in the mess room for coffee and a snack and then turned in, full of contentment that sometimes made us feel vaguely guilty, as though we had not yet won the right to have this much peace.

I was lying on my bunk one night, listening to the crash of rain and the sounds of the storm that blew up suddenly after supper, when I heard a vague shout from the dock, but I couldn't make it out. Then there came a loud rapping at the door, and when I shouted, "Come in!" Sholom appeared, dripping and excited.

"The steward is dead!"

That brought me onto my feet. "What happened?"

"I don't know," Sholom said, still out of breath from running. "I was in a little bar when that agent, the one with the beard, came in and said, 'Get the Captain. The steward is dead.' I grabbed a cab, and here I am. That's all I know."

I grabbed a raincoat, and we hustled down the gangway and into the cab. We groped slowly to town through the downpour. "He's in a hotel," Sholom said. "The agent gave me the address." And he handed a slip of paper to the driver. It took a long time to get there.

The cab pulled up in front of a small hotel. As we entered, the clerk took one look at us and gestured upstairs. On the second floor we found an open door and a room filled with people. The agent was there, and Gingi. Two uniformed policemen were making an itemized list of everything in sight. The bed was in disarray. On the far side of it, on the floor on his back, was Dave, his head turned toward the wall. In the middle of the room were his shoes, one of them lying on its side, as though he had removed them and tossed them aside carelessly. On the dresser was a bottle of cognac, two-thirds empty. And spread out on a dresser were a number of galley knives he had brought ashore to have sharpened.

"What happened?" I asked Gingi.

He shrugged. "I'm not sure. But you can draw some conclusions. Dave had a girl here with him. Apparently the girl was too much for him."

One of the French cops made a sly remark, and a chuckle swept the room.

"What did he say?" I asked Gingi.

"He said, 'There are few better ways to die than the way Dave went.' "

"Is the girl being held?" I asked.

The policeman understood sufficient English. He said to me, directly, "No, Captain. We allowed her to go. The heart of your steward apparently just stopped."

Gingi asked, "Where are his papers?"

We looked through his clothes and wallet. In a closet was the steward's coat, and in a pocket, his wallet. But it contained only some franc notes, nothing in the way of identification. "His papers must be aboard the ship."

"You'd better go and look for them," Gingi said. "I will stay and handle this part of it."

So I rode through the noisy night to the ship again. In the steward's room I found a pack of old letters and the odds and ends of documents a wandering man accumulates and are somehow taken to explain his presence on the earth. Among the letters I found several from the French girl in Cairo, and I made a note of her name and address so that we could write to her. And there was an older letter, quite old in fact, from a girl in Oregon, and at the end of it was written, "I love you." There was a union book with the dues paid up for the year. And a notification from the Congregation Ben Samuel to the effect that his father had been properly buried. Next to that was a paper officially certifying the death of his mother. I noted that her religion was listed as Lutheran. So Dave was half-Jewish after all. I gathered all the papers together and rode through the rain again to the hotel.

I found Gingi waiting in the lobby. "They removed the body for an autopsy," he told me. We went out in the rain again to try to find the bureau where the steward's death could be legally certified and the formalities completed for the private voyage he had undertaken.

The next day Dave Wurm took over the cooking. He came up with some soggy pancakes for breakfast, and the coffee was bitter. But none of us had any appetite anyway.

In the afternoon I was required to be present when the body was placed in a coffin: the French officials had to be assured that this was *our* steward and not anybody else's sailor. After I convinced them, a French tinsmith closed the cover of the metal box and soldered the joint that sealed the cook out of this world.

Back aboard the ship we all discussed the matter of the funeral services and finally agreed that since Dave was studying his catechism, he might well be laid to rest with Catholic prayers. None of us could think of any harm it would do him.

On the day of the funeral a cavalcade of taxis lined up on the dock, and all of us, except a few who had to be left on the ship, rode slowly into town and up to the ancient cathedral. We were a strange-looking lot, the men of the *Paducah*. We did not have enough decent-looking clothes for all of us to be dressed up at once. There had been considerable swapping and lending. And now we had tall men in short pants and small men in oversized coats. I was the only one aboard who owned a black necktie.

So the priests chanted in Latin over the body of the man who had a Jewish father and a Lutheran mother and whose last aim in life had been to settle down for a few final years of comfort with a Catholic wife in a town in Egypt and who seemed happiest when he was drinking whiskey and singing a cowboy ballad.

We filed out of the dim cathedral and followed the coffin to the cemetery, where arrangements had been made to keep it in a vault for six months. That should be time enough for his body to be claimed—if there was anyone anywhere concerned enough to claim it. All of us crowded into the squat building heavy with the musty odor of death. The place was filled with hundreds of tiny coffins, all of them only two or three feet long. An attendant explained that these contained the bodies of babies of refugee Spanish Republicans who were waiting to bury them fittingly in Spanish soil when again they could call it their own. And as I walked out into the sunlight, I thought to myself that the steward would have a lot of democratic little shipmates on his final voyage.

12 ✳ Arrivals

Late in the afternoon, just before quitting time on a day some three weeks after we tied up to the dock, I made a round of the ship and found the *Paducah* transformed drastically. Rough board bunks were being built into every available square inch of her. Gedda and Henry, the Scot, were getting their loudspeakers up, placing them so that not a single person aboard the ship would ever be out of reach of the sound of a voice from the bridge. Sheet-metal workers were installing a ventilating system that would direct fresh air into every remote corner. But there were so many bunks being built that I was amazed. And at the stern rail from one side to the other, with a partition separating them into two groups, were toilets hanging over the sea.

When I found Moka on an upper deck, I asked him, "How many people do you intend to bring aboard?"

"Fifteen hundred," he said calmly.

"Fifteen *hundred*!" I shouted. "On this ship? They won't be able to move. They won't be able to breathe. I carried troops during the war, and we crowded them, but never like this. Hell, it's impossible."

"Crowded, yes. Impossible, no. Believe me, friend," he said, "we are not new at this. We know what we are doing. First of all, even if we stacked the people in rows, they would be better off than where they are. I don't know if you have seen the camps we are taking them out of. If you haven't seen them, you cannot imagine it. And you can't be told what it is like because you won't believe it. It's beyond understanding. Only if you have lived in them will you know. That's what the ships are for, so that no person, anywhere, in any time ever on this earth, should be forced to live like this again.

"Think of it this way, too: these ships are the hopes and the very life of hundreds of thousands. We can carry only a small percentage of these, but by carrying those few we literally save the lives of all the others. So long as they know the ships are running, they have something to hold onto. Without the ships they would have nothing, no vision of anything but the barbed wire before their faces. Our ships, these poor little old tubs, are a lifeline for all of our people. They sustain themselves with these symbols of a new life."

"I'm sorry," I said quietly. "I didn't stop to think before I opened my big mouth." He was still standing there at the rail looking off across the river as I walked away.

There was a change in the French workers' attitude toward us. I mentioned it to Heavy, who replied, "They've gone cold on us." The friendliness was gone. The pace of the work had slowed. The Frenchmen no longer congregated in the crew's mess room to swap their cigarettes for ours and to exchange a glass of red wine for a cup of American coffee.

"It can mean only one thing," Moka said. "We must have a meeting of the crew at once."

When the men were assembled, Moka wasted no time. "There is something wrong with the French workers," he declared. "Do any of you know what it is?"

The room was silent, and the men exchanged puzzled glances.

"All right," Moka said. "We must act quickly. Whatever you are doing, drop it, and find out what's wrong with the Frenchmen. Mingle with them. Talk to them. All of you by now must have made friends among them. Ask them. Don't be too obvious about it, but find out. We must know today before it's too late. The captain and I will be in his room. As soon as you learn something, report to us immediately."

In my room we waited nervously. It was Martin Gooen, the radio operator, who reported first.

"I've become good friends with that young boy who runs the electric saw," he said. "So I asked him what was wrong. At first he wouldn't talk. But when I pressed him, he blurted it out. 'Why do Jews help fascists?' he asked me. All the men have been told that this ship is being fitted to carry arms from the United States for French fascists."

Moka rocked back and forth on my bunk with his arms around his knees and grinned. "So they've arrived," he said. "First they create an atmosphere of suspicion, distrust, and hostility. Then the act of violence. But this time we can beat them. Thank you, Martin," he said, and he hopped off the bunk and strode out of the room. Martin followed.

In a few minutes Moka was back with an elderly French workman, a gaunt-faced old fellow with an enormous white mustache. "This man," Moka informed me, "is the trade union shop chairman of the ship workers.

I'll have to tell him what we are doing." And he began to explain patiently in French.

I watched the old man's face as he sat down. It was wrinkled in a mixture of curiosity and suspicion. Moka pounded away. The old man lifted his eyebrows. Moka produced the plans of the work and a drawing of how the ship would look when all the refitting was done. And then he told him of the *Pan Crescent*, another refugee ship. She was sunk in Italy when a magnetic mine was mysteriously attached to her hull. Fortunately, the water was not deep, and it was possible to save her. The old man's face sharpened with interest. When he got up, he was smiling grimly, and he shook hands with each of us with a solid grip. "*Bonne chance*," he said and walked out.

In a little while the whine of the electric saw and the pounding of hammers halted abruptly, and the ship went quiet. Moka and I looked at each other. What now? We hurried out on deck. Back on the fantail the French workers were clustered around the old man, who was standing on a bitt and talking to them quietly, from time to time pounding a fist into a palm to emphasize a point. When the meeting broke up, the men went back to their work—and as they passed us, they looked at us and smiled.

"Well," Moka announced two days later, "tomorrow the replacements will come aboard. A mate and a cook."

"We need a third mate, too," I reminded him.

"Can you promote someone from the crew?" he asked. "It is difficult to find trained officers here."

"I could promote Sholom. But I want him to stay on deck. I'll need him there. Of the others, either George or Heavy could handle the job."

"Which will be the best?" Moka asked.

"Well, they're both good men. But Heavy has been to sea longer, and he's made the trip before. Heavy would be best."

"Good. Then Heavy will be third mate."

When they came aboard, the replacements—two Spaniards—didn't waste any time before getting to work. They were eager to be doing something, as though they had a need to prove to themselves that they were still a part of something and capable of useful effort. The new chief mate, Miguel Buiza, was addressed as "Don." He was a thin, tall man with a high-domed, gaunt face that looked ascetic even with the neat pencil-line mustache. Francisco Romero, the cook, was short and fat and bald.

Neither of them knew much English, but we introduced ourselves. Don Miguel wanted to acquaint himself with the ship; with a pencil and a notebook he leaped in and out of lifeboats, listing and checking their contents and inspecting the boats for their safety. Then he went prowling everywhere. Romero, whose name was promptly cut down to "Chico," blasted into the galley in a big white apron and a high white chef's hat. The whole crew cheered him; we were sick of David's sad cooking, though we had to give him kudos for trying. Dave had been in the combat engineers in Europe in World War II, where his cooking experience had been KP duty—peeling potatoes and washing dishes.

On the evening of the day the Spaniards came aboard I was standing at the rail watching the French shore workers go down the gangway after their day's work. Buiza and Romero watched, too. Suddenly, Buiza uttered a sharp exclamation. Turning, I saw him pointing toward one of the workmen and speaking excitedly to Romero, who stared at the workman with hatred.

"*Capitan*! That man. You see the one?" Miguel called to me, pointing again. "That man is a spy. We know him well. He is for Franco a spy!"

Later, with an interpreter, we got the story. The man first appeared at meetings of Spanish Republicans in Marseille. Several men sent into Spain to work with the guerrillas were arrested just over the border. To prove their suspicions of him, the Republicans allowed the purported spy to get papers bearing fictitious names but genuine addresses in Bilbao. Within a short time the houses bearing those addresses were raided by the Guardia Civil.

Moka had the man discharged at once. It struck me that the man was lucky. Judging from the look of hatred that clouded the face of Don Miguel at the sight of him, I was convinced that if Buiza had encountered him face to face, he would have killed him.

Sunday came with its quiet, and there was no sound of work to disturb the ship or the nearby woods. And I was beginning to feel restless. I thought all of us were, especially Moka, although he hadn't spoken of it. We all were anxious to get on our way, to get on with the thing that had brought us here, to get it done. Thinking of it too long in anticipation was making us nervous. But the construction work still went on, and we did not know yet when we would be ready to sail.

Around eight o'clock in the evening, Gingi sat down alongside me on the bench in the mess room, where I was having a cup of coffee.

"I'd like to tell you about your new Chief Mate Buiza," he said. "His full name is Miguel Buiza Fernandez Palacios. He was commander of the Spanish Republican Navy. He came from a noted Seville family and was a career naval officer. When Franco revolted against the legal Spanish government, Buiza was one of the few regular naval officers who stayed with the republic. I heard he was a liberal Republican, something like one of your Democrats in the U.S. In short order he became Vice Admiral, Spain's highest naval rank, and then chief of staff of the navy. When Franco won, Buiza took his fleet to French-controlled Bizerte and surrendered it to the French.

"It has been a honor to offer work to him. After World War II started, Buiza, who was living in Oran, offered himself to the French Foreign Legion. He was accepted and given the rank of captain—the only time in Legion history that such a commission had been offered to a new recruit. Buiza's Spanish Legionnaires fought from North Africa up the Italian boot to the final defeat of the fascists. His was one of the most decorated units in the French army."

13 ✳ *"We Forget Nothing"*

All day long the bunks were built and the installations were made. The *Paducah* was slowly being transformed into a crude passenger ship. At night the crew went ashore, and we dawdled through the long French meals and went to the American movies with French dialogue, took our walks in the woods, went fishing at Le Barre, and waited and waited until we would be ready to sail.

Moka called another meeting of the crew.

"What is it this time?" I asked.

"I'd rather not talk about it," he said solemnly. But in the mess room he, Gedda, Tabor, and Gingi laughed loudly among themselves while waiting for the men to assemble. When they were present, Moka spoke.

"It has come to us," he said, "through our own channels, that most of you have contributed to a fund being collected for a poor girl in Biarritz."

This was the first I had heard of it, but the men exchanged embarrassed looks. One of the men spoke up.

"She told me she'd been in Dachau and that her mother and father were both killed. And she wanted to go to Palestine. So we gathered a little money among ourselves to help her out."

"I can't criticize your intentions," Moka said. "But your destitute girl is an old acquaintance of ours. She's a British agent. I must warn all of you again to be on guard and to be careful. Stay away from that girl. For Jews who really need help, there are several organizations. Relieving distress is hardly your responsibility. That's all."

But Henry, the Scot, had a word. "Ye've soft hearts," he said, looking at the men, "and soft heads to go with them. But ye've touched me, and I cannot bear to think of the girl in need. Give her this for me." And he laid a button on the table. The other Shou-shous stepped up and added a streetcar ticket, the stub of a movie ticket, and a torn one-franc note, and they walked out solemnly. The men grinned sheepishly, and the meeting was over.

The construction work went on. Now a shore gang began ripping out the partitions between the two mess rooms and the galley.

"What's this?" Baird, the chief engineer, asked at supper time.

"They're going to combine the crew's and the officers' mess rooms to make more space."

"You mean we'll eat with the sailors and the black gang?" The black gang was the engine room workers.

"Sure," I replied.

Baird studied it. He was unusually young to have a chief engineer's license, but he was competent and did his job all the way. The chief had strict standards, and he was obviously distressed at the thought of the risk to ship's discipline for the officers to eat in the same room with unlicensed personnel. He looked at me; I grinned back at him. Finally, he said, "Hmmph," and fell to eating.

But later he asked, "How will we sit?"

"I don't know. I haven't thought about it."

"Well," he said, "I think we ought to have a separate table."

"OK," I said.

Changing the subject, I said, "I heard a funny story today. A Greek shipowner bought himself a vessel in the United States, and on his way back to Greece with her he stopped at Gibraltar for oil and water. The British convinced themselves that it was a Hagana ship, and they sent a party of soldiers aboard to seize her. The Greek screamed, 'Piracy!' and raised such a bloody big stink that the British withdrew their soldiers. But they didn't want to take any chances. Before the ship left, someone opened the sea cocks and scuttled the ship right in the harbor. Now the Greek is suing for everything he can dream of. The beauty of it is that it was his ship and had nothing to do with the Hagana!"

Moka laughed.

"I just hope we won't have to put into Gibraltar for anything," I added.

After supper Moka and I went out on deck to smoke and to watch the dusk settle over the woods. A police car bounded up to the gangway and stopped with a jerk. Two cops got out and opened the back door. Heavy stepped out. His clothes were torn, and his face was bruised. Two more cops followed him out of the car. The lot of them came clumping up the gangway. Silently, Moka and I led them to my room. I asked Heavy what happened, and one of the cops began talking excitedly. I shut him off and turned to Heavy again. He tried to grin, but the result wasn't too good: one side of his face was puffed out.

"Guess I'll have to borrow some money from you, Captain, to pay these dogs off. Had a hell of a time talking them into bringing me to the ship. And then they sent four of them along." He glared at the cops, and one of them started up again.

"Tell him to shut up," I said to Moka. "Tell him we want to listen to Heavy first."

The cop subsided sullenly, and Heavy continued.

"Aw, it's nothin'," he said. "Last night I won a hat full of francs at the casino at Biarritz. Then I had a few drinks, and it was late, so I went to the Grand Hotel to spend the night there. When I asked for a room, the clerk called me '*chien*'—a dog—and said something in French that I wasn't sure of. So I asked him if he could say it in English. So he said, 'We have no room for dogs.' That's what I thought he said the first time. So I just leaned over and let him have it. He went down like he was shot. I guess that made me madder than ever: he didn't give me time to hit him again.

"On the wall behind the desk there was a board with all the hotel keys on it. I reached over and grabbed the board and went outside, and I scattered the keys all over the street. Then the jerk came to and ran out and hollered, 'Police!' And I decided not to run. Hell, I was the guy that was insulted. When the cops came, they didn't understand English. So when one of them grabbed me by the arm and started jerking, I hit him, too. It was a beaut while it lasted. But they locked me up."

Moka questioned the cops, and one of them produced an itemized list of damages. Moka translated it for us: "Replacement of keys—five hundred francs. Medical treatment for hotel clerk—five hundred francs. Fine for disturbing the peace—one thousand francs." It totaled about $170 U.S.

I counted out the money, handed it to the cops, and got a receipt. "What happened to the francs you won?" I asked Heavy.

He tried to grin again. "I don't know," he said. "These cops must have rolled me."

"You weren't drunk, were you?"

"Well, not very," he said with the same feeble grin.

"I ought to log you for letting yourself get arrested."

On the way out, one of the cops made a declaration.

"What did he say?" I asked Moka.

"He said that if they have any more trouble with this man, the fine will be doubled and he'll get a jail sentence."

"The only thing I'm sorry about," Heavy said, "is the way that clerk went down so fast. I wanted to work him over."

Moka and I rode into Bayonne with Don Miguel to meet his friend Pablo, who had just come out of Spain. We got off at the square and walked past the cathedral and beyond it the ancient citadel, centuries old but still garrisoned with soldiers. Buiza took us to a small cafe, where we found a table with a red-and-white checked tablecloth. We all ordered co-gnac from a waiter with a moon face and eyes that protruded like a frog's. A man walked in, saw Miguel, and came toward us. The left sleeve of his coat was empty, and the end of it was tucked into the pocket. He nodded and sat down while Buiza introduced us. Pablo's skin was very dark, his jet-black eyes topped by heavy black eyebrows, and there were deep hollows be-tween the high cheekbones and the square jaws. It was a harsh face.

"How is it in Spain?" I asked.

"*Malo*," he said. "*Todo es malo*. Everything is bad."

When the waiter brought the cognac, Pablo lifted his drink and said, "*Salud!*" And looking at me, he added, "To the Americans of the Interna-tional Brigade."

"That seems like a long time ago," I remarked.

"For exactness, it is eleven years," he said. "But, *hombre*,"—he smiled— "we forget nothing. We do not forget one single thing."

"To remember everything isn't pleasant," Moka said. "But he's right. If we ever allowed ourselves to forget, it would be like dying. I have known some who have decided to forget everything. They are as useless as dead men. They have made a peace with their own doom."

"That is true," Buiza said. "But also to remember means to hate. I have thought much about this, and it is still sometimes strange to me, but if one does not know how to hate properly, he does not know how to live properly in this world. I think that the man who cannot hate cannot truly love, either."

Sitting with these three men, I felt like an innocent; Moka with the weight of the memory of six million murdered Jews and a continuing war for a patch of land to live on, the Spaniards with the memory of Guernica and the tiny coffins stacked in a vault because not one of them could yet lay claim to three feet of free earth of their own to serve as a grave.

"Ay, *hombre*," Pablo said with a friendly grip on my shoulder, "I drink to the Americans of the Brigade. They taught me English, them and the British. They were good men. I fought with them, and I know."

Lightening up, he proposed, "Let's drink to the American cigarette." With chuckles, we downed the drinks.

"What are conditions like in Spain now?" I asked. "Buiza says you have just. . . . "

"Let us not speak of that in a public cafe," Pablo said quickly, glancing about the small room. "Ears grow long in this part of the country. What should I tell you? We have an old slogan: '*Resistir y fortificar es vencer.*' How would you make that in English, Miguel?"

"Hold out and fortify and you will win," he said. "And there is another saying we learned in the days of the war: '*Hay que tomar la muerte como si fuera aspirina.*' You have to take death like an aspirin."

"Between these two," Pablo said, "we live. Let us drink and talk of other things."

So we talked about the merits of Spanish women over French women, but we couldn't reach any conclusion. The women of each country seemed to be different in their values, personality, appearance, and courage.

We ordered more cognac, and the Spaniards talked about the coming bullfight, and then we went home to the ship. Pablo waved his one arm at us as we parted.

14 * Not a Game

I wandered around below decks watching the carpenters work. The *Paducah* was becoming a jungle of bunks crammed into every available space from deck to overhead, from bulkhead to bulkhead, with only the narrowest of passageways between them. It was going to be rough on people crowded into these quarters, but Moka insisted that it would be better than what they were used to having. That was hard to believe, but I did. Still, I wished they wouldn't be so crowded; I liked to think of myself as a humane skipper with a happy ship.

Up on deck I stopped and watched a man with an acetylene torch cut a neat round hole in the steel deck plate. Later a ventilator pipe would be run through the hole to carry air to the crowded bunks below. The torch with its hissing blue bullet-flame ate cleanly through the steel with a little splutter of hot sparks. As I watched, I heard Sholom's low whistle, the whistle that could mean only one thing. I turned and looked. Coming up the gangway with Gingi was a dark-haired girl, and waiting to greet them were Moka and Gedda. I walked over, and Gingi said, "Good morning, Captain. I'd like you to meet Maia. She might be your special radio operator."

"How d'you do?" I greeted Maia. "Special radio operator?"

"We're installing a special radio below decks," Moka said. "Once we're in the Mediterranean, we'll be in constant touch with our own shore station. We need our own operators who know Hebrew and our codes. Hebrew is a great secret service language; so few people can understand it." He grinned.

"You wouldn't guess it from looking at her, but Maia has made three trips through the blockade already," he added.

Indeed, I wouldn't have guessed it. She was a very pretty girl and appeared far too young to be running blockades. But these Hagana people were always surprising me with their quiet competence, which seemed so casual and offhand. Maia smiled at me and said nothing.

"Do you mind if I show her the ship?" Gingi asked.

"Of course not. Do you want me to lead the way?"

"That won't be necessary," he said. "I can find my way around. Remember, I helped draft the plans for refitting her."

As they moved away, Sholom walked up. "Did I hear somebody say she would be our radio operator?"

"She might be," Moka said, smiling.

"Oh, brother," Sholom said. "Why didn't I think of it before? That's what this ship has needed right along, a radio operator like her."

"Who is she?" I asked Moka.

"She's from Germany. The only survivor of her family. She was three years in Auschwitz. After the war she got out and came to Palestine in the illegal immigration. During the trip she established herself as a leader of the people. She had strength, and she had courage. We're always looking for people like her. There aren't many, but the few who came through the German camps with their strength and their courage intact are the best people of all. Nothing can break them. So we trained her as a radio operator. She's been captured twice by the British; once she got through."

"You said she *might* be our operator," Sholom said. "What do you mean, *might*?"

"We have another ship almost ready to sail. She'll go out on whichever one leaves first."

"Can't we hurry this damned work?" Sholom cried.

In the afternoon they sent a taxi down to the dock for her. She was going out on some ship now in Italy.

I asked Gingi where Morgan's new ship was.

"She's on her way here from Sète, a small French fishing-tourist port in the Mediterranean."

"Be here soon?" I asked.

"Tomorrow in the afternoon," Gingi said. "And she may have created some trouble for us. The French were trying to put a claim on her for damage to the docks. A subterfuge the British instigated. But she slipped out without a pilot or clearance from the port. They may try to seize her here, and us along with her."

The next morning Gingi came aboard just after lunch and called Moka and the other Shou-shous to my cabin. From his face and manner we could tell that he was agitated.

"We may have to sail soon," he informed us. "We'll try to finish the work here, but we must be ready to leave at a moment's notice. I've already arranged for fuel and water to be delivered as soon as possible. The British are increasing their pressure on the French government."

"Where will we go from here?" I asked. Gingi looked at me in a manner that reminded me of Moka's firm reply to me once before when I had asked a question—"We will know when it is time to know."

But Gingi said simply, "We don't know yet. You may even have to sail before we know. In that case, you'll get your orders by radio."

"What brought this on?" Moka asked.

"A second ship at Sète. An American ship," he said, "the *Warfield*, an old riverboat. She's carrying 4,500 refugees, the biggest vessel we've ever run. I don't know if you're familiar with the port of Sète. I've been there. Its harbor is surrounded by a breakwater, and the only outlet to the sea is like a jigsaw puzzle. There are three parallel seawalls, a breakwater at right angles to them, and an extremely narrow channel for an exit, with many shallow places. We offered a French pilot one million francs to take her out, but he refused."

"What happened?" I asked.

"The American crew decided to take her out themselves. They let go the lines about two o'clock in the morning. They ran aground twice and ran into one of the seawalls once. It took them an hour of twisting and turning to reach the narrow channel, and most of the time they thought they would never make it. When they did get into the Mediterranean, two British destroyers and a cruiser were waiting for them. They're following her now. They'll attack as soon as she reaches the territorial waters of Palestine. And now we can expect them to tighten up on the *Paducah*."

"What's our name for the riverboat?" Moka asked.

"*Exodus 1947*," Gingi said.

The *Exodus 1947*. She was on her way to Palestine, and we would hear more about her in the coming weeks.

When we left my cabin and walked out to the deck, all of us noticed a well-dressed young man on the dock. Wearing flannel slacks and tweed jacket and hatless under the bright sun, he looked like a tourist as he strolled slowly up and down, looking the *Paducah* over very carefully. Gingi spoke to Moka in Hebrew. Without a word Moka set off at a fast walk for the gangway. The young man stopped when he saw him approaching, then turned and took off at a dead run up the road. Moka ran after him. They both disappeared around a bend.

"Who was that?" I asked Gingi.

"I don't know."

"But the way you spoke to Moka I thought—"

"I never saw the young man before in my life," Gingi said. "I simply told Moka to go down and find out what he wanted. When he ran, he told us all we need to know."

In a few minutes Moka returned, out of breath.

"Well?" Gingi said.

"He had a car waiting for him. Another man at the wheel with the engine going. British diplomatic license plates." He slapped the ship's side in disgust.

In the afternoon we called the crew together and divided them into two watches. Shore leave was cut down to a few men at a time. The French workers began to work overtime, using bright cluster lamps after dark.

Next night the sound of a shot snapped me awake. When I rushed out to the deck, Moka was leaning over the rail with a pistol in his hand. I could hear the sound of a small boat pulling away, and voices speaking excitedly in French.

"Maybe the British, and maybe not," he said. "Not taking any chances. I shot in the air and told them to get away from here."

The next day the police guard at our gangway was doubled, and everyone leaving the *Paducah* or coming aboard was searched. The gendarmes were apologetic about it. "It is orders," they murmured as they gave us a quick frisk and examined any packages we might be carrying. We submitted passively, but none of us liked the procedure.

During the war the French had experienced the humiliation and the fist of German occupation. Because of this, some of the French, both in the government and the population, could understand the plight of the Jewish refugees and were sympathetic to the ship and its crew. They had, after all, given permission for the ship to be refitted in Bayonne. But there were others who had different views.

Gingi brought the local newspapers aboard and translated the headlines for us. It was charged that we were loaded with munitions. We were called a threat to the peace of Bayonne. It was reported that the British Admiralty had complained that France was giving active aid to the illegal immigration to Palestine.

"This is only the beginning," Gingi said. "These attacks will become stronger, but only in a section of the press, the extreme right-wing papers that are susceptible to British pressure. Nevertheless, they will try to drive us out of the harbor. We'll have to hurry."

Two dignitaries from Paris boarded the *Paducah* with a police escort. It was necessary to sign a document declaring that the ship would not take aboard in Bayonne any Jews bound for Palestine in violation of British immigration quotas. The two officials were embarrassed. They assured me that they personally had the greatest goodwill toward us, but this, unfortunately, was a matter beyond their control and related to the diplomatic relations between two sovereign powers. Surely I could understand that in such affairs one was compelled to abide by international agreements. With an apologetic shrug they laid the document on my desk. I signed it readily; it had not been our intention at any time to receive passengers in this port, anyway. The two officials seemed relieved. They shook hands with me warmly, but before they left, they glanced skeptically at each other and at me, as though the suspicion had occurred to them that they were being tricked and the *Paducah* might after all be a threat to Bayonne and to France herself.

Next day a string of oil cars was brought up the railroad tracks on the dock. Our hoses were coupled, and the pumping began. In the afternoon a large packet of French charts was sent aboard. We opened them in the chart room and found that they covered the Aegean and the Black seas. This was the first inkling we had of where we might go next. We left Dave Greer there to study them; he would be our navigating officer.

Later in the afternoon Gingi came aboard and into my cabin with Moka.

"We've just received the details of the arrival of the *Exodus* in Palestine," he said, looking closely at me.

"What happened?"

"There was a battle," he said. "The Americans fought like—well, they fought like heroes. It's a word I don't like; it's overused and misused. But sometimes it's the only word that can be used. I think this is one of the times.

"They were headed toward Gaza, about twenty miles offshore—not yet in territorial waters—when the British challenged them. British destroyers, one on each side, rammed her together. Our report says they caught her on the rise of a swell, and then she hung in the air between them for a moment before settling back into the sea. They tossed strings of firecrackers aboard and fired tear gas, to cause fear and panic. Eighteen British soldiers, armed with pistols and clubs, boarded her at the boat deck. One boy, a young immigrant orphan, was shot point-blank in the face and killed instantly when they went aboard. The people fought back—with potatoes and tins of food. The American officers and some of the sailors barricaded themselves in the wheelhouse. The soldiers fired through the door. Then they broke in, swinging their clubs. They hit the first mate in the head. Later he died in a hospital ashore from a fractured skull. His name was Bill Bernstein.

"Most of the crew was captured and locked up, but six men held out in the wheelhouse and steered a course for Haifa. Finally the soldiers captured the wheelhouse, but some of the crew made their way aft to the steering engine. They disconnected the cables to the wheelhouse and steered with the engine itself. The British tried to put more boarding parties on her, but the *Exodus* zigzagged so they couldn't make it. Then the destroyers began ramming her systematically. When it became clear that they would sink her with all 4,500 passengers, the crew called for a truce. The British conducted her into Haifa.

"According to our reports, at least four persons were killed: three passengers and the mate. We don't know how many were hospitalized. Five destroyers and a cruiser were used against her—an old, unarmed riverboat loaded with women and children. The attack lasted three hours. The entire city of Tel Aviv has shut down in protest."

When Gingi left, I called the crew together as if it were a usual "coffee time" and told them the story. "Talk it around," I told them. "Tell everybody aboard what happened. Give them all the details. I think a lot of us had the idea we were playing a more-or-less polite game of hide-and-seek. Well, it's not polite, and it's not a game. Everybody aboard and ashore, where you have your new friends, should know it."

It was nearly ten o'clock at night when Gingi came aboard again, a thin young man with him. "This is Ben Kulbersh, your special radio operator," Gingi said. "You'll have to sail no later than daylight. The British are taking out a warrant tomorrow to seize the ship. We should finish loading the oil at four o'clock. A pilot will come aboard at five."

"What's our next port?"

"We don't know yet," Gingi replied. "I've cleared the ship through customs for Livorno, Italy, and that's the way the papers are made out, but you won't go there. Lay a course for Alborán Island. Before you get there, we'll radio you your destination."

Don Miguel, Dave Greer, and I went to the bridge and studied the chart. Alborán Island was a tiny spot of land in the Mediterranean about one hundred and forty miles due east of Gibraltar, and almost exactly midway between the coast of North Africa and Spain. We left Dave there to plot his course.

All night long the work went on, and the big hoses from the oil cars pulsed with the steady beat of the pumps. The French shore workers were sweating under bright cluster lamps and floodlights putting the last touches to their work, spiking in the last of the uprights for the wooden bunks, welding ventilating pipes in place, and finishing the job of making our mess rooms into one. Moka made a hurried trip into town by taxi and came back with a bulky package. He stowed it away in a corner under the bunk in his room. Sholom and the entire deck crew prowled fore and aft, cleaning up the litter of the shore workers, lashing down all heavy objects, and making everything secure. On the dock the gendarmes stared at us curiously.

A little after four in the morning the pumping was finished, and the empty oil tank cars were shunted off the dock. We started up our gyro-compass, its rotor humming, and set its repeaters on the bridge to the heading of the *Paducah* at the dock. We tested the steering gear and the whistle and the engine-room telegraph. Down below, the engines were turned over slowly as the steam pressure rose in the boilers. We were all ready, and I went to my cabin to relax a bit before the pilot came aboard.

But I did not even get my shoes off before Don Miguel and Greer were both at my door. "The gyro," Greer said. "Something is wrong. She oscillates and won't settle down."

I was alarmed at the thought of making this long run using only our magnetic compass. It had a variable error, changing capriciously day by day; we had to compensate for it on every new heading, and we could never be certain of our true course.

If the gyro was oscillating, the trouble was probably in the rectifier tubes. I crawled down the narrow ladder into the generator room. The heat down there hit me like a blow. I removed the black metal cover and found the base of the tubes to be a mass of rust. I could see where moisture from the sweating steel overhead had dripped into the box.

Back on the bridge, I told Greer, "Shut her down. We'll have no gyro from here on." We would be dependent on the erratic magnetic compass.

The first small streaks of dawn were showing when the pilot came aboard. Solemnly Moka and I shook hands with the old foreman of the French workers, and solemnly he wished us good luck. Then he herded his men together, and they trooped down the gangway with their tools. We said good-bye to Henry Tabor, the Scot. Moka and Gedda embraced when they parted. Gingi was the last to leave the ship.

All of them stood in a tight knot on the dock and waved as we pulled slowly out into the river, turned around and headed downstream. It was full day by the time we crossed Le Barre and stopped to let the pilot off.

15 ∗ Out of Command

For a long time after we dropped
the pilot, I stood on the bridge and stared back at the land mass and the
peaks of the Pyrenees and watched them dwindle as the *Paducah* pulled
steadily away. I felt no elation at our success in escaping one jump ahead of
the British. I had felt elated when we cleared New York and put to sea, and
again when we sailed from Horta with Carley staring at us from his office
window. These had been small personal triumphs, and they had made me
feel good. But now I felt that we were being pushed away, driven off, and
that every door was closed against us. I had first felt this sensation when
Carley came aboard in Horta and in his cold, clipped, precise manner had
let me know that we would get nothing from him. A thought had flashed
through my mind: it was like being locked out of the world. We had confronted the same closed door in Lisbon. Now, in Bayonne, another door
had been slammed shut against us. It seemed to me that I was discovering
what it meant to be a Jew. Now I, too, was a Jew, and the *Paducah* herself
bore a curse, and we were driven from one closed door to confront another
closed door. Well, if that was the way it was, by God, we would pound and
pound on the closed doors until we crashed them open.

Sholom came down the deck with the wash-down hose, Eli behind
him dragging its weight along, the strong stream clearing the decks of dirt.
I called Sholom, and he handed the nozzle to Eli and came up to the
bridge.

"The new mate," I told him, "doesn't speak much English. And he'll
be pretty busy up here on the bridge anyway. So you'll have to take most of
the responsibility for the deck work."

"Yes, sir," said Sholom. "As soon as I finish washing down, I'll cement
the hawsepipes. Everything's under control, Captain."

"Good. I just wanted you to be on your toes and not wait for the
mate."

He went back down to the deck and took up the hose again.

I went into the chart room and Miguel went out with his sextant to take a bearing on the sun. When he came back, I instructed, "Make a true course of 270 degrees, applying your compass error." He nodded and set to figuring the problem. I went below. On our port side the coast of northern Spain bulked up, and I thought of Don Miguel and Romero the cook. They had their closed doors, too. It struck me that half the world was busy trying to shut the other half out.

Supper was a noisy affair now with everybody eating in one mess room. Chief Baird had won his point, and the officers had a separate table. But sitting at it as officers were Heavy and the three men the chief himself had promoted, Gutmann, Brettschneider, and Kohlberg. The whole division between officers and men was pretty well broken down, and to my mind that was the way it should be. Conversation was general between both tables.

After supper I was lying in my bunk reading when I heard a shout on the bridge.

When I entered the wheelhouse, Don Miguel pointed to the steering wheel and shook his head.

"She doesn't answer," Dave Blake, the wheelsman, said. "I have her hard right, but she's still swinging left."

I took the wheel myself and sent Blake to inform Charlie, the first engineer. I put the wheel midships and let the ship drift. There was no danger, for we were far off the coast, but already I could see us piling up on the rocks if this happened while we were among the islands in the Aegean.

Blake came back and took the wheel again. After a time Charlie came up to the bridge. "It was a burned-out contact again," he said. "But there's nothing to it. Just takes a few minutes to replace it."

"Can't it be fixed so that it won't burn out?"

"No," he said, "not without major replacements. But I've got plenty of spare contacts."

"But if this happens when we're in a tight spot," I told him, "we can drift into disaster while you're putting in a new contact."

"Aw," Charlie said, "I wouldn't worry about it."

He wouldn't worry about it. I was fuming as I walked back to my cabin.

Before breakfast in the morning the chief knocked on my door and came in, sat down in my big chair, and swiveled it around to face me.

"Bad news," he said.

"What's wrong now?"

"There's a leak in the starboard condenser. We're taking seawater into our fresh water."

"Damn! Everything happens to us. What do we do now?"

"I started up the evaporator, but it has a very limited capacity. If we can't fix the leak, we'll have to put in somewhere for more fresh water."

"What are the chances of fixing it?"

"Charlie's working on it now. The only thing we can do is shut down the starboard engine, take the head off the condenser, and pack it with sawdust. Then we hope that the sawdust will find the hole and plug the leak."

"I guess the old ship is just showing her age. Well, you can stop her any time you like; we're well offshore." The chief left, and I banged my fist on my desk in irritation. Then I walked back to Moka's room to tell him about it. I was beginning to lean more and more on his calm intelligence. I had confidence in my own judgment and skill, but I had a lot of respect for the easy way he confronted a tough spot.

"Well," he said cheerfully, "we'll see if they can fix it."

"But if they can't, we'll be in trouble. We don't dare put into a Spanish port with our Spaniards aboard. And we've got a thousand miles of Spanish coast to cover."

"That's so," Moka said. "But let's wait and see if they can fix it. If they can't, then we'll worry."

An hour after breakfast the chief came to my room. "Well, she's packed. We'll wait a couple of hours, and then take some tests and see if we plugged it or not."

While I waited, I worried. I could think of no safe way to go into a Spanish port without our two Spanish Republicans being discovered, and discovery would mean imprisonment for them at least, and most likely a firing squad. I didn't like to think that their lives were at this moment depending upon a grain of sawdust looking for a hole to plug.

I was also worried about Heavy. Heavy hadn't said anything, but I knew that he was worrying, too; his face showed it. And he went about his work quietly, not with his usual exuberance. I wondered if it wouldn't have been better to have left him in Bayonne. He had been caught running the blockade before, on the *Ben Hecht*; if captured again, he might face a 10-year sentence. Why should he deliberately risk that? Why hadn't we given him more serious thought before we sailed? It was too late now; there was no way for him to turn back from here.

I was pacing the bridge when the chief called up through the speaking tube. "I think she's fixed," he said. "The salt content has dropped."

But on the morning of the day we were to go through the Straits of Gibraltar the sawdust gave way, and the salt content of the boiler water jumped way up. We stopped the ship at once, and fresh sawdust was packed into the condenser. When we got under way again, Moka and I went up to the chart room.

"We'll have to go through the straits at night," he said. "We must try to get past Gibraltar without the British seeing us. No telling what they will attempt."

I computed our distance from the straits. "If we slow down now, we should be off Tarifa about midnight. That means we will pass the Rock at two in the morning. That ought to be as good a time as any to slip past."

I called the chief through the speaking tube and told him to reduce our speed to a hundred and twenty revolutions a minute. We coasted along waiting for time to pass.

After lunch the chief came to my room again. "Well," he said, "she's still leaking. We didn't get it plugged."

"We've got to go through the straits tonight. Can you keep her going till we get into the Mediterranean?"

"Yes. But we'll have to blow down the water tubes with steam a couple of times each watch to clean them. That takes a lot of water. And it's hard on the men down there."

"Keep her going till we get inside. We'll figure something out then."

It was three o'clock in the afternoon when we heard the hum of a plane. After a while we spotted it, flying high and heading directly for us. At first I didn't pay much attention to it, for it was not unusual to see planes over these waters. But when this one was directly overhead, it circled us and began descending. As it came down, we could see that it was a big four-engined bomber, and as it got closer, we could see its markings: the round bull's-eye of the Royal Air Force. It dropped lower and lower in large circles, and all hands were out on deck staring at it. And then I held my breath for a moment; it seemed the plane was going to drop something on us. Some heavy object to damage us. As it went by, it made a shuddering blast of sound. At the moment the plane was directly abeam I got a perfect sight of it as though a camera shutter had tripped in my mind to fix the image there, seemingly motionless, for one whole second. Three men standing in the waist window stared at us with totally expressionless faces, like faces seen in a dream. Now the plane rose and circled and came back for another run, aimed straight at us with a rising roar of engines. The memory of wartime raids on ships was still vivid enough to make me tremble a little as this plane came charging at us as though on a bombing run.

"They've got a camera. They're taking pictures," Bailey Nieder cried from the deck as the plane went by the second time. After a third run—the three faces still staring blankly at us through the waist window—the plane climbed to several thousand feet and flew in loose circles above us. Moka, standing beside me on the bridge, swore softly in a language I didn't know.

"We might as well put on full speed ahead," I said. "There's no chance of sneaking through now."

"Might as well," he agreed.

I gave the order; the *Paducah*'s engines were boosted to their normal one hundred and fifty revolutions a minute, and we headed for the straits at our customary ten knots. Late in the afternoon we raised the yellow tops of the Atlas Mountains in Morocco, and then, a while later, we could make out the flat plains of the Spanish mainland off our port bow. The plane kept us in sight all the time; it climbed high and flew toward the land until it was a scarcely distinguishable speck, then came racing back to buzz us in a frightening dive that cleared our little signal mast by no more than ten feet, so that the slipstream swept the ship in a sudden burst of wind.

Dave, the second mate, was the first to see the second plane; he pointed it out coming toward us low on the water, and it flashed by us almost at deck level. Now the two of them made sport of us, diving and buzzing, and we were seized by a rage that was heightened by our helplessness. Sholom was standing forward by the windlass, and as one of the planes drummed over us, he shook his fist at it in a gesture that was silly in its impotence. Now the second plane leveled off and came roaring in at us. Dave Wurm ran to a can of galley garbage and picked out an old catsup bottle and heaved it at the plane's propellers as it flashed over. But the bottle made a futile little arc and fell into the sea with a mocking plop. The expressionless faces in the waist window stared at us, like something out of a weird nightmare.

Five miles off the entrance to the straits we sighted a small, trim ship coming toward us. Through the glasses we made her out to be a destroyer, mean-looking in gray battle paint. She must have been running at maximum speed, for she came up very fast. She was really a beautiful craft, every line of her combining grace and power perfectly proportioned, but to us she looked hard and malevolent. She bore down upon us and suddenly wheeled and slowed in a marvel of maneuverability, placing her directly abeam, paralleling our course and matching our speed, not more than thirty yards off. Her decks were crowded with curious sailors, and her bridge was a cluster of officers' uniforms. Among them were two men in civilian dress.

A strange figure in a bed sheet with a Turkish towel wrapped around his head like a turban appeared on our boat deck. It was Wurm dressed as an Arab parading up and down the deck under the eyes of the British destroyer crew.

Even some of the Englishmen on the destroyer broke into laughter. And for a brief moment the two crews shared the joke.

Then Heavy shouted a warning. "Don't let them get a good look at you. Those are CID men." He was referring to the Criminal Investigation Department agents in civilian clothes. "Later they'll try to identify the crew members."

Across the water, through a loudspeaker, came a crisp voice: "What is your destination, *Paducah*?"

Moka grabbed the megaphone and yelled back, "Livorno, Italy!"

The destroyer maintained her position on our beam, and we were studied and examined from stern to stern through binoculars and telescopes. Then she dropped back some fifty yards astern of us and slightly to one side of our wake, and there she stayed. "She'll tail us all the way in," Moka said. "And she'll keep a little offside our wake—they're afraid we might drop a cable over to foul her propellers.

"Well," he added, "maybe later we *will* try it."

The planes had disappeared now that the destroyer was on us.

I looked back at the little warship and thought of the many times during the war when I had prayed for an escort like her.

The sun set, and night came on as we plodded toward the straits. Would they try to stop us at the Rock of Gibraltar? Or would they let us through? The night was so clear that the chain of lights circling the Spanish coast on one side and Morocco on the other danced and glimmered as though alive. Dead ahead of us was the swift-flashing beam of the lighthouse on Tarifa Point on the Spanish side. Behind us glowed the navigation lights of the destroyer, red and green on the sides, yellow on the mast. In the darkness in our wheelhouse, tension was high. Miguel took repeated bearings on the light ahead of us, checking and rechecking, wary of the westward current that could drive us toward the rocks. Moka leaned on a porthole ledge and peered intently ahead. I paced back and forth, four steps one way, four steps back. The wheelhouse clock ticked loudly.

The cry from the man at the wheel was like an explosion. "She's dead!"

I leaped over to verify it for myself: the wheel was hard right, but the *Paducah* was swinging slowly to the left.

"Stop both engines!" I shouted. Moka and Miguel both jumped to the telegraphs. I ran to the engine room speaking tube and called frantically for Charlie, "The steering gear—." But before I could say anything more, he replied, "Right," and I knew he was on his way to fix it. But the dark coast seemed right under our bow, and the *Paducah* was swinging slowly into it. In an effort to control her, I gave new orders: "Full ahead port engine, full astern starboard engine," but the propellers had little effect. The rudder must have jammed all the way over when the wheel went dead. "Stop both engines."

Miguel hoisted on our little mast two red lights six feet apart in a vertical line, which in international code means, "Out of command." The *Paducah* lost way and gradually stopped swinging to the left, but now we were drifting helplessly. I cursed everything about the ship and the men who built her. The sudden silence of the ship with her engines stopped was eerie; the ticking of the wheelhouse clock was like a slow drumbeat. The lights of Tarifa were so clear and so close that we could make out details of houses under street lights, and we could see a cafe with people walking past it. By now we had swung ninety degrees off our course, with our bow pointed directly toward the shore, but we seemed to be drifting back out through the straits. The clock ticked away. Far behind us the destroyer stood off, waiting to see what happened to us, and the thought that the men aboard her were looking for us to pile up on the rocks was infuriating. Damn it, wouldn't Charlie ever get that contact replaced?

I was almost ready for the shudder as the ship struck bottom when a shout came from aft, "OK. Gear fixed."

"Full astern both engines! Wheel hard left!"

Slowly, terribly slowly, the *Paducah* began to back off and to turn. When we were well clear, I ordered full speed ahead. We brought her round on her course and through the straits once more. We took down the red lights. The destroyer resumed her position on our stern. With a handkerchief I mopped the sweat off my face.

We passed the Rock of Gibraltar, the light on Point Europa flashing alternately red and white. Some time later, the shore lights of Melilla on the Moroccan side faded away into the night, leaving only a dim glow on the horizon, and we were in the calm Mediterranean. We set a course to pass a little to the north of Alborán Island.

I called the chief in the engine room through the speaking tube. "Keep the engines full speed all night," I told him. "We'll worry about that leak tomorrow. I want to get as far away from Gibraltar as I can before we slow down."

I turned to Moka. "Let's go down and get some coffee."

"Captain," he said, "I need some coffee."

16 * From the Mediterranean to the Black Sea

Moka came to my room before breakfast. "We got our orders by radio last night," he said. "We're going to Varna in Bulgaria, on the Black Sea."

"Varna! Well, we'd better check on that leaking condenser and see if we're going anywhere. You ever been in Varna?"

"No."

The chief came up to breakfast from the engine room, dirty and sweating and angry. "She's still leaking," he reported. "We'll try packing her with sawdust again after breakfast. That's all we can do."

"And if that doesn't work?"

"We'll have to get more water. We can keep going if we blow down the tubes two or three times every watch and keep the salt off them. But that takes a lot of water, and we don't have enough."

By mid-morning we knew that the sawdust hadn't worked.

The chief, Moka, and I gathered in the chart room and studied the coast of North Africa. Oran and Algiers were big ports, and they were French territory, but the British were bound to have large consulates there, and that was not good. Farther along the coast, around the point of Cape de Garde, was Bône. It was not a very large port, and it was far enough from the big centers to give us time to get in and out before British forces could be sent to interfere. And Baird insisted that we dare not go beyond

Bône because we might run out of water. We studied the spot on the map marked Bône until finally Moka said, "We'll try it."

We computed a new course that would take us two miles off Cape de Garde so that the destroyer following us wouldn't know we were putting in to the coast until we made a sharp turn straight for the port. We computed the distance and slowed our engines by five revolutions a minute to time our arrival at about seven-thirty in the morning. With luck we would be able to run in, get our water, and sail again before dark.

The black gang had a rough time now; it was not easy work blowing down the tubes. Two or three times during every four-hour watch we could hear the sharp, angry hiss of steam, and vicious black smoke belched out of our two stacks. The men coming up from the engine room as dirty as chimney sweeps and sick with exhaustion dropped on the deck to lie for a long time in the cool air before they could muster enough energy to go and wash up.

And our food was running low; we had left Bayonne in such a rush that we didn't have time to stock sufficient supplies. One of the black gang turned up with a case of bleeding gums. We did not know whether it was an infection or a vitamin deficiency, but all hands were given a cup of canned orange juice from our dwindling stock of it, and we put the afflicted man on a daily ration.

Late in the afternoon of the day before we were due off Bône the air became damp. By sundown every surface was wet to the touch. There was a high overcast blotting out the stars, and the night was black and muggy. At first the light on Cape Bougaroûn shone brightly, but within a few hours the mist began to settle down on the coast and the horizon ahead of us was blurred, then lost. I put on a sweater and oilskins and went up to the bridge to spend what looked like a bad night. Normally the Bougaroûn light could be seen for thirty miles, but when we were no more than three miles off, the mist thickened and blanked it out. That was when we missed our gyrocompass; depending on the magnetic one with its varying error gave all of us the creeps, for we might be heading on a course that would take us farther in toward the already close and dangerous shore. Close to the water, visibility was good; it was only over the land that the mist had settled down like a blanket. Behind us we could see the lights of the destroyer tailing us closely.

We ran for three and a half hours after we passed the Bougaroûn light, until we judged we should be off Cape de Garde, but the beacon that should have been there didn't show through the mist. We ran nervously for another half hour, and still we raised no light. If our calculations were correct, we should have cleared Cape de Garde five miles back. But maybe we had been bucking a current we didn't know about. If we made our change of course for Bône before clearing the cape, we would be on the rocks in a matter of minutes. We ran for another half hour. I felt like a tight knot of nerves. I had to make a decision. I argued with myself that our calculations couldn't have been so far off that we hadn't cleared Cape de Garde. I would have to chance it. Just as I was about to give the order that would swing us in toward the coast, we saw a flicker of white light. Then we saw it again: it was the beam on Cape de Garde. But it was on our starboard bow, and it should have been behind us. A quick bearing showed we were one mile off the rocky coast. I had a tremendous urge to turn and run for deep water, but I controlled it; with luck and extreme caution, we would be safe enough this close in, as long as we could take our bearings on the lighthouse. But the destroyer behind us took no such chance. As soon as she picked up the light, she turned and headed offshore, then continued to tail us at a safer distance. When the light was abaft our beam, I gave the wheelsman the new course. The *Paducah* made a sharp and sudden turn. Instantly the destroyer swung in, too, and she began to blink a signal, beaming her powerful searchlight on a small cloud well in over the shore. We spelled out the words as the dots and dashes flashed. But it must have been coded, for it made no sense to us. Whom could she have been signaling? Were the French taking messages from British warships? But even if the whole British navy were being called out, we had no choice but to put in to Bône.

Daylight broke as we made an approach to the port, but the mist persisted. We could see through it no better with the sun up than we could in the dark. We made careful calculations, and when we reached a point that should have been abeam of our destination, I stopped both engines and made a ninety-degree turn before we lost steerageway. Now Bône should have been two miles directly ahead of us, but we could see nothing but a blank wall of moisture. The destroyer stopped, too, and stood off idly watching us. If only we had plenty of time, we could have lain here and waited for the mist to lift. We couldn't do that, yet it was difficult to make the decision that would send us probing forward in this soup. If we were wrong, we would pile up; visibility was zero, and we would be on the rocks before we saw them. While I was hesitating, Moka walked up to me. I looked at him: "Should we go in?"

Without hesitation, he grunted, "Yes!"

"Slow ahead both engines," I ordered, and the *Paducah* crept forward. The destroyer didn't follow this time; no foolhardy risks for her. Slowly she drifted out of sight. We could feel the lift of rising swells as the water below us became shallower. We stared ahead so intently our eyes watered with the strain. I found it difficult to breathe deeply.

When we saw the town, it didn't seem real; it was like a mirage. But it was directly ahead of us; we had hit it on the nose. I felt like shouting back to the destroyer lost in the mist: how do you like *this* for navigating?

When the pilot came aboard, he asked, "What are you coming in for? Food? Water?"

"Water," I told him. "You seem to know about us."

He laughed. "The British consul has been waiting on the dock for you for the last hour."

But when we tied up, there was no one on the dock who looked like a British consul, only a few Arab longshoremen idly looking us over. Moka and I walked up the road that led from the dock to the main street, a cobblestone thoroughfare between low yellow buildings. The sun was merciless, and we were bareheaded. "Let's buy some hats," Moka said.

The girl in the shop showed us brown hats and gray hats and yellow hats and sun helmets. Then she brought out two straw hats of blazing white with dazzling red and yellow and blue ribbons. They were louder than trumpet blasts and drum rolls. We laughed and bought them and wore them down the street as though we were carrying banners.

We found an agent who was glad to sell us water and assured us the pumping would be done before dark. On the way back to the ship we stopped at a shaded table in front of a little cafe and ordered wine. As we sipped it, a little crowd of bootblacks and miscellaneous, curious young Arabs congregated and stared at us, but none of them offered to shine our shoes. We were, in this world, political figures. After a time one of the biggest of them, muscular and tough, walked up to our table and spoke to us in a tight voice in Arabic. It sounded nasty and mean. Moka stiffened, but he nodded and smiled. When the tough character finished his speech and walked back to his group, we finished our wine and left.

"What did he say?"

"Oh, the usual thing." Moka shrugged. "Dogs of Jews, and so on."

At the dock a cluster of well-dressed Europeans was staring at the *Paducah*. As we came up, a man in the uniform of a French colonel approached us. "These gentlemen," he said, indicating the group of civilians, "wish to know why you came to this port and how long you intend to stay."

"Tell the gentlemen," Moka replied, "that because of engine room trouble we came here for water, and we are leaving before dark."

"That is all we want to know. Good-bye." He returned to his group, and the lot of them moved off toward the town.

In the afternoon a British cruiser and two destroyers came up and lay off the entrance to the harbor. The cruiser lay farthest offshore, but the destroyers were in close. Later we learned that the destroyers shadowing us in the Mediterranean were the HMS *Tocogay*, the HMS *Mermaid*, and the HMS *Cardigan Bay*. Standing at the rail, Moka and I watched them. "I just remembered," he said. "About two weeks ago a small fishing boat loaded a hundred and fifty Moroccan Jews somewhere along this coast and managed to get through. The British must think we came in to pick up passengers. When they see that we didn't, they'll think they scared us out of it. I don't think they'll bother us. But look at the show of strength. Don't you think they could find something useful for their navy to do?"

The sun was already behind the hills when we sailed. The warships were not in sight. But in a few hours one of the destroyers was on our tail again.

Next morning it was clear to our escort that we were not heading north for the Italian port we had given as our destination. The destroyer pulled up alongside, and the crisp voice came over the loudspeaker: "Still going to Livorno, *Paducah*?"

I grabbed a megaphone and shouted back: "Yes. We're taking the long way round." The destroyer fell back again.

The second day out, the engineers fixed the leak in the condenser. But by that time we had discovered that the water sold to us in Bône was bad: every man aboard was stricken with diarrhea. I ordered that no water be used for cooking or drinking until it was boiled.

But now it was full summer, and summer in the Mediterranean is a glory of high sun and blue water and nights as soft as purple velvet. A sort of happiness settled over the *Paducah*, a sense of having met and settled the last obstacle between us and the thing we were to do. Moka and the deck gang went through the ship stenciling numbers on the bunks, and the ship was cleaned up and polished in preparation for our passengers. It seemed that there was nothing before us now but clear skies and easy sailing. And nothing behind us but the British destroyer.

All day long and part of the night music blared through our loudspeakers. When the Spaniards were on watch, we got wild and exciting flamencos sung by La Nina Valiente, whose records Romero, the cook, had brought aboard. Sholom played Yiddish records he had brought with him. There were songs in French that some of the men had bought in Bayonne. There were American folk songs, and lots of American popular music. We had on board several albums of Palestinian songs and dances, but Moka had ordered that these be saved for the passengers. The music rolled incessantly, and I was reminded of Henry the Scot's warning to me that I would curse the day he came aboard to install that "fearful system of sound." But now, with the sound system, we had a stock reply to our destroyer every time she pulled alongside and repeated her insistent question: "What is your destination, *Paducah?*" For answer we played a Dinah Shore record titled "Welcome, Welcome," the volume turned up full. We kept the record going until the destroyer dropped behind and again took up her position astern of us.

Every evening, Ben Kulbersh, our second radio operator, conducted a class in Hebrew. Progress seemed to be slow. However, Dave Blake, who studied the language alone, without benefit of the class, was now able to conduct simple conversations. Buiza studied English. At night most of the men took their mattresses out and slept on deck, under a great bright moon. Often we sailed so close to the islands crowding the Aegean Sea we could see the campfires of the shepherds and hear the bleating of goats.

Drowsing in a hammock I had slung on the flying bridge over the wheelhouse, I heard Heavy and Moka talking in the quiet night. "I've never turned a shovelful of dirt in my life," Heavy was saying. "My old man was a fisherman in New Bedford. I was practically born on salt water. I've never worked anywhere but on salt water. Lots of sailors dream of buying a farm for their old age. Not me. I like the water."

"The land is good, too," Moka said. "I remember the first time I went out as a boy to work in an orange grove with a hoe. It was a summer day, and the sun was hot and bright, and the ripe fruit on the green trees, I thought, was better than jewels. Who could eat jewels? And the smell of the earth as I turned it with the hoe was finer than any perfume. I remember I threw down the hoe and began eating oranges. I ate twenty-two of them, walking around under the trees and spitting out the seeds. And I thought that everywhere I spit a seed a new tree would grow. I felt like a giant or a god."

I fell asleep in my hammock in the quiet night.

We approached the Turkish straits, the Hellespont on our port bow and Cape Kumkale on our starboard. As we pushed toward the entrance to the Dardanelles, Buiza on the bridge looked back at the British de-

stroyer and spat over the side. "And so in this way the great British civiliza-
tion conducts itself."

"Think she'll follow us through the Dardanelles?" I asked.

"That pig-boat?" He spat again. "Not to the Black Sea. I think this
bravado is only for the Mediterranean. They think they own it. With us
she's brave: we have no guns. But in the Black Sea she's not so brave.
Watch. She'll run away like a dog."

He was right. As we entered the narrow strait, the destroyer, the *Mermaid*, hauled up and lay motionless in the calm water. Someone turned our
loudspeaker on, and the Dinah Shore record blared "Welcome, Welcome."
The destroyer turned slowly and steamed away from us. "You see?" Buiza
said. "They have no *cojones*, no balls, for the Black Sea." After a moment
he added, "But when we come back with women and children, then they
will be brave."

By the time we passed Gallipoli and started into the Sea of Marmara, a
strong north wind slowed us down. Chief Baird notified us that our fuel
tanks were so low we were in a crisis. Fariello proposed that we put a starboard list on the ship to make the oil accessible and have the men form a
daisy chain with buckets, cans, anything that would hold oil, and carry it to
the reserve tank.

Slipping and sliding, all available men went into the fuel tank, where
they became covered with oil. The buckets and cans were scooped full and
passed along to one man who poured the oil into the reserve tank. This
went on until no more oil could be taken.

We continued through the Bosporus and into the Black Sea. Ahead of
us the chart showed miles and miles of areas heavily shaded in red. These
were the minefields. We picked our way carefully up the coast toward Bulgaria, and because of the mines we had to take a long, roundabout course
toward Varna. It was midnight when we approached the entrance to the
channel. We had radioed ahead, announcing our arrival, and we edged up
as close as we dared toward the mine-free channel and then waited for
a pilot.

He turned out to be a young Russian with blond hair and a snub nose,
trim in his naval uniform, and with practically no knowledge of English. I
called Moka up to the bridge to serve as interpreter.

"We won't go in during the dark," the pilot informed us. "Mines break
loose and drift into the channel. It is swept clear every day, but at night
it is risky."

"Should we stay where we are?"

"No," he said. "There is a current here setting in toward the shore. We had better go another two miles out, away from the minefields."

We turned around and ran for twenty minutes, and then we shut down the engines to lie there until daylight. We left Buiza to stand the night watch and to take a periodic check on our position, and Moka and I went to my room with the pilot. We brought in coffee and sandwiches, and I opened a bottle of cognac to spike the coffee.

"Many Russian pilots on this coast?" I asked through Moka.

"No. I'm the only one left."

"Is Varna a nice town?"

"It's not what you'd call a sailor's town." He smiled. "No girls. Not like the Romanian ports."

"Are you married?" I asked.

He frowned. "Not now," he said. "My wife and little girl were killed in an air raid in Leningrad."

I didn't say much after that. But Moka and the pilot talked all night in Russian. In the morning we made the thirty-mile run into Varna and tied up to a dock. We all felt something like relief. Here at last we would take the people aboard.

17 * Waiting, Waiting

The morning passed and nothing happened. I was sleepy from being awake all night, and so were most of the other men. We did only the work that was absolutely necessary. From our decks we could see little of the town; there were some trees near the dock, but they seemed old and gray, and they hid from us any view of Varna proper. All we could see was the immediate area of the port, and it looked like any other port, dirty with a network of railroad tracks leading down to the water's edge, the railroad cars bearing markings in all the languages of the Balkans as well as in German. We wondered what we would find here, on the other side of what had become known as the Iron Curtain.

Our lunch was a sorry meal of thin soup and potatoes; we were nearly out of provisions. In the early afternoon a little man, no taller than five feet and quite emaciated, came aboard and introduced himself as the chief of the harbor police. Moka's knowledge of Russian enabled him to understand most of the man's Bulgarian. When they ran into difficulties, they switched to French. I was handed a packet of small cards, and Moka explained: "They're passes for shore leave for the crew. Merely for identification purposes."

I must have shown surprise, for the little police chief smiled understandingly, and Moka translated. "Your men can go anywhere. There are no restrictions whatever. We hope you all have a good time while you are here."

"Ask him if we can get any food."

"He says that's not his department. His job is just to issue passes and look after the security of the ship. But he says some people from Sofia will come aboard some time today. They'll know about food."

I walked out to the deck with the police chief when he left. At the foot of our gangway I discovered a very large young soldier with a rifle. The police chief looked like a dwarf beside him, and the soldier drew up and snapped off a sharp salute as the chief passed him. This must have been what he meant by the security of the ship, I thought.

It was nearly sunset before the Sofia people, three men, arrived. A pale, middle-aged fellow led them into my cabin. "*Shalom!*" he said. "*Shalom!*" I replied, using the only Hebrew word I knew. We shook hands, and he continued in rapid Hebrew. When he finished, I shook my head apologetically and asked, "Do you speak English?"

"Yes. But you don't speak Hebrew?" When I shook my head again, he seemed quite taken aback. Just then Moka shouldered into the room, and they greeted each other warmly. Explanations were made.

"This is Dov," Moka said, introducing the pale fellow. "He is a journalist and one of my people."

Now Dov introduced the other two men, both of whom had heavy black mustaches. He seemed a little embarrassed by them.

One of them was Peter, an immense fellow better than six feet tall, with tremendous shoulders and a rough, broad face. His eyes were keen, and he had a big grin. He represented the Bulgarian government, and he spoke English with a thick accent. The third man was Emil. He was not so big, but very dark, with a crop of wild, uncombed black hair. Emil, I was told, would stay aboard the ship. He would serve as our agent and as a liaison with the local government officials. He knew no English, but he spoke excellent Hebrew, which surprised Moka. Emil explained that he was a merchant seaman, an anti-fascist who had escaped a death sentence imposed upon him by the government of old King Boris by jumping ship in Palestine. There he had worked in a fishing collective and learned the language. He and Moka, it turned out, had several mutual friends.

"What about food?" I asked.

"We'll supply you with the same rations our sailors get," Peter informed me. "I think it will be adequate. People who work get the heaviest rations."

"How soon can we get some of it aboard?"

"A cartload will arrive today. We knew from Chaim that you were short."

"Who's Chaim?" I asked.

"He's the Hagana chief for the Balkans," Moka answered. "He is in touch with Gingi in France."

"You fellows have quite an organization," I said admiringly. Turning to Peter, I asked, "What about oil?"

"That's a big problem," he said. "There's none in Bulgaria. Not a drop that we can tap. We are negotiating to get it from Romania. It might take a little time. But that's the only thing that might hold you up. The people are ready; we can have them at the ship on twenty-four hours' notice once we get the oil."

"Are the British in a position to interfere?"

"Yes," Peter replied promptly. "Their power is limited, but they can trouble you. The Bulgarian people abolished the monarchy and declared war on Germany, but our official status today is still that of a defeated enemy country. The Romanians need hard currency, and they are being paid well in U.S. dollars for each passport for the refugees. There is an Allied Control Commission in Sofia with Soviet, American, and British representation. The acting chairman is a Russian, General Tcherepanov, and he has two votes, against one each for the other two members, but under certain conditions the individual members can issue independent orders that must be obeyed. The Russians and Americans have been supporting the immigration to some extent. Though they are under pressure from the British to prevent embarkation of the refugees, the Russians are not interested in helping British foreign policy in the Middle East."

Later we learned that the Bulgarians also wanted U.S. dollars and were paid for every passenger.

"Any danger of an attempt on the ship?"

"It's not likely. But just to be sure we have posted a twenty-four-hour guard on the dock. You've seen the soldier?"

"Yes, I've seen him. I'm glad he's on our side."

Peter and Dov left to return to Sofia. As they went down the gangway, a creaking little farm wagon pulled by an old and weary horse came lumbering down the dock. It was loaded high with grapes and melons, lettuce, onions, peppers, tomatoes, and fish. Sholom and some of the deck crew spotted it, and when it pulled up at the foot of our gangway, they set up a shout that aroused the entire ship. Romero came out of his galley, looked, and gave a lusty Spanish cheer. All hands raced down the gangway, and some of the men hoisted the bewildered peasant cart-driver to their shoulders. The others began carrying the food aboard. We realized then how hungry we had been.

In the evening I went ashore with Moka and Emil. As we passed the soldier at the foot of the gangway, he nodded and said, "*Drasti.*" I nodded and repeated, "*Drasti.*" Then I turned to Moka. "What does *drasti* mean?"

He laughed. "It's a greeting. It means hello, good-bye, anything. Like our *shalom.*"

I asked Emil how conditions were ashore. "Are you asking as an observer of social phenomena or as a sailor?" Moka translated.

"As a sailor," I laughed.

Varna was a neat little city. Its streets were clean, and they were lined with two- and three-story buildings that were modern and well built. The shops we passed seemed well stocked with clothing and furniture and staple goods. When I mentioned this to Moka, Emil seemed to understand me, for he told Moka, who translated, "It's not bad, but it's not too good yet. When the Germans left the country, they took with them everything they could carry. They stripped the stores and the factories and the farms. The new government got a clean start."

In the early evening the streets were crowded with promenaders, old and young couples, boys in pairs and girls in pairs. It was like Mexican and South American cities where everybody comes out in the cool of twilight to walk and to greet friends and neighbors as the day fades, a pleasant custom largely unknown in American cities. At the far end of Varna there was an immense park, and to enter it we walked under great arches supported by white pillars. The whole world seemed calm and at ease as we strolled through the trees with the water of the Black Sea visible far beyond and below us.

Emil led us to a huge building called the Casino. It was filled with hundreds of small tables at which people were sitting and eating small fried fish served with tomato salad and drinking white wine. We found a table and were served the fish and salad and wine, which apparently was the Casino's standard—its only—food offering. A small orchestra broke into an American jazz number. It wasn't too bad, but it wouldn't draw any crowds on West Third Street in Manhattan. The atmosphere of the Casino was one of complete relaxation. It was so big it seemed that most of the town was there. We nibbled at the delicious little fish and drank two bottles of the tangy white wine while the orchestra played jazz. For the first time since I boarded the *Paducah*, I felt thoroughly relaxed and at ease. I was also dog-tired from being up all the night before. When Emil suggested a visit to Varna's biggest nightclub—"It has the hottest swing band in the Balkans," he told us—I begged off and found my way back to the ship and turned in.

The first thing I heard in the morning was one of the sailors in the passageway outside my cabin. "It's a hell of a town," he was complaining. "No girls, no nothing. At ten o'clock at night it's so dead you could fire a cannon down the main street and not hit anybody. And nobody can understand English. It's the worst place I've ever been to."

At breakfast the chief engineer was worried. "We need oil," he warned me. "If we don't get some today, we'll have to shut down the plant. There'll be no lights, no blowers for the galley, no cooking."

"I'll see what I can do," I told him.

"Can't run a ship without supplies. Never made such a trip. Running out of water and oil and food all the time. What's the matter with these people? They think we can operate on air?"

I knew he knew better, so I let him sound off. His problems were basic to the success of this voyage. He had a right to complain. But the problems were not easily solved.

Emil assured us later that he would get us some oil before night, and he went ashore at once to look after it.

Moka had a shore gang at work putting the finishing touches to the preparations for our passengers. I was in his cabin when he hauled from under his bunk the package he had brought aboard the night we sailed from Bayonne. It contained hundreds of cards, each bearing a number, and a quantity of cloth strips inscribed in Hebrew. They looked like armbands.

"What's all that?" I asked.

"Each passenger, coming aboard, will be given a card with a number. The number will correspond to the number on a bunk. Our crew will be divided into squads and will lead the people to their proper stations. There will be no confusion, and everyone will find his place."

"And the colored strips?"

"We will organize several groups from the passengers to perform special functions. They will wear these for identification." He held one up. "This says 'Master-at-Arms.' This one says 'Fire Squad,' this, 'Food Squad,' and so on."

"Looks like the whole operation will be well organized."

"It has to be," he said. "We've learned that from experience. But the armbands and the special squads have a deeper importance. This will be the first time in many, many years that any of these people will have even the slightest measure of social responsibility or social obligation. Now, with their own squads, they will be in charge of themselves and responsible for themselves. You'll see for yourself how much that means to them. I've seen old men weep just because we put a band around their sleeves and told them, 'Now you are in charge.' They've forgotten that it's possible for them ever again to be anything but hounded and destroyed. They've been driven so low that they can be reborn with an armband."

In the afternoon the same little groaning cart that brought our food came creaking down the dock, loaded this time with twenty drums of oil. This should make the chief happy, I thought. But when he saw it, he exclaimed, "Diesel oil! Dangerous."

"It's the only thing we could get," I told him.

"Well, I don't like it. If the firemen get careless and don't watch their burners and the fires go out, this stuff could blow the ship up."

"We'll warn them to be careful."

"I still don't like it."

"How long will the twenty barrels last?"

"A day and a half," he said.

It took us a long time to transfer the oil from the drums to our tanks with our small electric pump, but we would have lights and hot meals for another thirty-six hours, anyway.

Two weeks passed and there was still no action from Sofia. We had long since done everything possible to prepare the ship for its passengers; there was nothing left to do but wait, and the waiting was beginning to have its effect upon us. The chief engineer had simply withdrawn into silence and the privacy of his cabin, appearing only for meals and then going back behind his closed door.

The men went their separate ways. Dave Gutmann told me that they had made a new friend, the son of George Dimitroff. The father had defied Hitler at the Reichstag fire trial in 1933, when Hitler first came to power. Young Dimitroff, who sought out the young Americans, told seditious jokes about the Russian occupation of Bulgaria. One Sunday Dimitroff took our sailors out to a country inn, where they all had too much to drink. Back in town at the Astoria Bar, George Goldman started throwing tables and chairs. When his companions couldn't quiet him, several men held him so that Heavy could knock George out. But at the last moment, Heavy stopped. "I can't hit the son-of-a-bitch," he said.

When the Bulgarian police arrived and took George into custody, the guys sobered up fast. Later, a quiet George was led back to the ship. He was a model of decorum for the rest of our stay in Bulgaria.

All of the crew, myself included, were feeling the strain of inaction. We had been at a high pitch of anticipation when we docked in Varna, and now we were bored and nervous, tired of the waiting. As an additional burden we still carried the scars and the inner turmoil of World War II in our bones and were seeking some outlet to relieve the tension.

Twice we ran out of oil, and for days we had no lights, no hot coffee, no cooked meals. The weather turned cold, and the soldier at our gangway wore his greatcoat now. When we had no oil, the ship lacked warmth and all of us shivered. We ate cold salads and cold food out of cans and at night groped in the dark or burned candles.

Now, we were out of oil a third time. At supper we sat in the cold gloom of the mess room and munched on sandwiches made of Spam and the coarse black Bulgarian bread, washing it down with red wine. We thought moodily of the dreary night ahead without warmth or lights and wondered how long, how long, we must wait and wait.

There was no talking during the cold meal. All of us were unhappy, but nobody wanted to gripe out loud—there was still that much morale left. Larry Kohlberg attempted a joke, but nobody laughed. Larry had an unusual ability to sense the mood of the men and to win their respect. Though he came from a wealthy family, he accepted dirty jobs as they came and sought no privileges.

When they finished eating, some of the men carried bottles of the red wine back to their rooms, and everybody simply disappeared into his own quarters.

Late in the evening I was pacing up and down the deck, both to keep warm and to try to make myself tired enough to sleep. I was startled by Dave Wurm's voice raised in anger, sounding harsh in the night, a suggestion of fright in it. It was unusual for Dave to raise his voice. But now he was shouting, "Let him alone!"

I heard Heavy's voice, thick and mumbling. "He's my buddy, I tell you! I just seen him look in the door. Just now. Hey, McElroy!" And Heavy stumbled out on deck, weaving from too much wine. "Hey, Mac, where are you, Mac?"

Dave, following him out, rushed to me, his eyes large and his expression pained. "McElroy was his best friend," Dave whispered, a note of horror in his voice. "They were torpedoed during the war. McElroy was killed."

Heavy lurched a few feet and stopped by the corner of the deckhouse. "Hey, Mac, you old bastard! Where you been? Jesus, I thought you run out on me. Let's find a joint where we can get some beer and talk." He chuckled drunkenly. Then he shouted, "Hey, Mac, don't leave me!" He slid down the side of the deckhouse and lay prone, sweat beading on his face.

Dave ran over, kneeled, and placed his hand on Heavy's shoulder. "It's all right, Heavy. Mac says he'll be back later."

After a moment, Heavy said, "It's OK, Dave. I'm all right."

Together Dave and I got him back into his room and wrestled him into his bunk.

It rained for three days. When it stopped and the sun came out, it seemed brighter than it had ever been before. It warmed up the old ship, and we got another load of oil, so that the lights were on again and hot meals were served and there was heat in our cabins through the cold nights. But every evening, when the day was done, all of us seemed to want to get off the ship as quickly as possible and to stay away from it as long as possible. There was still no word from Sofia. It seemed to us that we had been born on the *Paducah*. This trip started as long ago as we could remember, and it would have no end. All of us would die on the *Paducah*: she would be our tomb. And every evening after supper we ran away from that.

There weren't many places to go in Varna. Most of us congregated at a nightclub called the Astoria, the place that had what Emil called "the hottest jazz band in the Balkans." I didn't really like the place, but it had music and lights and cognac and entertainment and hostesses. All of it added up to a spurious, artificial gaiety, but any kind of gaiety was welcome those days.

I was sitting at the bar on a high-legged stool one night slowly sipping vodka, making the drink last because I did not want to drink too much. I watched the girl acrobatic dancer, a contortionist. I had never liked contortionists. When the act was finished, George Goldman ran out into the middle of the floor, bowed elaborately in all directions, shook his hands over his head in the classic boxer's pose, and then ran off. He got a bigger hand from the audience than the performer had.

As the band started up and the dancing began, two young militiamen bearing rifles and side arms entered and looked the place over very carefully. Then they walked toward me. They were very young and in need of haircuts. They looked like farm boys who hadn't been in those ill-fitting uniforms very long. What did they want from me? They took places beside me at the bar.

The thinner of the two spoke to the bartender and nodded toward me. When he was finished, the bartender, who knew English and was my friend by now, smiled and translated. "He wants you to know," he said, "that the people who come to the Astoria are not representative of our country. He says the real people of Bulgaria can't afford to come here."

The young militiaman smiled, looking very much like a shy farm boy now, and spoke again. "Most of our people," the bartender translated, "can't read or write. We are learning, but it takes time. We haven't had our own government for very long. You American sailors have culture." And the young militiaman smiled at me the way I suspected he would smile at a big brother.

I was so embarrassed by the thought that to him I represented culture that I felt like pushing aside my vodka, climbing off my high bar stool, and apologizing for being there. But all I did was smile self-consciously and ask if I could buy them a drink. The young man who did the talking shook his head and patted his rifle. "He cannot drink on duty," the bartender explained. Both young men smiled seriously, saluted me stiffly, and strode out.

The incident reminded me of Sholom and his girlfriend and of her effect upon him. Those days he took exceptional care of his appearance, spending a long time dressing and shaving and combing his hair and fussing with his necktie and shining his shoes. Once dressed, he was in a great hurry to get ashore, where he stayed until dawn, but he always came back sober.

"What's with Sholom?" I asked Heavy.

Heavy grinned and said, "Didn't you know? He's got a girl."

"So? He's had girls before, but he didn't stop being a roughneck."

"This is a different kind of girl," Heavy said. "I've met her: she's really something. Serious, studying to be an actress—she wants to go to Hollywood. She's interested in 'art,' and she thinks that Americans are all highbrows. Sholom's just trying to live up to her idea of him. She regards him as a gentleman of refinement. So he wears neckties and shines his shoes and takes her to the opera and the museum of art."

"I don't believe it."

"It's true. He comes back cursing and swears he's going to leave her and get himself a girl he can have some fun with. But he doesn't leave her. Next day he can't wait to get ashore to see her again. I won't be surprised if he begins to like opera and art."

"Worse things could happen to him," I told Heavy.

The streets were dark, and there were not many people on them as I walked toward the ship. But a movie house suddenly splashed the sidewalk with light as the doors opened and people spilled out. Among them was a familiar long figure, Moka. With him was a girl. "Good evening, skipper," he said when he saw me. He introduced the girl: "This is Tania. She doesn't speak English. You're going to the ship?"

"Yes."

"Come and walk in the park a bit."

In the quiet park we could feel a light wind rustling the leaves. There was a moon, a small one, no more than a quarter, but it gave enough light to put a sparkle on the water seen far off through the trees. Walking along, none of us speaking, we heard music, and following the sound of it we approached three men sitting on a bench. Two of them had mandolins, the other a guitar. We sat nearby and listened.

The men did not speak. When they finished a song, there was silence for a moment or two, then the guitar sounded a couple of chords, and they swung into another song. From time to time I recognized a French or Spanish or Italian song I had heard, but most of them were Slavic and unfamiliar to me. All of them, even the gayest, seemed to have an undertone of sadness.

After a long time Tania spoke. "She said the musicians are sailors," Moka translated. After another period of silence, she spoke again. "She says one out of every ten persons in this country plays a musical instrument." I thought of Sholom's girl, and of the young militiamen, and of their belief in American sailors as men of culture.

Tania told us she had a little cart and a mule named Enraptura. Her family had a vineyard on the side of the hill beyond the city where the grapes were ripening and there were pecan and walnut trees. "It is so clear you can see for miles," Moka translated.

The moon was far down toward the horizon when we got up and walked away. But the three musicians were still playing as we passed out of hearing. In all the time we had sat there, not one of them had spoken a word. Through their music, it seemed, they had developed a communion deeper and closer than possible with the spoken language, and I felt envy. Americans, I thought, rarely got this close together.

When we left the park Moka asked me to walk Tania home; he had a late meeting with some Shou-shous. He said his goodbyes.

The girl and I walked along in complete silence. Tania was a beautiful girl. Her hair was long; in the twilight her eyes looked black. I hadn't realized how tense the delays and obstacles of the last weeks had made me. I had been left with a dried-up feeling, as though I had just been sitting on the ship and withering. I thought how wonderful it was just to walk in the park under the trees with a girl, and I wanted to lengthen these warm moments.

If only I knew more Bulgarian, but I knew only one word, and I was saving that. Apparently she didn't know even one English word. When she stopped before a house, we looked at one another and laughed. Then I said, "*Drasti,*" and she replied, "*Drasti.*"

18 ✳ *On the Run Again*

It was a cold morning, but I did not stay in my cabin. After three weeks I was sick of that room, and I was getting sick of the *Paducah*, and I was even getting sick of the whole city of Varna. It seemed we had been beside this grimy dock for at least a year. But if we were sick of waiting for the people to come aboard, how sick must the people be of the waiting they had done. Patience, I told myself. That reminded me of Mayor Fiorello La Guardia of New York City. He used to speak every Sunday on the radio and tell his listeners: "Patience and fortitude." And that reminded me of the war years. I didn't want to think of that time, so I walked down the dock and watched the crew at work.

As much to keep the men busy as for any other reason, I had ordered them to shift the ship's big life rafts to get them more evenly distributed.

They were cumbersome things, nearly impossible to handle because not enough men could get a grip on them. So Heavy had hit upon the idea of lowering them into the water with a winch, floating them to where they were wanted, and then heaving them aboard again. Emil, our Bulgarian liaison man, had practically made himself one of the crew, and it was he who took off his shoes and socks, rolled up his trousers, and rode the rafts down and guided them through the water. He seemed to enjoy it, although it struck me that the water must have been terribly cold. The job took most of the morning.

When it was done, all of us sat in the mess room drinking hot coffee and talking. Emil, speaking in Hebrew with Peter Gilbert, one of our oilers, translating, told us of a friend of his, a fisherman, who used his small fishing boat to take Jews rescued from Germany to Palestine during the early part of the war.

"Where is he now?" someone asked.

"Oh," Emil said, "the fascists executed him."

"Just for carrying Jews?"

"*Just!*" Emil repeated. "Isn't that enough? You don't understand the nature of fascism or you couldn't ask such a question. You Americans are lucky: you've never lived under fascism. Still, you would be better off if you understood it better. To fight fascism, you must fight *every* part of it, every one of the things it stands for. And to fight *any* part of it is to risk execution. To the fascists, anyone who defended Jews was necessarily anti-fascist. Therefore they shot him. It is very simple. Yet it is hard for many people to understand."

In the evening I went to the Astoria. I stayed quite late. I spent most of the evening talking to an Englishman I had met at the bar. He told me he was a correspondent for a liberal weekly in London. "I met some of your crew here last night," he said. "Fine fellows, they are. All of them American?"

"Everybody aboard is American."

"Not many American ships put in here," he said.

When I made no answer, he laughed in a friendly way. "I say, old man, I'm not trying to pump you. Don't blame you for being a bit standoffish in this part of the world, but you needn't fear me. Just making conversation. Shall we have a drink?"

We had a drink, and after that one more, and the Englishman talked, mostly about his experiences in the Balkans.

"Most amazing thing," he said, "is the volunteer youth brigades. Thousands and thousands of them, boys and girls, have produced absolute miracles of construction, railroads, dams, things of that sort. And without any of the usual incentives you or I would readily understand—no pay, no immediate gain whatever. And the movement even has international appeal," he continued. "Here in Bulgaria, for instance, we have a British group. They call themselves the Major Thompson Brigade."

"Who's Major Thompson?"

"Oh, he was one of our hush-hush fellows. You know, a liaison man with the underground. You had them, too—what did you call them? O.S.S., I believe. Major Thompson parachuted into Bulgaria during the war and organized partisan forces and coordinated their work with the Allied armies. He was quite taken with the people here and kept a diary of his experiences. It has been published in England and is tremendously popular. Inspired all sorts of young people to come here and help rebuild the country. Quite a remarkable movement."

"Where's Major Thompson now?"

"Oh, he was captured by the Germans toward the very end of the war. They executed him. But I daresay he'd be flattered by the brigade named after him. They're all youngsters in it, and quite enthusiastic. They live in tents, and they work like coolies. At night they sit about a fire and sing songs, and they're quite keen about folk dancing. And they're all studying Bulgarian. They fancy themselves somewhat as 'cultural ambassadors of goodwill,' as one of them put it."

"Sounds like a good thing."

"Oh, I daresay it does no harm. They're all quite young, you know. I suspect in time they'll develop a genuine sense of responsibility. Now they're at the adventurous age. Be quite awkward for them, though, should war occur."

This stuffy bastard, I thought. "Should war occur," just like that.

"When did you last do something useful?" I asked him.

"Eh, what's that?" he said.

"And what are *you* doing to prevent a war from occurring?"

"But, I say—"

"You say crap," I told him, and I climbed off my bar stool and walked out. I supposed he was staring after me with his mouth open, but I didn't look back to see. I didn't care. And I was fed up with the Astoria. I told myself that I wouldn't come here again.

Rotter, Bergman, and some of the other men were in the mess room when I got aboard.

I drew a cup of coffee from the urn and sat down.

"You fellows in the Astoria last night?"

"Yes, we were there for a while."

"Meet an Englishman there?"

"Yeah, a correspondent. We had some drinks with him," one of the men said. "Seemed quite a decent guy for an Englishman. He even said he was sympathetic to immigration to Palestine."

"You told him we were going there?"

"Well, he talked about it. He seemed to know we were going there."

I exclaimed, "I don't trust that guy. He's a phony."

The next morning Moka went ashore to meet with the Bulgarians. When he returned he was hatless as usual, his fierce black hair as conspicuous as a flag. He grinned and waved when he saw me.

"Anything new?" I asked.

"Not yet. But later today we will have some decisions."

That afternoon the harbor police chief came aboard and talked for a long time with Emil. Then they came to my cabin, and I sent for Moka. Moka's eyes brightened as he talked to them. Then he translated.

"Well," he said, "our old friends have started to work on us again. The chief here has had a phone call from the British member of the Allied Control Commission. He demanded to know what this illegal Jewish ship was doing in the harbor."

"What did the chief tell him?"

"He said he knew of no illegal Jewish ship. He told him that the *Paducah* is a Panamanian ship with an American crew, that she is waiting for oil, and that there are no passengers aboard her."

"What can happen now?"

"Anything. We'll probably find out today."

"I think I know where this came from," I told him. I explained about the British correspondent for the liberal weekly in London.

Early in the evening Peter arrived from Sofia. "Flew down," he said. "We haven't much time. You'll have to be out of Varna by eight o'clock tonight."

"That's impossible," I argued. "We haven't got enough oil to turn the engines over. And where will we go?"

"I know you have no oil," Peter answered. "Emil told me. But we'll scrape together enough to get you fifty miles down the coast to Burgas."

"What happened?"

"The British member of the Allied Control Commission found out about the ship. He demanded that you be expelled from the harbor. The opposition of the Russian neutralized the Englishman, but then the Englishman issued an independent order. And, unfortunately, we must obey it. But we'll just shift you to Burgas, and if he issues another order, we'll simply ignore it and let him go whistle. I'll go ashore now with Emil and find you some oil."

The ship came alive as the men sprang into the work of preparing to sail. Even Romero violated his own rationing system and made a full urn of fresh coffee. We were on the run again—we were always fleeing from one place to another, looking for a haven and never finding it—but we were glad just to have something to do. And we were not really running this time: we were going only fifty miles, and then we were going to stand fast, defiantly, until we did what we had set out to do. We were all grimly pleased at that prospect.

Up forward, Sholom turned the windlass over slowly, testing the gears; the steering engine clattered in its deckhouse on the stern as the steering was checked; the navigation lights were snapped on and off and on again to see that all were functioning; and on the bridge Dave Greer studied the chart and plotted a course to Burgas.

And now down the dock came a small switching engine with an oil tank car behind it. Peter came aboard grinning. "It belongs to the municipal government," he reported. "I cut through two weeks of red tape and simply 'requisitioned' it. The tank's not full, but there's enough in it to take you down the coast."

We hooked up our little electric pump to the tank car and began the painfully slow process of transferring the oil to our tanks. By seven o'clock it was clear that we would never make the eight o'clock deadline.

"We must make it," Peter said. "If we obey this order to the letter, it will placate the British; they will feel their power, and that will make them happy, and being happy, they'll probably overlook the fact that their order was obeyed only to the letter and not in the spirit. I'll be back soon." And he ran ashore again.

In fifteen minutes he came clanging down the dock riding a big shiny red fire engine, the firemen all grinning under their polished brass helmets. The fire engine's pump was hooked up, and the oil surged aboard us in a thick stream. It was five minutes to eight when we cast off our lines and backed slowly away from the dock. Peter waved gaily. "I'll see you tomorrow," he shouted.

We made the run easily, as though we were the Staten Island ferry, and by four o'clock in the morning we were tied up and secure alongside a dock in Burgas. After drinking a cup of coffee, I turned in to get a few hours' sleep.

After breakfast Moka, Emil, and I stood at the rail and looked over the port. To my surprise it was almost exactly like Varna; for a moment I had the eerie feeling that we hadn't gone anywhere, that we were still at the same dock and nothing had changed. The harbor installations were identical, even to the shape and size and length of the piers. Emil explained: "It is because the Germans built these ports from a master plan. My country was under German influence for a long time. Our kings were of Saxe-Coburg-Gotha. All of Bulgaria's professional men, doctors, lawyers, engineers, scholars, were educated in Germany. And German capital dominated the country."

Early in the forenoon Peter came aboard with several men and found me with Emil and Moka drinking coffee in the chart room.

Peter introduced us to the harbormaster, a middle-aged man wearing a uniform heavy with gold braid, who nodded curtly and did not offer to shake hands. Next was a tall, athletic-looking fellow, chief of the harbor police, who shook hands with a warm grip that was so strong I winced with pain. The third visitor was Gregor, a slim, alert young man with a mustache and a fresh flower in the lapel of his carefully pressed jacket; he would be our local agent. He always looked so handsome and so well tailored that some of the crew later dubbed him "the best dressed man in the Balkans."

The Bulgarian officials were an odd mixture of holdovers from the old imperial regime and communists from the new government—an arrangement that did not work smoothly, I quickly found. There was a sharp exchange in Bulgarian between the harbormaster and the chief of police. "What was that about?" I asked.

Moka grinned. "The harbormaster said he would have nothing to do with this illegal ship, and the police chief said he would put him in jail and throw away the key if he didn't help."

"I'm returning to Sofia today," Peter said before he went ashore with the group. "I'll do everything I can to get you enough oil for the trip as soon as possible. Don't worry about anything—you won't have any trouble here. The second ship, the *Northland*, is due in about one day. Your two ships will run together for the final trip into the Palestinian coast."

In the evening we went ashore. We found a large casino like the one in Varna, and it served the same tender little fried fish and tomatoes and white wine, and there was a park, and a place with a hot jazz band. But I was not attracted by any of it; I was weary of waiting, and of passing time drinking vodka in a nightclub because there was nothing else to do. Five months had passed since we sailed from New York.

In the morning after breakfast a shaggy-looking man, heavy and big-boned, with a large head topped with a shock of curly black hair, came aboard and asked for Moka. When he found him, the two men looked at each other silently for a moment and then embraced closely, like brothers meeting after a long separation. "This is Chaim," Moka introduced him to me, "one of the Hagana chiefs in the Balkans." Chaim looked me over searchingly as we shook hands, as though weighing and judging me. There was something about the man, an air of wisdom, of solid good sense and total knowledge—his eyes conveyed the impression that he knew every-thing—that made me hope he would find me worthy. The two men went off immediately to Moka's room, talking together as they walked down the deck and laughing, happy just to be together.

At lunchtime Chaim ate with us, his big, shaggy head dominating the mess room and his presence exciting the men's interest. His appearance made it easy to think of him as a romantic hero, and surely a Hagana chief in the Balkans must have had incredible adventures. Even Chief Baird was less reserved than usual and looked upon our guest with some deference.

Chaim spoke excellent English. "You've all heard about the *Exodus*?" he asked.

"Yes," I replied. "She sailed while we were still in Bayonne. Gingi there brought us the news of the battle."

"Well, the battle, yes," Chaim said. "That was one thing. They killed three of the passengers and the American mate. But have you heard about her since?"

"No, we haven't heard anything."

"Then I shall shock you with the news," he said. "She carried forty-five hundred passengers, you remember. Well, at Haifa they transferred all of them to three prison ships. The *Empire Rival*, the *Ocean Vigor*—idealized names, aren't they? Perfect names for floating dungeons—and the *Runnymede Park*. That's the most ironic of all. Runnymede, the place of the signing of the Magna Carta, the charter of liberty.

"Anyway, all of us supposed that they were taking the people to Cyprus, as customary. Even the British soldiers put aboard for the trip thought so, and they took with them only enough personal equipment for an overnight run. But they didn't go to Cyprus. Instead, they went to France, to Port de Bouc, not far from where the people had embarked. And on one of the ships the officer in charge ordered all books in Hebrew or Yiddish to be burned, which included religious books.

"As soon as they anchored in Port de Bouc, a British officer ordered that no food or water be sent to the ships. Our own organizations in France supplied them with food. The British said, in effect, 'This is where you came from. Now get off.' The people replied, 'We will get off these ships willingly only in Palestine. Not in any other place.' The attitude of the French was, 'If they come ashore here voluntarily, we'll do what we can to look after them. But we cannot force them to disembark.'

"The British thought about it for a time and then issued an ultimatum. It's brief. I have memorized it. To me it will stand as one of the worst declarations of perfidy, evil, and shame of all time. 'Those of you,' it said, 'who do not begin to disembark at Port de Bouc before eighteen o'clock tomorrow, August 22, will be taken by sea to Hamburg.' The three ships are on their way now to Germany. Not one passenger left the ships willingly in France, and in Germany they will have to be put ashore by force."

It rained for three days, and for three days we did not see the sun. It was a cold rain, and the whole ship was chilled. Everything was soggy to the touch. We stopped caring about the rain; we stopped caring about anything. We would never get dry again, we would never get to Palestine, we would never get home, we would never see the sun again. And to hell with it all anyway.

The *Northland* arrived in the rain and gloom. It was larger than we were and a better-looking ship. We saw her in the harbor, but before we could visit her, she heaved up her anchor and sailed out a different channel. Later, we learned that the harbor authorities had moved her to a special security anchorage because they needed the docks for commercial ships. I wondered how Morgan was doing as skipper.

Emil sat in my cabin on the third night of the rain and played a guitar and sang a song, gloomy and tragic. Moka and I listened in dejection.

"That's one of the favorite songs of my country," Emil told Moka when he had finished, and Moka translated for me. "It's a very old song, from the time of the Turkish rule. In those days the Turks took the strongest and best of our young boys to Turkey and there trained them as soldiers until they lost all memory of their childhood, of fathers and mothers and sisters and brothers. Then the Turks would send them back as occupation troops, so that we enforced our own oppression. This song is about such a young man. When he returned to Bulgaria as a soldier, he fell madly in love with a beautiful Bulgarian girl. Eventually he discovered that she was his sister. They both destroyed themselves. That is our song."

Melancholy settled over the three of us. We said goodnight, and the other two went to their rooms. I crawled into my bunk and turned out the light. Even the blankets felt damp. I could hear rainwater gurgling in the scuppers out on deck.

By morning the rain had stopped, but the skies did not clear. Nothing dried, and it was bound to rain some more.

After breakfast, Gregor, the Bulgarian government agent, came aboard. "The oil will arrive tomorrow morning," he told us. "And the people will arrive tomorrow night."

All day long the sky remained overcast, gray, and damp-looking, as though at any moment the rain would gush again. Sholom and his sailors wandered over the deck, doing things that didn't really need doing— everything had been long since done. The men seemed to be under a compulsion to do something. Wherever they could, they made work for themselves. They checked the ventilators, they checked the lifeboats, they checked the rafts, they removed lashings and put them on again, convincing themselves that they needed tightening. Heavy, as third mate, was busy about the bridge. There was nothing to do there either, but he checked the clock with the chronometer, and with a rag he rubbed up some of the brass work, and he looked at the canvas dodger furled now under the bridge rail, and then he fiddled with the halyards on our signal mast. Don Buiza and Dave Greer spent the afternoon in the chart room, checking and rechecking the run down through the Aegean Sea and into the Mediterranean and then east to Palestine. Prowling over the ship, Moka examined everything, checked everywhere. Even he could find nothing to do that hadn't been done. In the afternoon he sat in his room organizing his numbered cards and the colored armbands.

I poked my head into the chief's room and found him lying on his bunk reading. "The engines are ready," he said tersely in answer to my question. He turned back to his book, but then said, with warmth in his voice, "Well, I guess I'll go down and look around anyway," and he got up and put on his shoes.

Late in the afternoon I made a round of the ship myself. And deep down in one of the holds I found Dave Kellner praying silently in his phylacteries and *talis*. His eyes were closed, and he didn't see me. I walked away as soundlessly as I could.

In the evening there was a great rush for the washrooms. Everybody aboard bathed and shaved, and we all put on clean clothes. And then we settled down to wait. This would be the last night that the *Paducah* belonged to us. We were all keyed up as high as we could go with anticipation. But with the anticipation I had a feeling of dread, too: we were waiting now to take aboard a cargo of misery. It was as if a terrible army were coming to possess us. We wouldn't even be the *Paducah* any longer. We would be the *Geula. Redemption.* I repeated the word over and over to myself as I fell asleep.

At dawn the tank cars came clattering down the rails of the dock and clanked to a jerking halt. The sky was still overcast, but it was not raining. Sandwiched in between the two tank cars was a flatcar, and on it was a large diesel-engine pump—and Peter, who leaped off and came aboard. It took all hands, including Romero and the mess men, to unload the pump from the flatcar and set it up. We got it coupled and running before breakfast. After breakfast we connected a freshwater hose to a coupling on the dock. We could almost see the ship settle deeper and deeper as the oil and water poured into her. In the afternoon a horse-drawn wagon loaded with food— fresh vegetables, meat, and bread—stopped at the foot of our gangway. Behind it was another wagon, and behind that still another, a long wagon train of food. Again all hands without distinction went to work carrying it aboard.

Late in the afternoon I went to the bridge and studied the harbor. I estimated the distance from the end of the dock to the clear space of the harbor where a ship could turn, and from there to the opening in the breakwater leading to the sea. For an hour I studied these distances, and the dock's position relative to channel and to breakwater, until I could close my eyes and see it all as clearly as if they were open, until the whole layout of the harbor was marked on my mind like a map drawn to scale. If we left this dock at night, in the dark, I wanted to know my way through the harbor. I did not want any miscalculations here with a shipload of people. When I was certain I could be blindfolded and take the *Paducah* out, I went below again.

The night was totally dark; neither stars nor moon could filter any light through the thick clouds. But every light on the *Paducah* was burning; we were lit up as if for a festival. All of us had been standing on the decks for a long time, not thinking anymore, just waiting, and then someone shouted in the dark, "Here they come!" It had just the sound we somehow knew it would have. It was almost as though we had heard it before, as though we had gone through all this in another time, another place.

The train of cars glided down the tracks and stopped. There were no lights in the cars and no sign of people anywhere. It was oppressively quiet. Peter, Emil, Chaim, and Dan, a Hagana man who had just came in from Sofia, walked out of the darkness into a pool of light on the dock, crossed it, and walked on into the darkness again.

Forward, near the first car, Moka stood with most of our crew, which had been divided into squads. Quietly he gave final orders. He dispatched one group down the train, one man to take his post beside each car. We had run out two extra gangways; at one was Leonard Rotter, at the second Eli Bergman, and at the third George Goldman. Behind each of these was a group of men who would guide the people to their places. Moka posted what he called the "separation squad." Its job was to take from each passenger all excess baggage for which there would be no room in the holds. "Be as gentle as you can," he told this group, "but be firm. If they don't want to give up their bundles, just tell them that the more bundles there are, the fewer people we can carry. And be sure to impress upon them that each person will get his own property back."

Moka was called from the dock: "Telephone. From Sofia." He jumped down the gangway and was onto the pier and away into the dark interior. It was five o'clock.

In ten minutes he was back. Full of something new, he jumped up the ⟨gang⟩way. He didn't wait to seek privacy. "Captain," he said, "the *Northland* ⟨is leaving in an h⟩our. She'll be loaded first. We'll have to move out of this ⟨berth. We can't⟩ load here."

⟨…⟩s. He looked at me, as if expecting that ⟨…⟩ reason that these orders couldn't be ⟨…⟩ near disaster of plans fouled up by the ⟨…⟩ orders.

⟨…⟩ ship's rail.

⟨Where do⟩ we move?" I asked.

⟨…⟩ right where we are. Just move far enough

⟨…⟩ to do. We were going somewhere. With all ⟨…⟩d to Sholom, "All hands back aboard. Half ⟨…⟩f aft. We'll put three men on the dock f'w'd ⟨…⟩es. Start them moving our head line up to the ⟨…a⟩fter spring line f'w'd about eighty feet. We'll heave the ship forward on the spring, slacking all after lines. And when the men are able, have them move their after lines forward to the next bollard. Same forward. But we'll have the spring line move us."

There were some Bulgarian Communist officials on the dock, some of whom understood English. All seemed a bit shocked and perhaps pleased to see an order executed so quickly and efficiently. Apparently they were having trouble getting anything out of their naval establishment.

As the ship moved forward, I was moved by the effort that this crew of young volunteers, former innocents to the sea, was displaying in moving the ship. As the after lines tightened with the ship's forward movement, they were slacked off and the big bights, the eyes in the rope, were lifted and moved ahead to the next bollard. And the same thing was happening to the forward lines.

The key was the inch-and-a-half spring wire; it was taut and singing a bit as it took the strain from the winches and moved the ship forward.

We moved four hundred feet and secured to our new position.

Moka approached to apologize. "There's a reason for loading the *Northland* first. We want to load as many people as we can into her, and then we'll take the rest. When we get close to the Palestine coast we may want to bring the ships together and move our people into the *Northland*. We could then return the *Paducah* to Europe and save it for another voyage."

The only illumination on the dock was the glow from the *Paducah*'s lights. It was not very bright and produced weird shadows. We could hear the sound of the water as it lapped against the piling of the dock.

We had coffee and thought about what small but important thing each of us might have forgotten.

Then the *Northland*, like a ghost ship, quietly slid opposite the empty place on the dock, and her heaving lines quietly came leaping into the light. Our crew grabbed them and pulled until the weight of the heavy mooring line was dragged across the black water. Dripping onto the dock, the bight was dropped over the bollard. The big lines tightened, and the *Northland* came alongside and was secured.

Gangways from the *Northland* clattered onto the cobblestones of the pier. Men took up their positions.

Moka shouted in Hebrew to the bridge of the *Northland*. Getting a hoarse reply of acknowledgement, he waved to our sailors. "You can give a hand to the crew of the *Northland*. But don't get in their way."

Capt. Rudy Patzert in 1947.

Moka Limon, the Hagana commander who joined the crew in Bayonne.

Walter "Heavy" Greaves, a veteran of the run to Palestine who was promoted to third mate for the second leg of the voyage. (J. G. Seruzier)

The *Paducah* steams past Gibraltar. This photograph was apparently taken by British intelligence. (U.S. Naval Historical Center, Naval Imaging Command, Washington, D.C.)

The *Northland* and the *Paducah* moored at Haifa, their passengers still aboard. (Clandestine Immigration and Naval Museum, Haifa)

Members of the *Paducah*'s crew on the seawall at Biarritz, France. *Left to right*, Lou Ball, Reuben Shiff, and Al Brownstein. Ball and Shiff later joined the Israeli army and were killed during the 1948 War of Independence.

At the pier, the "welcome" to Palestine. (Clandestine Immigration and Naval Museum, Haifa)

British reinforcements board the *Paducah* after she was towed to Haifa. (Clandestine Immigration and Naval Museum, Haifa)

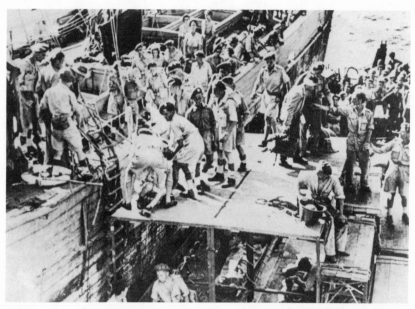

Passengers of an unidentified ship are forced to disembark. The raised platform was built temporarily alongside the ship. (Clandestine Immigration and Naval Museum, Haifa)

Disembarked passengers about to have their baggage searched. (Clandestine Immigration and Naval Museum, Haifa)

The baby aboard the *Northland*. (Clandestine Immigration and Naval Museum, Haifa)

British soldiers examine the immigrants' possessions on Haifa pier.
Confiscated canned goods and utensils lie on the ground. (Clandestine
Immigration and Naval Museum, Haifa)

Northland passengers wait as their bags are searched. The ship was renamed the *Jewish State* on the way to Palestine. (Clandestine Immigration and Naval Museum, Haifa)

A British ship used to take refugees from Haifa to Cyprus. Note the cages and barbed wire. (Clandestine Immigration and Naval Museum, Haifa)

Xylotymbou, the main detention camp on Cyprus. Detainees in Camp 65 line up to enter Camp 66. (Clandestine Immigration and Naval Museum, Haifa)

Tent mates on Cyprus. *Left to right:* Miguel Buiza, Antonio Chirri, Francisco Romero, Rudy Patzert, and Enrico Lopez and Howard Edmondson from the *Northland.*

Syd Abrams (*left*) and Eli Bergman in the Xylotymbou detention camp, October 1947.

Paducah and *Northland* crew members who were held in the Athlit detention camp and then moved to the Kiryat Shmuel camp. They remained in captivity the longest, until December 1947. *First row, left to right,* Albert Brownstein, Giuseppe Delfino, Sholom Kusnitzki, and an Italian seaman; *second row,* David Wurm, an unidentified Italian sailor, Eugenio Fantoni, and another Italian; *third row,* Eli Bergman, Jared "Rocky" Gibralter, Marvin Weiss, Lewis Brettschneider, Francisco Romero, Ernest Lipshutz, Miguel Buiza, and Charles Fariello. The three Italians were from a third ship, the *Af Al Pi Chen,* which had arrived in Cyprus a few days before the *Paducah.*

The "wild kids" and orphans from the *Northland* at Kibbutz Ma'aleh Hachamisha one year later. *Back row, center,* Irving Meltzer, radio operator. The boys called Meltzer their "American uncle." (David Nathan)

Blockade runners in Jerusalem in 1947. *First row, left to right,* Rudy Patzert and Ernie Lipshutz; *second row,* Larry Kohlberg and Sholom Solowitz. The other men are unidentified Palestinians.

19 ✳ The Ragged Line of Misery and Hope

There was a hush in which small sounds were extraordinarily clear—the lapping of the water, the splash of the *Northland*'s overboard sanitary line discharge, and the shuffle of feet coming toward us out of the dark. I had found a place at the side of the f'w'd gangway. Alongside me was a member of the *Northland*'s crew, Eddie Kaplansky. I had not been given a specific assignment, so I stepped back into the shadows, out of the light. I wanted to be out of the way, and, curiously, I wanted to be alone.

Now the first contingent of the passengers came into the cone of light. They were children, small children, five- and six- and seven-year-olds, squat little figures dressed fantastically in the cast-off clothing of adults, which made them look strangely old, an effect heightened by their solemn little faces, at once childlike and not childlike at all, but touched with fear and tiredness and sorrows usually known only by the old. The first of the kids reached the gangway where one of the crew was stationed. A tot, he bulged widely under the layers of rags and odds and ends of clothing wrapped about him, and he wore an old cap so many sizes too large that it almost covered his head and ears and neck. As he shuffled up the gangway with childish difficulty, the sailor, with a sound that was half laugh and half sob, scooped him up in his arms and clasped him fiercely to his breast.

And now, scores and scores of these tiny figures straggled out of the dark and struggled up the gangways. The men of the *Northland* picked up the smallest of them and carried them into the ship tenderly, as though these were their own small sons and daughters, their own flesh. I'm not a sentimental man—at least, I like to think that I'm not—and I couldn't remember when I had last wept, but there were tears in my eyes now. I was not ashamed of them when Eddie Kaplansky found me in the darkness and

119

stood beside me. "These are the orphans," he said simply. "There are so many of them, so very many."

I could not stand in the shadows any longer. I walked out to the dock and picked up one of the smaller girls, no more than three years old, to carry her aboard the *Northland*. She fought me like a little animal with a fear-driven strength. But I found that she was afraid not of me, but of being separated from her companion, a slightly larger girl. I took that girl by the hand, and carrying the one and leading the other, I went into the ship and to the compartment of bunks nearest the top deck that had been designated for the children, to keep them as near as possible to fresh air and sunlight—if this ship, at this time, could hope for sunlight.

There seemed to be hundreds of these tiny orphaned refugees. After them came the larger kids, fifteen- and sixteen-year-olds. But they were not kids at all, for they had been thrust into maturity without ever knowing that they had had no childhood. They came down the dock in marching order, erect and proud and singing. It was the first time I heard the "Hatikvah," the Jewish hymn of hope. They sang strongly, their heads lifted, and had a stately quality combined with yearning and determination. These boys and girls gave the song an overtone of fulfillment, making it almost a chant of victory as they marched up the cleated gangways and disappeared through the ship's lighted doors on the last stage of their terrible road to Palestine.

Far down the line of railroad cars there came out of the dark a cry in English from one of our men, pitched above the singing voices and cutting through them: "A woman is having a baby!"

No, I told myself, this couldn't be. This was too much, and I ran toward the sound. Inside one of the boxcars, in a pool of pale yellow light from a small flashlight, lay a woman with her eyes closed and her lips pressed tightly together. Over her bent an older man, a doctor from among the people. The birth was over when I arrived. The newborn baby was already bundled up and in the arms of the father, who mumbled unintelligibly. We improvised a stretcher and placed the woman upon it, and she was carried aboard the *Northland*, her eyes still closed and her lips clenched. The doctor took the baby and followed. The father, dazed, stumbled along behind. I put my hand on his shoulder, said, "Come with me," and I took him to Morgan's cabin. He sat in the big chair and clasped and unclasped his hands. I brought out a bottle of cognac and poured two drinks. I needed one as much as he did. Silently we downed the liquor. He looked at me with thanks in his eyes and managed a feeble smile. After a time he spoke in Hebrew, and I shook my head. "English?" he asked, and when I nodded, he said, "What name, the ship?"

"This," I told him, "is the *Northland*."

"*Northland*," he repeated, "*Northland*." He was silent for a moment. Then a small shudder shook him. "No! Not *Northland*."

I felt immediately what he was thinking. *Northland*, the place from which they had fled.

We found his wife in one of the sailors' rooms, the doctor with her. He assured me mother and baby were all right. I left the father there bending over his wife, who was smiling now.

The first fingers of dawn were visible when the last passengers, a cluster of fifteen or twenty, stood on the dock at the foot of one of the gangways. Joseph Almog, the *Northland*'s Hagana commander, led some of his crew members below decks to find space for this last little group. When Almog came back, sweating, this band was taken aboard, and the dock was clear. Somehow, 2,664 men, women, and children had been crowded into the *Northland*. The ship was 216 feet long and 30 feet wide. The *Northland* had performed many tasks during her years with the U.S. Navy's Bering Sea patrol. She enforced the law for the Justice Department; gathered military intelligence for the Navy; carried mail for the Post Office Department; carried teachers to their posts for the Interior Department. And now, on perhaps her final voyage, she was packed with passengers, refugees from the societies of Europe and Asia, who were seeking a new life in a new land.

The action now shifted to the *Paducah*. Most of the crewmen who were still aboard making last-minute preparations—Buiza, Greer, the cook, and his helpers—now came to the ship's rail and looked down on the developing drama.

I watched the first turmoil of people in their motley mix of clothes, human shapes distorted and thickened by an abundance of skirts, pants, jackets. A continuous line of people entered, boarded the ship and disappeared, led to their bunks deep below. The ship seemed to devour them.

Starting down a ladder to one of the holds, I met Rotter coming up. "It's pretty hot down there," he warned me. This compartment was already filled, and it *was* hot, and very crowded. Most of the occupants were elderly people. The bunks were built in tiers of three and in pairs, with narrow passages between them. Utterly exhausted, many of the passengers were in their bunks, their tired faces gleaming with perspiration in the dim light. But others were full of animation, keyed to a nervous excitement.

The compartment hummed with talk, and there was an air of quiet jubilation. Two women sitting on one of the rough board benches stripped two sleepy, sweating children of their undergarments. They paid no attention to me as I squeezed past them. A group of older men, bearded, were arguing with great energy. They paused briefly to look me over, then continued, amplifying their words with vivid gestures.

I was a stranger to these people, and I had a quick feeling of not belonging, of being an outsider, observing all the signs of misery but not really knowing it, not really feeling it, scarcely even understanding it. I made my way to the ladder and went back on deck.

Still an endless line shuffled down the dock, emerging out of the darkness into the dim light. After pausing at the "separation squad" to surrender their bundles, which joined a huge pile on the dock, they clambered up the gangways and disappeared into the ship.

One of the Shou-shous on the dock was talking to a group of young people, ragged and wild-looking, their hair long and unkempt, all of them thin to gauntness and possessing an air of reckless savagery. They looked like a pack of young wolves.

"Where did they come from?" I asked.

"From Romania," the Shou-shou told me. "They're our 'wild kids.' There are many like them all over Europe. They went into the *lager*, the camps, very young. There's an old saying: 'He who lives with wolves usually learns to howl.' It's true in their case. When these kids got out, they knew how to howl, all right. And they found themselves in a world completely torn apart. They lived, but don't ask how. They fought and they stole and they did rough things, but they lived. In Palestine there is hope for them. In a land of their own we might reclaim them."

Their leader was listening with an expression of mocking curiosity, as though saying, "Who the hell do you think you are?" But there was also apparent in his face a grudging respect for this obvious new authority.

Later one of the Shou-shous told me, "They could give us trouble, but I don't think they will. We will keep them together and give them responsibility as a group. I think they'll be all right as long as they have some authority and the challenge of a job to do. Anyway, it'll be a new experience for them. Their leader's name is Label . . . he's a tough one."

Sholom was working in a four-man "separation squad," and I stopped to watch. An older woman with an enormous bundle approached, and Sholom spoke to her in Yiddish, pleadingly. She looked at his young and anxious face with her wise eyes and with a little shrug silently handed him the bundle and walked toward the gangway. Sholom, sweating, threw it on the growing pile. A young woman with a baby in one arm and a bundle in the other was stopped by one of the crew. She shook her head worriedly and spoke to him, but his Yiddish was inadequate. He moved to take the bundle from her, but Sholom roared at him, "She says her kid's diapers are in there, damn it! Let 'er keep it." But Moka, who seemed to be everywhere at once, came up. With a friendly smile he took the woman's bundle, opened it, found the diapers, and handed them to her, then retied the bundle and threw it on the heap. The woman went aboard with a smile, and Moka darted off. Men wearing black bowl-topped, broad-brimmed hats and long black coats, bearded, and with paises—the lock of hair growing down in front of the ear—shuffled up to the squad and surrendered their bundles, most of them very small. An unusually large woman with a fat face spoke appealingly to Sholom in a low voice. He started back from her as though she had struck him. Forgetting his Yiddish, he shouted in English, "Get out of here!" The woman sneered at him and passed on.

"What was that about?" I asked.

"What, that old witch!" he said. "She wanted to know if she could buy special quarters and food for herself! The people you meet!"

From the dock, as out of a cave of darkness, the endless line of people emerged to pause at Sholom's group, then move on toward the oasis of light, toward the gleaming round portholes and the bright rectangles of the doorways. It seemed, as the night dragged on, that all of humanity, troubled, beaten, and worn, was filing out of the blackness and pouring into the *Paducah*. I wondered how in the world could she hold them all.

The night was far gone when I went to my cabin to seek a little corner of quiet where I could sit for a moment and try to deal with my emotions. But it was not quiet in my cabin; a troubled hum of voices came down the dock from the *Northland*, and I could hear shouts from the dock as the people still poured aboard. I wanted to rest, I said to myself, in the midst of people who had not known rest in their lifetimes. Wheels clacked on the rails as a boxcar was emptied and shunted down the track. A fresh car loaded with people was moved into position by the gangway.

A woman appeared at the door, her face twisted in worry and voice full of agony. I could not understand her words, except for the name Mendel, which she repeated over and over. It seemed that Mendel was lost. From awkward sign language I gathered that Mendel was not very big, about three feet tall, and with this information I sat the woman in the skipper's chair and went to look for him. It would give me something to do. Wandering through the holds, crowded, hot, and smelling now of human bodies, I squeezed my way through bunks where there was scarcely room to pass and asked repeatedly for Mendel, but could not find a child who was three feet tall and lost. Finally I returned to the cabin, but the woman was gone.

I went out on deck and stood at the rail for a long time, watching the people come aboard, until I no longer saw individuals with separate faces and different backgrounds and private dreams and personalities but just a mass of humanity bearing a burden too heavy to carry and looking for nothing at all in the world but a home.

One of the Shou-shous came up the gangway to the boat deck. "Where do all these people come from?" I asked him.

"About eighty percent of them are Romanians who were interned in slave labor camps by the Nazis. Others fled from the Germans into the Ukraine, where they were interned when the Nazis occupied the Ukraine. Still others went further into Russia and were not captured by the Germans. Some took part in the partisan operations against the Germans. The rest are Hungarian Jews who were either in slave labor camps or in death camps."

After one hour I could see that the ship had sunk deeper into the water, perhaps a whole twelve inches.

A wave of exhaustion swept over me. Half hypnotized by the repetition of watching the people board, I went to my room and lay down.

Dave Greer shook my shoulder gently. "Time," he said. "We've about finished loading."

I scrubbed my face in cold water to erase all sleep. Now it was time to be awake.

Chaim, Peter, and Emil were standing with Moka on the dock by the gangway. Joining them, I shook hands with Peter and Emil. Dov grasped my hand in both of his and gave me a long, searching look, as though trying to find in my face the explanation of why I, a non-Jew, was doing this. Chaim grasped me by my shoulders and gave me a quick, strong hug, then turned and walked away. The others followed. Moka and I went aboard, and the gangways were rolled onto the dock, where they fell with a clattering finality.

I asked Moka, "How many?"

"One thousand, three hundred and eighty-eight."

Don Miguel, Dave Greer, and Heavy were waiting on the bridge.

"Everything ready?" I asked.

"Ready," Heavy said.

"Is the *Northland* ready to go?" I asked.

"They are following us out," said Buiza.

"Are our engines ready?"

"Yes."

"Fore and aft. Stand by to let go," I said, and the Spaniard left the bridge to go to his post on the fo'c'sle head; Dave, the second mate, went to the stern. Heavy walked over to the engine room telegraph. I nodded to him, "Stand by on engines." He pushed the brass handle down and up, and from the engine room came the tinkling reply as the small arrow moved to "Stand by."

The decks were so crowded with people that the crew had some difficulty moving about.

The lines were let go fore and aft, and we were free of the dock. "Slow astern, starboard engine. Wheel amidships," I ordered. We could feel the vibrations as the propeller turned, and we backed off, turning into the harbor.

The people were pouring up on deck now, crowding every available space. Silently they watched the gap widen between the ship and the shore. From far down the dock Peter, Emil, Dov, and Chaim gave us a final wave. As we passed through the breakwater into the sea, the sun was just detaching itself from the horizon. Dave Wurm, who was coiling down a line on the fo'c'sle head, suddenly straightened up and, in a thin but clear voice, began to sing the Jewish song "Hatikvah," or "Hope." Slowly at first, then faster, like a fire spreading, the people took it up. Standing straight and facing the sun, the men, the women, the young people, the kids lifted their voices over the sea, and they sang.

20 * Through the Minefields and the Straits

For six hours we picked our way through the minefields. For the entire time, I sweated with nervous tension. Before we sailed, Emil had told us that a year ago a ship had struck a mine in these waters and gone down so swiftly that all aboard were lost. We constantly checked our positions with our chart and the still-visible coast. Even with a lookout posted on the fo'c'sle head and another on the bridge, I strained my eyes looking for any object in the water. When we were finally in the clear, I was exhausted, not only from the tension of passing through the mines, but from the long, almost sleepless night so filled with emotional strain. But I reminded myself that everybody aboard was as tired as I was, and some, perhaps, more so.

I left instructions on the bridge that I was to be called if anything unusual, no matter how minor, occurred and went to my cabin. I found on entering the passageway that most of our men had given up their rooms to women and children. I looked into Moka's room and found it crowded with small children, about fifteen of them, ranging from one to four years old, and a young woman who was apparently their nurse. I withdrew hurriedly and went to my own cabin, now the only spot of privacy aboard the ship. I wondered whether I, too, should give up my room and sleep somewhere on deck. But I couldn't do that. Until we reached the coast of Palestine, mine was the big job. I would be on the bridge almost constantly, needing to snatch whatever sleep I could, whenever I could. Besides, my cabin was more than my room; it was the ship's office, its safe filled with the ship's papers, and I couldn't turn it into a dormitory. But maintaining such luxurious privacy in the midst of so much crowded suffering seemed indecent.

I didn't turn in right away but sat at my desk and wondered about the new problems of the ship—the feeding and care of fourteen hundred persons, including infants, kids, broken adults, and the old. I told myself that this was not my worry; my only worry was to get the ship through. All the rest was Moka's department, and I had nothing at all to do with it. Nothing at all. Except that, as a human being, I was unable to shed my responsibility.

While I was sitting there, Moka came in, carrying a tremendous stack of papers. "The passports and exit visas for each passenger," he said, dumping the lot on my bunk. "We'd better put them in the safe. The customs men at Istanbul will want to see them."

"Expect any trouble from the Turks?"

"No," he said. "They're not in a position to do anything, one way or another. They'll simply get us through their waters as quickly as they can, and then try to forget that we were ever there."

"Where are you sleeping now?"

"You looked in my room? It's full of kids. Oh, I'll find some place to spread a blanket."

I decided to take a look around before I turned in. I went first to the galley, where I found five young girls in aprons. "My assistants," Romero said with a big smile. "They help."

"But I thought the people had their own cooks. Moka told me they would do the cooking for the passengers. All you have to do is cook for the crew."

"The galley isn't big enough," he said. "Besides, why should they work? With my helpers I can feed everybody. It's simpler this way."

"How many hours a day does that mean for you?" I asked him.

"Who knows?" he shrugged. "What are hours? When I am helping people, I feel good. Hours have nothing to do with it."

I left him there with his five girls and his steaming pots. I knew the job he had undertaken would mean at least sixteen hours a day of furious labor. As on army transports during the war, we could serve the passengers only two meals a day. Even so, it was almost a continuous process, with the people going single-file past the serving line with their mess kits. When the last person in the line had been served, it was almost time for the second meal to start. The crew had to be fed three times a day, and between times the small children got milk and chocolate in the mess room.

I didn't get far before I gave up my attempt to make a tour of the ship: it was far too crowded to go walking about. The passengers occupied almost every inch of deck space. There were endless lines before the water faucets, installed at points near the rails; the people stripped as far as decency would allow, and even though the water was cold, unheated sea water, they washed in it without complaint.

Some women had formed a broom brigade and were sweeping up the quarters below decks. Another group of women had commandeered the crew's wash buckets and were bathing all the orphan infants aboard. But most of our passengers were listless, sprawled motionless on their bunks, some of them sleeping in utter exhaustion, the wakeful ones staring at nothing with unseeing eyes, remembering all the things they would never be able to forget. I pushed my way through the crowds to my own cabin and closed the door, and I fell asleep as soon as I hit the bunk. It seemed that I had been awake for a week.

Music on the loudspeaker wakened me. It blasted through the ship with a strident quality, and I recognized it as one of the Yiddish phonograph records brought aboard by Sholom. One of the more religious crew members had told me that they were too suggestive, but Sholom was very fond of them. I wondered, as I lay on my bunk, if we should play them. Unwillingly, I climbed out and went to find Moka.

"What about this music?" I asked him.

"Most of the people don't understand it," he said. "The songs are full of American idioms and double meanings which they can't get. I don't understand them all, either."

When I suggested to the bosun that his records might not be appropriate, Sholom looked at me pityingly for my failure to appreciate good, bawdy singing. With surprise on his face, he said, "You know, these Jews, wherever they come from, the Sephardim, many don't understand Yiddish. They use Spanish."

But we switched to the Palestinian music Moka had provided. "They'll hear plenty of that," Sholom grumbled as he gathered up his records. "What they need is something lively to pep them up." He went below shaking his head.

The weather was perfect. There was a high, bright sun that gave just enough warmth to take the chill out of the autumn day, and the Black Sea was as calm and smooth and green as the top of a billiard table. From the bridge the old *Paducah* looked like a Sunday excursion steamer, her decks crowded with sunseekers on a weekend holiday—except that a close look revealed the ragged clothes, the gauntness and the ugly scars, the numbers tattooed on the forearms, and the pain in the eyes that looked big because the faces were so shrunken.

I remained on the bridge all day, pacing back and forth on the starboard wing. I wished I could go below and sleep, but I knew I couldn't: the ship was too noisy, and I was too excited. Looking at all the accumulated misery of the throngs on our foredeck, I wondered if I would ever rest easily again or if, for the rest of my life, I would be haunted by guilt for what had been done to these people. It seemed to me as clear as the thin, bright sunshine that the crimes committed against the Jews had not left any of us untouched, and the guilt, somehow, was upon all of us. If I had been asked to explain it convincingly to someone who had no such feeling, I suppose I would have failed, yet it seemed unarguable to me at the moment.

The afternoon passed. I ate supper hurriedly and returned to the bridge. At sunset we approached the Bosporus. It grew totally dark before we reached the pilot station, and a battery of powerful searchlights was directed upon us, the bluish glare throwing long shadows and casting a black silhouette of the ship upon a sheer cliff on our far side. Though the searchlights were an aid to us, I resented them. I stared moodily at the monstrously distorted shadow of the *Paducah* as it slid along the cliff side, silent and ghostlike.

The Turkish pilot was nervous when he came aboard, but he said nothing beyond the commands necessary to guide the ship, and I asked him no questions. He seemed to relax a bit after several cups of coffee and a pack of American cigarettes. We made our way silently down the Bosporus. A brooding quiet settled over the ship. The only sounds were the low hiss of the water along our sides and the intermittent rumble of the steering engine on the afterdeck. At Istanbul the pilot maneuvered us into position, and as we dropped anchor, the sudden clattering of the chain sounded like an eruption, something unexpected and dangerous. Then the silence closed in again while we waited for the customs and immigration men to come aboard.

In my cabin I removed from the safe the great stacks of exit visas and passports and placed them upon the desk. Moka came in, but we didn't speak; we just sat and waited. After a time, two Turkish officials were shown to the cabin. They both looked a little pale, as though they had seen something that frightened them.

The British had tried to put pressure on the Turkish government to stop the ship by claiming that it was not seaworthy and that the passports of the passengers issued in Bucharest had forged Uruguayan visas and were therefore invalid. But the Turkish government had to watch its step because of the Russian presence in the Black Sea and the Dardanelles.

Neither of the Turks sat down, and I didn't invite them to be seated. I felt a vague hostility toward them; I was weary of uniformed men, men with the power and authority to say, "You can't go there, you can't do that." If I wasn't careful, I knew I would yield to the temptation to take these two and pitch them out of my cabin on their heads, brass buttons and all. Whether they sensed my antagonism or not, they did nothing provocative. Instead, they were exceedingly polite.

"You have many people aboard," one said.

"Yes," I replied. "We have many people aboard."

"I am afraid, Captain, there is a question of ship safety. You must be overloaded."

"Whom are you representing when you make a charge like this?" I asked.

"Only the Turkish government," the senior pilot answered, his face blank.

"Is there anything I can do to satisfy you that this is a safe ship?" I asked.

"We will have to discuss this matter with our officials ashore," he said.

"When you leave," I said, "you must release the information that we have 1,388 people on this ship, with limited sanitary conditions and limited food. Many people, around the world, will be watching. If you keep the ship here, we'll soon have a crisis of sanitation and lack of food."

Both officials were quiet. They wrapped some cord around the large bundles of passports and left the ship.

Looking back over our stern, I saw the *Northland* slowly coming up toward the anchorage. I watched the splash as her anchor clattered into the black night sea. The officials did not go ashore, but headed for the *Northland* and boarded her.

We settled down to wait and to speculate about what the night would bring.

The *Paducah* lay anchored just inside the blockade chain that stretched from a breakwater in the north to another in the south and separated us from the Black Sea, which lay on the far side of the chain.

As I waited, I lay down on my bunk and quickly fell asleep.

Greer, the second mate, suddenly called, "Here comes the chief pilot."

I reached the rail and looked down at the pilot's small boat. Climbing the few ladder rungs to the rail, he swung his legs over and came up to my room. With a surprisingly jaunty smile he said, "OK, Capitan. Here's your clearance."

He handed me a single sheet of heavy, official-looking paper covered with Turkish script.

I was too dumbfounded to do anything but shake his hand and say, "Thank you."

As he was leaving I asked, "Has the *Northland* also been cleared?"

"Yes," he said. He stopped at the rail and called up, "Your pilot for the Sea of Marmara will be here shortly."

Good as his word, the new pilot came aboard.

All night we sailed the Sea of Marmara. When we were well clear of the land, I turned in, but I did not sleep, in spite of my tiredness. I tossed and turned for a time, and then, wearily, put on my clothes and went to the bridge, where I paced back and forth and listened to the murmuring sounds sifting up out of the swarming quarters below deck.

We were an uneasy ship with an uneasy cargo. It occurred to me quite suddenly that I was thinking of myself in relation to the passengers with a new, complete identification, as though I were one of them, fleeing from a terrible past. Why this new attitude, I asked myself. I was not one of them. I was not fleeing from my past; when this trip was done, my responsibility, self-assumed and limited to the navigating and running of the ship, would be over. I would go home again. The barbed wire and Bren guns were not for me. Those experiences were for the Jews, and I was not a Jew. "And being for myself only, what am I?" There it was again. Hadn't Emil told us that under the fascists in Bulgaria anyone caught aiding the Jews had been executed? That you couldn't oppose a piece of fascism without opposing every manifestation of it? And to oppose any part of it was to risk your life. The barbed wire and the Bren guns could have been for me. I *was* one with the passengers of the *Paducah*. I was committed to their side. What happened to them happened to me, happened to all of us. We all shared, both the pain and the promise. And it struck me that there was enough of both to go around; no man needed to suffer a want of either.

By morning we were entering the narrow strait of the Dardanelles.

We stopped the ship, which was quiet for the moment. Then there came the babble of voices as the passengers crowded the decks to stare at the Turkish coast in the early morning light. Luckily, there was land on both sides of us, and the people were distributed more or less evenly. I had a haunting fear that sometime, somewhere, something would cause everyone aboard to crowd to one side of the ship. Their weight wouldn't capsize her, I thought, but it would be enough to give her a dangerous list.

We dropped a rope ladder over the side, and a pilot climbed aboard. He made no secret of his distaste as he shouldered his way through the crowd to the ladder leading to the bridge. "Insulting bastard," I thought to myself, taking his attitude as a personal affront. When he greeted me with a "Hallo," I replied brusquely. We gave him coffee and cigarettes but discouraged conversation. After a few minutes he gave up trying to talk and limited himself to orders to the man at the wheel.

And then it happened. Syd, the wheelsman, called out, "Captain, she's not answering. I think she's dead."

We were just off Cape Canakkale at one of the narrowest points, and the currents ran dangerously swift. I leaped to the telegraph and rang both engines to a stop, then hollered down the speaking tube for Charlie to fix the steering engine.

Greer called in a low voice to Syd, "Put your wheel, midships and keep it there for now."

Syd nodded calmly, midshipped the wheel, and stood quietly back from it. He had become an experienced wheelsman.

"Ai, ai," yelled the Turkish pilot, grasping his head in both hands in frightened impotence. "Over there, Captain," grabbing my arm with one hand and pointing with the other. "That buoy, underneath, it's an American Liberty ship. She went out of control right here and cracked up on a rock. Ai, ai!"

The *Paducah* had lost nearly all headway by now, and the current was sweeping her rapidly toward the red buoy and the land. I leaped to the telegraph and rang for full speed ahead on the port engine and full speed astern on the starboard engine to turn the bow away from the coast. Under my breath I cursed the old ship and her dilapidated steering gear, and cussed Charlie for his slowness. And for good measure I cussed the Turkish pilot for his uselessness.

The ship shuddered as her propellers, thrashing in opposition to each other, bit into the water with maximum power. For a moment it seemed as though the vibration would open some plates. But slowly our bow stopped swinging in toward the land, hovered motionless for a moment, and then, gradually, began swinging offshore. Now I rang new orders on the telegraph: "Full speed astern on both engines." Then I shouted down the speaking tube: "Give 'em all you've got! Strain 'em!"

By the time we had worked our way back toward the middle of the narrow channel, Charlie appeared on the bridge and announced cheerily that the steering engine was repaired. Seeing his casual attitude, I realized that only the few of us on the bridge knew how close we had been to tragedy. Fariello went below and I turned to the Turkish pilot. "All right, she's yours again." He nodded, but the fear remained in his eyes. I walked to the far end of the bridge to get as far away from him as I could.

"Both engines full ahead," said the pilot.

I went below, so tired that I stumbled as I walked toward my cabin.

21 ✳ *The British Return*

Dave Wurm brought the news to me in my cabin. "Do you want to see the bride?"

"Bride?"

"Yes, we're having a wedding this afternoon. Fellow met the girl in Auschwitz."

"Sure, I'd like to see the bride. Does the skipper get the right to kiss her?"

Dave grinned. "You'll have to see the bridegroom about that."

Deep in the ship, on a shelf-bunk, the girl sat, rosy-faced and excited, her bridegroom, thin and gaunt but radiating happiness, beside her. They were so engrossed in each other that they hardly saw Dave and me.

Label, the Romanian "wild kid," and his gang were practicing songs for the wedding. Martin Gooen rigged up a loudspeaker connection on the foredeck so that the wedding could be broadcast to all those people who had to stay below.

The afternoon was ideal for the wedding, the sun warm and glinting off the calm sea. From the bridge Moka, Miguel, and I leaned over and watched the preparations. Lacking the wedding hupeh canopy, a prayer shawl was substituted. Menachem Keller, the Hagana radio operator, stood by with his broadcast hookup. Label led his young men and girls in joyful dancing. Then the wedding party, headed by a dignified old rabbi, passed through the mass of people to the canopy. There was such a press of spectators that the bridegroom was pulled under the canopy with difficulty. The bride wore a neat white dress with a white veil over her face. The people pressed in so close that I couldn't see the details of the wedding. I could see an older woman with tears rolling down her cheeks.

"What's that?" Miguel asked. I looked where he pointed. Out on the horizon was a ship with the neat, trim lines of a destroyer. Was it Greek or Turkish, or were the British back?

With great speed the destroyer steamed across the sea toward us. Through the glasses I could see the Union Jack hanging from its flagstaff. So they were with us again. They probably had some agent in Istanbul watching to let them know of our return to the Aegean.

With deadly grace the destroyer came alongside, and the people who were engrossed in the wedding became conscious of it. A silent feeling of hate, so intense it could almost be smelled, rose from them. With bitter eyes and grim faces they stared at the destroyer. At twenty yards from us, we could see the British looking us over through powerful binoculars, scrutinizing our faces, our clothes, the layout of the ship.

The rabbi who was conducting the wedding ceremony stopped his singing of the service, raised a clenched fist, and shook it at the destroyer. Then, regaining control of himself, he continued with the service.

From the destroyer came a metallic voice over a loudspeaker: "What is your destination?" Dave Gutmann grabbed the Dinah Shore record, "Welcome, Welcome," set it on the record player, and switched the loudspeaker system from the wedding to the record. The jazzy voice boomed out over the sea, drowning out the destroyer's loudspeaker. As her sailors lined the rail and stared at us blankly, the destroyer wheeled and fell in astern of us.

There had been no real prospect of escaping the pervasive arm of the British fleet. One of the Turkish pilots had already warned us that "everyone" was asking about the *Paducah*. But there was the small, ever-present hope: a dark night close to the Palestine coast, a moment's chance, a sharp turn left to swing the bow to shore, full ahead on the engines, a short sprint to the beach. We would drive the ship hard up on the sand and let as many as could slide down ropes and have a chance for freedom.

Now we had to recognize that a force greater than ours was controlling our destiny. We were not greatly surprised. There was no time to be disappointed; we had to prepare for the next steps.

Days followed nights in an even, peaceful flow. The weather continued to be beautiful. My worries were small ones, like the ship's listing in the mornings and evenings. Moka had designated the starboard side of the boat deck as the place where prayers might be said. And each morning and evening the men and boys, from five-year-olds to eighty-year-olds, gathered there. In their prayer shawls, *talis*, and yarmulkes, holding the Torah in front of them, they filled the ship with their cries. Early one morning Heavy, watching the passion and the sorrow of the prayers, commented soberly, "They give it hell, don't they?" It gave me a wrenching sensation to see a tiny boy carrying the sorrows of generations on his narrow shoulders.

The weight of the praying men and boys gave the ship a three-to-four degree list, the only time it shifted from its even keel.

One dawn, tired from a night's vigil on the bridge, I was struck by the thought that in my imagination I had seen such a picture of people. Awakened by the impact of the idea, I thought that I had not been there when these people left Palestine a thousand years ago, but I would be there when they returned.

The people settled down in the jammed ship to a new adaptation to their age-old pilgrimage. When off their watches, all our crew mingled with the people. Even the engine gang, who were isolated in the engine room, where no passengers were allowed, wandered among them. The other crew members were with them even while on duty, for the sailors had tasks in areas now occupied by the people. Even the privacy of the wheelhouse was invaded by Label as he broadcast to the passengers. His orders were brief. Besides telling the mothers of the milk and chocolate for the children, he often had to order some of the people to move from the sunny side of the ship back to the shade. Lovers of the rare sun, they followed it around to stay in its light and warmth.

The nights were glorious. There was a full moon, and the young people pushed their way into a group and sang in low voices. As I leaned against the bridge rail, listened to their songs, and watched the silvery moonlight on the placid sea, I enjoyed rare moments of internal quiet. The voices of the young people carried low over the passengers, some asleep, some awake.

We sailed south past the Greek islands of Mytilíni and Psará toward the Doro Channel, that ancient sea route. Low on the silvery, moonlit sea rose a sharp line of purple, the mountains that guard the sea gate of Doro. Then the flashing golden eye of the lighthouse on Cape Doro broke into the night.

Clicking on the chart room light, I unfolded American chart 3923, Aegean Sea, Southern Sheet—one of the most beautiful of all charts. Some lover of Greek history must have made this chart, some romantic mariner who journeyed in spirit with Ulysses over these sea roads, for it contained far more information than the modern mariner required. Here were the modern names of the many islands and, in italics, their ancient names. A profusion of details looked up at me from the chart: the names of tiny villages high on mountains, places no sailor ought to be concerned about; old volcanoes, now sunk, their burning hearts filled with fathoms of salty water, while fishermen took the fish from the green depths over the crater.

I thought of the fearsome monsters braved by Ulysses, and of the decidedly less fanciful but very real dangers faced by us. For us, not the giant Cyclops, but an empire grown old, struggling to keep what it had; not Erebus and the danger of Scylla and Charybdis, ancient destroyers, but the struggle of modern empires. Our passage, I thought, was more perilous than Ulysses' voyage among the ancient myths.

With rule and pencil, I drew our course—through Doro Strait and down through Zea Channel, ancient Keos Channel, toward Palestine.

I pushed my way gently through the crowded passageways of the ship. The pilgrims filled every space in which a person could lie, stand, or sit. Every movement of an arm or a leg had to be considered carefully and carried out slowly, lest one strike another person. The top tier of the three-high bunks was higher than my head, and men's and women's faces looked down at those below. Everywhere I went, people pressed against me. The mass of people on this ship made me feel as if this was not a ship carrying 1,388 people, but an entire world crowded with quietly suffering people. Here living was a struggle for fresh air, the battle to get to a latrine or a faucet, to prevent the jostling of a mess kit of stew and carefully bring the big spoon to a hungry mouth.

We passed Crete, then Cyprus, and the coast of Palestine was only a day's sail away. That night the destroyer that was shadowing us was joined by two more. The three fanned out, one astern of us and one on each beam. Our ship was silent in the moonlight; a new weariness caused by life aboard had overtaken the people. Many had not seen the sky since we left port a week ago. The smell of grime and sweat grew despite the daily struggle around the faucets. And the deck had accumulated a crust of dirt where people had walked and lived. In the last two days a new passivity had come over the people. The ship was their ship, but life was clenched into its narrow confines.

Meals were served with dexterity and hard work, twice a day. The children got special diets supplemented by milk and chocolate. The records we played over the loudspeaker system, a mixture of U.S. popular tunes and Palestinian songs, were one of the few sources of enjoyment, peace, and relaxation for the refugees. The Palestinian songs still were strange to most of the crew and the emigrants, but they had a familiar rhythm carried down through centuries with some old, some new, words. The most often played, most enjoyed song was Dinah Shore's "Welcome," which had a special meaning for all, passengers and crew.

I had learned to recognize a few faces—those of the nurses, the doctors, the pretty girls working in the galley—but for the most part the people remained an anonymous mass. Still, among them were those I wouldn't forget. This evening Moka asked me if he could use my cabin. When I agreed, he asked me to stay.

"A rabbi is complaining about a woman," he said. "Apparently she is working as a prostitute. At least she is sleeping, quite publicly, with different men." As an afterthought he mumbled, "Where the hell could she sleep?"

In a minute she came up. Her face was battered and her clothing wretched. She must have been young, but her teeth were gone, her nose was askew, and she had an expression of indifference. I saw the tattooed numbers on her arm. Moka spoke to her in Yiddish. I could understand that he was expressing the complaints against her and asking for an explanation.

She shrugged her shoulders and, to our surprise, smiled at him. She spoke softly, betraying no great emotion or urgency to deny or affirm, and she allowed us to have our opinion as if it did not concern her. The heat of her body filled the little cabin. I saw pity in Moka's face, but he had to play some moderating role between her and her shipmates. I could understand that he was warning her, and then he allowed her to leave. He got up with a shiver.

"We've got a last bottle of champagne in the frig," I said. "Let's kill it."

Hanging a towel over my porthole and shutting the door so that we wouldn't feel the eyes of some passerby on us, we got as many of the crew as we could into the room.

On my bunk sat Heavy, his face lined, his eyes tired. Next to him were Sholom, a new life in his tough body, and Miguel, as quiet as ever with his haunting face. Brettschneider looked emotionally exhausted, but Moka seemed as fresh physically as at the beginning of the voyage. I pulled the cork with a pop and caught the foaming liquid in water glasses. There was enough for everyone to have a small drink. A unified, hardened gang of men now manned the ship. The struggle to make this voyage a success had joined crew and pilgrims.

"A toast!" Moka held his glass up. "To Eretz. And to its people." The glasses clicked solemnly, and the toast was downed.

22 * Capture

Morning brought bright heat. We had been sailing south for six days, and that peculiar quality of the sun and sea in the tropics was with us this day. We were eighteen miles off the coast of Palestine, still outside territorial waters. But this was the day we were going in. Now we had four destroyers around us; one more had joined the pack during the night.

In the midst of the growing tension and heightened activity on the ship, I found myself on the bridge staring at Cyprus on the chart of the Eastern Mediterranean. We believed this would be our place of internment. Curious, I searched the island, looking for some clue that might give me an advantage to escape or to master some unknown danger. But the chart offered nothing more than the island's geographical location.

I was concerned not only about being sent to the detention camp on a remote island but about other possible penalties. There were some in the British Foreign Office, we had been told, who wanted stiff jail sentences for American captains and crews in order to discourage other seamen. Heavy, Brettschneider, and Gutmann had been warned at Acre of a jail sentence if they returned on another ship. But despite these threats crew and passengers had committed themselves. There was now no alternative course to sail.

The word was passed to all hands to change their clothes. Sholom was our outfitter, taking our American khakis and blues and handing us Romanian pants, shirt, shoes, coat, and cap. A bunch of kids gathered, and he passed our American clothes out to them. In my cabin I piled the things to be disposed of on my bunk. Menachem, the Hagana radio operator, gave my books to someone who was able to read English. I held up the straw hat

I bought in Bône. A wide-eyed kid in a giant's coat that reached to his ankles stood in the doorway. He stared unbelievingly as I admired the hat. I motioned him to put it on. He took off his barbarian piece of a Romanian cap and put on the straw hat. It transformed him; he was now a human being with dignity. I tried on his discarded hat. If the British ever recognized me in this cap, I would acknowledge that they were as superior as they conceived themselves to be.

Below, in the galley and storerooms, squads were distributing the remaining food to the people. Army canteens were filled with water. The children were loaded down with the last of the milk and chocolate. Label was running around carrying out Moka's orders, his gang of wild kids working like beavers.

Then it was time to clear out the chart room, a painful operation. The sextant went over the side, as did all the charts and the chronometers. "The British look for loot," Moka had explained. "We won't give them anything."

Plans were made with the engineers to inflict sufficient damage to the engines so that the British wouldn't be able to get them running and sail the ship back to France: they would be forced to tow us to Palestine. The Hagana had abandoned the plan to transfer the refugees from the *Paducah* to the *Northland*. It would have been a risky maneuver, and there was not enough room on the *Northland* anyway.

Moka came into my cabin. "Well, we can't put up a resistance," he said. Tiny muscles in his jaw tensed in anger.

"Why?"

"Just received orders from Palestine. The British have built up a tremendous provocation in the press, saying we're heavily armed and that many casualties are expected." He banged the bulkhead with his fist. "Hagana says that with our cargo of old people and kids we would have too many casualties. So, we are to be captured peacefully."

Menachem, the Hagana radio operator, had rigged a tiny radio broadcasting station deep in the ship. He planned to continue broadcasting word of the British attack as long as he could. From our regular radio set in the chart room a program was organized for that afternoon, to be broadcast to Palestine.

Moka brought a flag from his cabin and unfolded it to reveal the Star of David in blue on a field of white. It was beautifully made, and I thought of some Jewish Betsy Ross laboring over it carefully, slowly sewing into it, stitch by stitch, the long memory of an ancient people. Taking the microphone, Moka announced the beginning of the ceremony of the raising of the flag. Wearily, people raised themselves from the deck and stood at attention. Sholom swiftly tied the flag to the halyard running to the top of the mast. Label and his gang led the singing of the "Hatikvah," and everyone joined in. The flag slowly unfurled in the breeze and rose to the masthead. Six-foot-long boards with twelve-inch-high letters were hung over the side. We were now truly no longer the *Paducah*; we were the *Geula*, Hebrew for "Redemption."

Twenty-five miles off the coast of Palestine we sighted land for the first time—the top of Mount Carmel. The news spread instantly throughout the ship. Men and women climbed dangerously up on the rail and the mast for their first sight of Eretz Israel. The ship listed with the weight as the people scrambled to catch a glimpse.

When we were ten miles off the coast we could see more of the mountain, with tiny white houses on its top. A British destroyer eased closer to us. We could see a platform rigged on its deck, level with our bridge. The purpose of the platform, I had been warned, was to facilitate the boarding of our ship by troops. Constructed of pipes and planks, it extended from the side of the destroyer for eight or ten feet. When the destroyer rammed us, the platform would hang over our deck, and the soldiers could quickly drop onto our ship. The destroyer scrutinized us closely, then drifted away. From Haifa, now straight ahead of us, another destroyer came out.

We threw our phonograph records over the side, Sholom and Heavy skimming them as far as they could. They read the names of the records aloud before throwing them into the sea. Now these, our most personal common possessions, were gone.

Seven miles off Haifa a destroyer came very close. By her leisurely approach we knew the British were not yet ready to attack. The destroyer's megaphone carried a voice loud and clear: "If you resist, the blood will be on your head. You are now entering territorial waters, and you are liable to arrest if you continue. I repeat, if you resist, the blood will be on your heads."

Of the crew, only Moka, George, and I were on the bridge, but it was swarming with Label's gang and other passengers to make it more difficult to identify the three of us. George had the wheel, Moka was standing by, and I watched our course. Sholom, impatient for the action to start, was striding around the boat deck, a pirate in a villainous cap and ill-fitting pants and coat. The other crew members had knapsacks and were dispersed among the passengers. Charlie had the engine throttle, and Brettschneider and Rotter were fireman and water tender. The chief engineer and some other crew members had stowed themselves in an empty water tank. They were going to try to evade the British by hiding there until everyone was taken off. Then they would slip ashore.

Five miles off Haifa Moka walked swiftly over to George at the wheel. "I'm not going to sail right into their arms like a sheep. Let's head down the coast." I directed George to swing the ship's head around till our course paralleled the coast.

"Here they come!" Sholom yelled. Looking aft, I saw a destroyer coming in very fast, heading for the ship's side. Soldiers in helmets and gas masks and carrying clubs and rifles were standing on the destroyer's deck. Moka nodded from his side of the bridge. "Here, too. Let's get out of here." I rang the telegraph to stop, the signal for those in the engine room to sabotage the engines and get out. George put the wheel midships, and the three of us strolled off the bridge. Pushing my way through the packed people, who were tense and stiff with anxiety, I lost sight of Moka and George. I did see Romero, the cook, sitting calmly among a group of people in a lifeboat, a knapsack in his arms.

A destroyer rammed into us, and the *Geula* heeled over heavily. The soldiers dropped from their platform, which hung over our bridge, onto the ship. Using their clubs as flails, they knocked down several of the men and boys standing there. From the deck of the destroyer a young sailor turned a hose on us. I was ready to brace myself against a stream of high-pressure water, but something else hit me—tear gas. I grabbed my throat and eyes. A woman alongside me threw her shawl over her child's head, hugging him to her, the tears flowing down her contorted face. A soldier with a Sten gun, his face hidden in a grotesque gas mask, strode down the deck. Through my tears I saw Sholom, as if in a dangerous comedy, heave a pail of water over the soldier. Sholom grinned as the soldier drew back and raised his gun. The bosun stepped back, leaped over some people crouched on the deck, and disappeared around the deckhouse. The soldier wheeled around in panic and gesticulated with his gun at some passengers close to him. But they were blinded by the gas. More soldiers came up. In parties of four and six, Sten guns at the ready, the soldiers filtered among the people.

The ship lost momentum, the engines went dead, and we took on a considerable list to starboard. We had been captured.

Sitting among the people with my cap pulled down over my face, the big coat's arms reaching to my fingertips, the pants barely reaching my ankles, my knapsack in my arms, I felt fairly safe. It took time for the fact to sink in: I was no longer captain. The bridge was no longer my domain.

Label roused me from my reverie with a stealthy nudge in my side. He motioned me to follow him. I was apprehensive about a British soldier who was staring at us, and I would rather have sat there quietly, but I followed. We went down the ladder to the main deck, where the people were still gasping for air as the sharp-smelling tear gas slowly dissipated.

"Doctor Moka, Doctor Moka!" one of the English-speaking nurses cried. I wondered what that meant. Moka pushed his way through the people to a corner of the hold. I could see the real doctors there, bent over someone lying on a lower berth. Label motioned me to stay among the people, and he walked over to the group. The people around me were angry. I understood someone to say, "Two babies are dead, killed by the tear gas." Two young British soldiers had taken off their gas masks now. Their faces were red, and they were nervous, their eyes panicky. Back to back, their Sten guns raised, they watched the people edging close to them, eyes burning with anger.

In Yiddish, in Romanian, the voices of the people were growing louder and more angry. A man shouted, "Kill the Britishers! They killed our children!"

Moka looked grimly at the angry people. He held his arms up and called out to them in Yiddish. I could make out that he was telling them to be quiet; fighting the British there would only mean needless harm to the people. The voices quieted down, but the hard look of hate remained on the faces.

Hours passed while the British prepared to tow the *Geula* into port. The inside of the ship was heavy with the odor of fearful people; the air grew stale. I could hear people sucking for breath in the oppressive atmosphere. A woman moaned as she shifted in the darkness. A child cried, its voice rising in a note of terror. The welling, hysterical wail sent a chill through my blood. By the light of a flashlight, I saw the mother trying to quiet the baby with her breast; the father stroked its arm. The panicky child's eyes gleamed brightly in the light. Then I heard Moka's voice softly cajoling the child. Handing the father the flashlight, he picked up the child, and with the mother and father following led the way through the people. The mother was haggard, her stringy hair falling over her gaunt, sweat-stained face. Wearily, the people looked up, then pressed their bodies back against others to allow Moka to pass.

As he went by, Moka leaned over to me. "No fatalities," he said. "Some babies were nearly suffocated by the tear gas, but they are recovering." A soldier's cockney voice shocked me out of my sweating apathy. "You can't get out!"

Moka answered quietly. "I'm a doctor. This child's very sick. I'm taking him and the father and mother out into the air." The soldier's protest died as Moka shouldered past him.

I grinned into the dark. Doctor Moka! A fine way to maintain organization and move around under the eyes of the British. I was starting to learn how the Hagana worked while prisoner of the British.

Moka returned. He flashed his light around, and it passed over me. He sat down beside me. "Pick a name you won't forget!"

A name! First name? I remembered the boy Mendel who was separated from his mother. But Mendel what? My friend Helen in the States— Levey! Mendel Levey was my new name. "Mendel Levey."

"OK. Here's the plan: we're giving you a girl who'll be your wife. You are tired and frightened and cannot speak. She'll speak for you. The British have already started the search for the crew. They're looking for single young men, especially those who are not with anyone."

Moka led me out onto the deck, now illuminated by the moon and stars. Label and his gang were gathered in a tight mass. They opened up, took me in, and surrounded me. Far off I could see the lights of Haifa. The ship was motionless. A destroyer was working itself into position to tow us. On our bridge a British officer leaned over and called to the fo'c'sle head, "Get that towline from the destroyer." Alongside of our group I could see a tight group of British soldiers conversing among themselves. The sound of English was strange to my ears. I had to remind myself not to speak English.

The relationship between the British officer on the bridge and the one on the fo'c'sle head was not good. The one on the bow grumbled back to the bridge, "I can't do anything with these people here."

From the bridge: "Well, move 'em out of there!"

Plaintive voice from the fo'c'sle head: "They won't move."

From the bridge: "Tell the sergeant. He'll move them."

A rumble of a voice in English: "Move away now. Come on. Out of here."

I could see a heavily built soldier with a big club nudging people away from the towing bitts. The people moved reluctantly, sullenly.

With the towline made fast, the destroyer started hauling, and at a speed of about six knots we moved toward the lights of Haifa.

Thankfully, I sensed the slight breeze on my sweating face; now air would circulate through the hot interior of the ship. It must have been hell down there.

A nudge, and a voice whispered in my ear. It was Lew Ball, who had been a Ranger in the U.S. Army during the war. "See that lieutenant there?" I looked and saw a young lieutenant. "I know him. Met him during the fighting in Europe. They're the Red Devils, British airborne troops. He's a real tough character."

"Better not say hello to him here," I whispered, twisting my lips in a wry smile.

I wondered where the rest of the crew was. We seemed to be pretty well spread out. I had seen only George, Lew, and a few others besides Moka, who was constantly traveling around, leading the sickest people to the fresh air of the deck, sending others back to the hell below.

Label whispered to me, in Yiddish, "Our radio is still broadcasting."

The faces of Label and of the girls and young men in his group seemed to have changed. And then it struck me; it was I who had changed. Before, as captain, I had felt sorry for these people, deeply felt their misery, wished to help them. But now I was one of them. Their problems were my problems. The more I was identified with Label and his gang, the safer I would be from detection by the British. What happened to them happened to me.

As we approached the lights of the Haifa breakwater, a leaden boom in the water made the ship shudder. Then another! They were depth charges to prevent anyone from slipping over the side and attempting to swim ashore. There was a viciousness in this. Depth charges had protected me during the war, when submarines attacked Allied convoys. Now, in the quiet night, they were being used against a worn-out people who were being towed into a Palestine port.

The voice of the British officer on our bridge called to the fo'c'sle head in a worried voice. "Have that anchor ready to let go."

The young officer on the deck looked over our anchor windlass with his searchlight. "I can't make out how it works. It's a decrepit piece."

For a second I could imagine Sholom charging out to the windlass, swearing at the Britisher for insulting it, and showing him how easily it worked.

Relaxed and confident, the young people around me carefully observed what was going on. The British soldiers were wearing what looked almost like football equipment—padded, high-topped leather helmets, leather arm protectors on their left arms—but unlike football players, they were carrying clubs in their right hands. They didn't carry the Sten guns as the first soldiers did. Tired and nervous, the soldiers talked about women and bars, the typical talk of occupation troops who hadn't experienced combat. They were fighting their battles against old women and children.

A tugboat took over the towing. I could see an American ship tied to a dock. What amazement there would be if I climbed dripping aboard that ship and went into the mess room and told the sailors sitting around that I had just escaped from the refugee ship!

With shouting and fumbling, the soldiers managed to tie the *Geula* to a dock. The town of Haifa rose up the slopes of a mountain, lights gleaming in windows. Here and there, apparently at strategic spots, searchlights blazed, lighting up groves of trees, houses, streets, in startling detail. The lights were so powerful that I imagined I could see a fly walking up the side of a house.

A gangway was put aboard from the dock. Several army officers came aboard and talked with the naval officer who had been in command. All naval ratings went ashore, and more Red Devils in their red berets climbed up the gangway.

On the far side of the dock I could see a large ship. From the silhouette she was a cargo ship, but apparently she had been converted to a troop carrier. Then I made out the barbed wire cages on her deck. It was a prison ship!

The *Geula* was a hubbub of officials coming and going. A short civilian spoke in Yiddish to a group of the people. My ears pricked up. An ally? Women in nurses' uniforms came aboard with milk, but before I could get a glass, a squad of British soldiers came up and ordered us down the gangplank.

Watching the line of our people going down the gangway, I saw a strange sight—bright red hair escaping from under a broad-brimmed black hat. It was Brettschneider with his red beard, disguised in the severe black clothes of a religious Jew.

Label steered me alongside a girl. "Marta," he whispered. The girl was almost as tall as I was, built heavy and strong. She must have been only about sixteen, for her face had that unaffected, wide-eyed look of a young girl. She must have been one of the kids saved by the Russians, for the girls from the *lager* didn't have her brightness. She looked at me and smiled to give me confidence. This was a curious switch of responsibility; she had been mine, but now I was hers.

Slinging the rucksack on my back, I followed Label down the gangway.

I was tired and dirty, no different in any visible aspect from the rest. At the foot of the gangway there was a gauntlet of British soldiers, lined up, shoulder to shoulder, on both sides of the dock as far as I could see. A large, mobile searchlight shone up the dock, radiating a fantastic bright light and projecting deep black shadows behind the soldiers. As we walked up the dock, our enormously elongated shadows ran on before us. It was a mad scene.

Soon some soldiers stopped us, took our rucksacks and bundles and threw them on a pile, and shoved us onward. Other soldiers separated the women from the men. Marta's eyes sharpened, and she protested in Yiddish as we were separated. But the soldiers shoved her one way and me the other. Soldiers stopped us and searched us quickly. Two steps further on, we were again stopped while a soldier with a spray gun shot DDT up our pants' legs, down our necks, under our arms, and into our hair. Smudged white, we continued down the dock. The man ahead of me was stopped by a young British officer. As he was interrogating, I realized that the British officer spoke both Hebrew and Yiddish. If he started to question me, I would be lost. Sweat broke out on me. Watching the officer, handsome and trim in his tropical uniform, his cheeks slightly sunburnt, question the small, whiskered man ahead of me in an arrogant fashion, I felt a growing hostility. Gaining no information, the British officer gestured him to move on. The officer stared into my face, but I was not stopped. Past him, my muscles relaxed.

The line turned, and we filed back up the dock to the gangway of the prison ship. Marta was waiting for me there. Grabbing my arm, she helped me up the gangway. Suddenly I found it was not an act to look bowed and weary.

23 * The Prison Ship

Soldiers were on both sides of the people, and we filed between them up to a wire cage. A door swung open, and we entered. Inside was a second, smaller cage, about twenty feet square, but the soldiers didn't allow us to stop there. On the far side was a hatch leading down into the ship. We stepped over the high step and went down steep stairs to the deck below. A passageway ran through the ship, with rooms opening off it on both sides. The soldiers below turned us into a room. Five people were already in it. On the bulkhead, a sign stenciled in black letters read "For Seven People." A soldier stood at the door and shunted people into the room until no more could be pushed in. Along the walls of the room, which measured about eight feet by ten feet, were wooden benches, secured to the deck with bolts. Standing on one of these benches to make more room, I counted thirty-seven people.

A little relieved to be out of the searchlight's blinding glare, I surveyed my captive roommates. Knowing very well what the procedure would be, my fellow prisoners had put on as many of their clothes as they could. They knew this would be all they would have left after the search. The men were wearing three and four suits each, and the women had put on dress over dress.

The heat of so many bodies in such a small room was intense. Leaning against each other in their weariness, sweat streaming down their faces, people crammed on the wooden benches. The younger people lay side by side on the deck, some in impossible positions under the benches, behind the feet of those who were sitting. The air reeked of sweat. A young British soldier wearing a worried expression stood in the doorway. He was only carrying out his orders, to see that we didn't leave the room, yet he seemed concerned. Speaking in German, he promised that once the ship was out of the harbor we could go on deck. I watched him warily. My German might fool someone who didn't speak it, but he knew the language far better than I did.

Marta shoved me and motioned for me to sit on the deck. It was wonderful to be able to sit down, for my legs ached. This had been a long day and night of tension and anxiety. Beside me was a woman with a baby in her arms. The baby's tiny face was bathed in sweat and covered with prickly-heat rash. As I watched the baby, its face slowly turned blue. The exhausted mother had closed her eyes. I spoke to her and pointed to the baby. Her face tensed. Tenderly she wiped away the sweat with her hand and gently rocked the child and hummed to it. The child's face seemed to soften, and the blue tint gradually disappeared.

An older woman half-sat against the wall, her head thrown back in utter weariness, the tendons of her throat taut with fatigue and age, sweat dripping slowly down her face and off her chin. She looked like she was dying. Half-panicked, I looked around to see if anyone was paying attention to her. A man shook his head at me in a quiet way and patted his hand gently in the air, motioning me to rest, indicating that the woman was all right.

On the white paint of the bulkhead I saw scrawled hundreds of names and messages; fathers looking for families, sons for fathers, daughters for mothers, in all possible combinations and permutations. Here were messages for all who suffered this fate to see—cries written on a wall!

After what seemed like a century, the ship started to move. I could feel the shudder as her propeller started to turn over. The soldier hurriedly disappeared from the doorway. Soon another man appeared there. He was small and terribly thin; his eyes were bright in a pale, whiskered face; the curly locks of the pais ran down in front of each ear. He looked carefully into each face and, seeing me looking at him, smiled gently. "*Suche meiner Bruder.*" Seeking my brother. He turned away with a tired, sad face, and was gone as silently as he had come.

Next a young man in old clothes appeared. He spoke to my cellmates in Yiddish, telling them that it was permissible to go on deck now. He motioned me to come with him. The mother with the baby went first; the woman had scarcely the strength to make the trip to the top deck.

The door of the inner cage was open, and we walked through it and out into a larger space, still within the outer cage. The cool night breeze blew the sweat away and restored my strength, and for the first time since the destroyer rammed us, I felt relaxed. I had passed one search. I wondered if they had caught any of the crew. People poured out of the doorway and into the cage in a never-ending stream. Sucking in the cool night air as if it were life itself, they sprawled on the deck.

A man and woman on their knees were clinging to the wire of the cage and gazing longingly toward the disappearing lights of shore. For them the lights were fading, perhaps forever, for they were old, and, as Moka had told me, these people could expect to spend one and a half to two years on Cyprus before being allowed by the British to enter Palestine under the quota. The woman was dry-eyed, but her face was unalterably sad. The old man placed a trembling hand on her shoulder and buried his head in his other arm.

Suddenly, Sholom's voice boomed out, loud and jovial. "Moka!" was all he said. He led me toward a corner of the deck where we found Moka. Quietly but triumphantly, we shook hands. We had come this far successfully.

"The bastards," Moka muttered.

"What?"

"The women were searched by Arab policewomen. They took wristwatches, everything. One woman was wearing her mother's locket, the only thing she had left. That was taken."

"How tough is the search on the other side?" I asked.

"Tough enough."

British soldiers kept watch from the far side of the wire. Suddenly, the outside gate opened, and a British sergeant-major carrying a little swagger stick walked in. He seemed quite drunk. Parading about, he shouted orders to the soldiers outside. "You four men, come in here. I want the women and children to have fresh air. Chase these men below." He looked around as if he were directing a charge against barbarians. Arms stiff at his sides, he hunched his shoulders forward and shouted at a man sitting on the deck, "You! Get up! You, get below! Women and children must have air." The seated man shook his head and disclaimed any knowledge of English. This infuriated the sergeant-major. He nudged him with his foot. "Get up, I say! Get up!" Reluctantly, the man rose, and a soldier grabbed his elbow and steered him to the doorway leading down into the ship. With a shove, the soldier sent the man clutching for the rail in order to keep from falling. Luckily, before he reached us, the sergeant-major got weary of his little exercise in chivalry and, taking the soldiers with him, left our cage.

With the sergeant-major safely gone, a soldier called in a low voice through the wire: "Here, maties, have a cigarette." He pushed a pack of English cigarettes through the wire. Surprised, I reached out to take them. The soldier had a pleading look on his young face, a face that had known work and hardship. I felt sorry for him. Some of the British soldiers showed their dislike of this detail and were unhappy with manhandling the refugees, especially women and children. Despite my predicament, I was thankful I was on this side of the wire and not on his.

Moka was stiff and hostile to the soldier and refused to take a cigarette when I offered one to him. Sholom was already asleep. Finishing the cigarette, I rolled over to sleep. I wondered what would happen when we arrived in Cyprus.

24 * Sneaking into Captivity

Dawn crept over the ship with a damp chill. The people lay about immobile, paralyzed by days, months, and years of weariness. I lit a cigarette from the English soldier's pack. The ship was moving slowly. Watching the water, I figured we were making seven knots, and this ship was capable of at least twelve. It was 130 miles from Haifa to Famagusta, the port of Cyprus, but at this speed we wouldn't reach Famagusta till after dark. I wondered why. Was it necessary to make arrangements for us in the camps there?

Waking up from a nap, I wondered where Moka had gone. Sholom slept on as if dead, his mouth agape. A cigarette stopped my hunger a bit, and I looked around. None of our crew was around, nor was my "wife," Marta. I recognized two of the nurses and the doctor from our ship. They were attending to a woman who was lying on a bundle of old clothes. I wondered how they got the bundle aboard. Holding the woman's hand was an older man. He looked as though he hadn't slept all night; his skin was yellow and wrinkled, his eyes luminous but sad. The woman was in pain, sucking in each breath as though it hurt.

One of the nurses had a tiny boy on her lap, his arms wrapped round her neck while he slept. The boy, very small, had pale, translucent skin. His face was appealing in sleep.

Outside the cage, at intervals of ten feet, British soldiers stood watching us, their backs to the sea. I hoped that the sergeant-major was sleeping off his drunk and that the hangover occupied him the rest of the day.

The sun climbed higher, its pale light turning yellow and warmer. People stirred. Sholom awakened with a rush, then sat up and yawned, his eyes sharp as they sized up the situation with a quick survey around the cage.

Heavy appeared and reported: "The Spaniards are in a room all the way forward. Rotter and George and Dave are on this ship. Couldn't find any more of the crew."

"Do you think they were caught?" I asked.

"I don't think so. This ship only has seven hundred people on it. The rest of the people and the crew are still in Haifa."

The nurses and doctor came over to sit by us. The little boy, now awake, was introduced as Peter. He spoke only German. "Peter was born in a Romanian *lager*," one of the nurses explained. "He's an orphan. A German-Jewish woman who knew only German protected him."

The child was like a kitten seeking affection. His arms fondled the neck of the nurse, Hannah, and she kissed him and stroked his arm. She was a very attractive woman of about thirty.

"Where were you, Hannah?" I asked.

"Biro-Bidjian."

"Biro-Bidjian?"

"Yes, in the Soviet Union. I escaped to the Russian side of the German-Russian border in Poland in thirty-nine. I worked in factories, on collective farms."

"How was it?"

"Hard work, but decent people. The war years they had very little, but they shared everything with us. That is, most of them. Always there were some with the creeping curiosity and poison of anti-Semitism."

"Were there many Jews who escaped Poland?"

"Yes. They were scattered all over the country."

"And your friend?"

"Haia, here?" indicating the other nurse. "She was in the Urals. She worked in a factory."

The sick, gray woman shuddered to a sitting position, then fell back groaning. The doctor walked over to her, grabbed her hand, and took her pulse, while looking intently into her face. Her quick gasps for air gradually resumed a normal rhythm; her strained face lost its fear and regained the resigned weariness. "Her heart is bad," Hannah said.

"Where did you learn English?" I asked.

"In school. Vienna."

"Vienna was your home?"

"Yes. I was visiting in Warsaw in thirty-nine."

"Your mother, father?"

"All gone."

The doctor was a short man with a dark brown face. He didn't have the air of a doctor, that confident poise you expected. "Where was the doctor?"

"Auschwitz," Hannah said. "You will probably hear stories about him. But don't believe them."

"Stories?"

"He had a terrible job. The Germans made him select those who were weakest for the gas chamber."

The words fell on my ears and stirred horrible thoughts.

"He saved many, but the families of those he sent can't see that."

"He's in an awful position."

"Not bad now compared to what it was!"

I found it easy to sleep, and that was the best way to pass the time. About one o'clock I was awakened by Sholom. "Chow," he said. Soldiers brought a tub of stew and passed it out in mess kits. It wasn't bad; it had bulk, and it stopped the hunger pains. Sholom went back for a second helping.

In the late afternoon we sighted the coast of Cyprus. The sun was caught on a purple range of mountains, and ahead we saw a low point of land, its yellow sand imperceptibly disappearing into the blue sea. As we came closer to shore, we could see many tents in orderly lines. It looked like a camp. We wondered if that was our future home.

The ship anchored about a hundred yards from the Famagusta dock. A big, flatbottomed barge was towed out to us by a little tugboat and made fast alongside. The soldiers started us moving in a file for the gangway. Marta's worried face appeared among the people, and she pushed her way to my side. At the foot of the gangway we were herded to the back of the barge as more people filed down, gradually filling it. With difficulty, four young soldiers carried the woman with the weak heart down the gangway on a stretcher. They had to maneuver back and forth gingerly, straining gently. Their awkward tenderness here among the hundreds they had humiliated and imprisoned would have been almost comical had it not been for the dying woman on the stretcher.

At last the ship was emptied; its human cargo stood on the barge. The soldiers and officers lined the rail and stared down at us solemnly. They seemed to be trying to grasp the meaning of what was happening, to understand how these people had become the enemy and the reason they had embarked on this terrible trip across land and sea, over many months, to get to Palestine.

The barge was towed to the dock, and we began to straggle ashore. Darkness had fallen on the dock and the town. The headlights of cars threw their lights on our path. We passed through another DDT spray station. Sholom growled as he emerged with his pants white with the powder.

We climbed into army trucks—I could make out the name Ford— and the tailboard was banged closed and hooked. The truck drove a hundred yards and parked in a line of trucks already filled with people. In a few minutes another truck pulled in behind us. Soldiers with fixed bayonets walked slowly up and down the line. Alongside of us was the shadowy bulk of some old castle, with a small passageway through the wall giving the impression of tremendous thickness. The headlights of a truck illuminated a stone figure of a lion standing on its hind legs, a banner in its paw. The headlights moved on, but the image of the lion stayed in my mind.

The convoy started up, and we passed into the night. Label, the "wild boy," and his girl sat on the truck floor, her arm around his shoulder. The other people I didn't know; they were vague, strange people journeying together. Marta stood, staring out into the night, her hands on the sideboards of the truck. To her the ride was an adventure. Youth has a wonderful capacity to accept all of life, to take bad after bad, never doubting that some good will come.

Skirting the town, the convoy went at a mad pace through the dark countryside. When the road curved, the headlights of the trucks behind us lit up barren, rocky ground; our headlights lit up the truck twenty-five feet ahead of us, the people swaying and shaken, stiff with weariness.

Mile after mile, we rushed along the country road. Houses were like shadowy thoughts; dim lights peered through small windows in the clay walls as we zoomed by. We went through a small town, past a cafe with men sitting in front. They stood and waved to us, clenching their fists in salute and calling out, "*Shalom.*" Welcome. I wondered who they were? Later I learned they were Greek Cypriots who were seeking independence from British Mandate rule. From the trucks we shouted back, "*Shalom,*" cheered by the first sign of a friendly people.

On the road a sign, glimpsed in the momentary swing of a truck's headlights, warned me that we were approaching the camp: "Headquarters

Camp . . . 3 miles." I learned later that this enormous collection of detention camps was collectively called "Xylotymbou."

Our truck pulled up behind another that had stopped in front of a Niessen hut. The hut was huge, at least two hundred feet long. When we jumped from the truck, soldiers directed us into a group of people. Marta held my arm so as not to lose me in the confusion. The only light was from flashlights, the headlights of cars and trucks, and the brief square of light when the door of the Niessen hut opened for a moment. A hand grabbed me, and I heard the friendly growl of Heavy: "Good, you made it."

Label appeared with two of his boys, who brought Romero and Brettschneider. As more trucks unloaded, I saw Sholom; Marta ran over and brought him into our group.

One of the Hagana Shou-shous came skirting the crowd and peering into the mass. Label gave him a low whistle, and the Shou-shou shouldered his way to us. "Who's here?" he asked in a low voice. We named ourselves. "They'll ask your name, age, country of origin, town of origin. Learn the order, and learn the answers in Yiddish. If they ask any more, act frightened and bewildered."

He turned to me. "What's your name?"

"Mendel Levey."

"Lavy, not Leevy. Age?"

"Fünf und dreisig."

"Country of origin?"

"Romania."

"Town?"

"What shall I say?"

"Ploesti."

"Ploesti."

"Good. All of you keep your wits about you. This search is going to be tough."

Label handed me a strange object. In the dark I could feel leather straps attached to a little leather box. Then I remembered the prayers on the ship. These were phylacteries, worn on the arm as a reminder of the history of the Jews. Label handed me a little cloth bag; inside I could feel a small prayer book and another phylactery.

A searchlight, half-blinding, flashed atop a high pole. It was a minute before I could see the high barbed-wire fence around us, fifty feet away to one side and stretching off into the dark. Romero smiled at me. "This far, Captain," he said, reassuringly. I wondered how he could be so confident.

With his bald head, the whimsical cast to his face, the fine lines around his eyes, he looked like a Spaniard to me, and nothing else.

A shushing sound from Label warned us of the approach of a British major. He walked up, in khaki shorts and khaki shirt with the pips on his shoulders denoting his rank. His face was round and red with a straw-yellow toothbrush mustache, and he wore a black beret. "I say! Do any of you speak English?"

A moment of silence, then Lew Brettschneider spoke, "*Parlez-vous Francais?*"

The major shook his head.

Lew continued. "*Habla espanol?*"

Again the major shook his head, his face turning a deeper red.

"*Sprechen Sie Deutsch?*" Lew asked. I almost laughed. I doubted whether Lew knew all those languages any better than the major did.

The major grew more indignant with each new humiliation by this Jewish barbarian who seemed to command so many languages. In desperation he blurted out, "I speak a dialect of a hill tribe in India."

Getting no answer from us, he turned and entered the big hut. And I laughed for the first time in days.

But a minute later soldiers approached us and separated men from women. The women went off into the dark, and we lined up in front of the door of the hut. The line started moving into the hut. Stretching and peering over the shoulder of the man in front of me, I tried to see what the routine was inside, but Heavy's bulk was in the way. He was the second man ahead of me. Heavy disappeared inside . . . then it was my turn.

A line of heavy wooden tables, end to end, ran to the far end of the hut, and behind them stood young, clean British sergeants. On our side of the benches stood more sergeants, each next to one of the refugees, some of whom were naked, others stripping off their clothes, some dressing and moving on to another sergeant.

I stood in the bright light inside the door waiting for orders. A sergeant motioned to me and spoke in Yiddish. "Over there." The words were jarring: I had come to think of Yiddish as the language of friends.

The young sergeant looked me over keenly. One of the bright intelligence boys! In English he told me to take off my clothes. Feigning ignorance, I stared at him stupidly. "Your clothes. Off!" He mimed the unbuttoning of the shirt and loosening of the belt. I took my shirt and pants off. I had no underwear. He looked my body over carefully and saw that I had no concentration camp tattoos. He looked into my face suspiciously and started to speak. There was a yell and an excited voice behind me. The sergeant and I turned and looked. One of the men from our ship, a tall, thin Romanian, was pointing and shouting at the British sergeant who had spoken Yiddish before. I could make out the words "Hitler espion" in the rush of excited speech.

A lieutenant walked briskly up. "What's going on here?" The Romanian poured out a torrent against the sergeant. "Who speaks English here?" the lieutenant asked of the whole room.

A mild man spoke up in a low, heavily accented voice. "I can speak a little English."

The lieutenant asked him brusquely, "What's that man saying?"

"That the man here"—the little man pointed to the sergeant—"was working for the Gestapo in Romania."

The sergeant turned worried eyes to the lieutenant, who carefully avoided them. "Nonsense," the lieutenant said. "Tell that man"—pointing to the tall Romanian—"that this sergeant was in the British army throughout the war." The lieutenant turned on his heel, passed close by the sergeant who was searching me, and said out of the corner of his mouth, "Tell Sirach to get out of here till this bunch is through. Someone else may recognize him."

My sergeant called to Sirach, "Sergeant, they have a job for you in Hut 3." Sirach, half-running, went down the long length of the room and out the door.

Turning, the sergeant kicked my foot. "Shoe off!" I bent over and untied my shoe, aware too late of my mistake in reacting to his English. In an effort to cover up the mistake, I also took off the other shoe. While I stood naked, the sergeant went through my pants' pockets, pulling out the phylacteries, prayer book, and a flashlight. He examined the flashlight suspiciously but saw that "Bucharest" was stamped on it. To justify his actions as he put it in his pocket, he said, "Dangerous. Could be used for signaling." He motioned me to get dressed.

As I was buttoning my shirt, I saw Heavy. He was still naked, and a sergeant and the lieutenant stood by him. He had typical sailor's tattoos on both arms, and across his chest there waved a tattooed American flag. The lieutenant took one look at the flag and ordered the sergeant: "Handcuff him and hold him for questioning. We seem to have a terrorist here." Heavy stood massive and quiet, sweat standing out on his face, neck, and shoulders, still stubbornly refusing to admit he spoke English, but unable to feign any other language. As a squad of British soldiers came on the double to lead him away, Heavy flapped his underpants in disdain.

Dressed, I went down the room and through the door. More soldiers motioned me to another hut. Inside was a British lieutenant sitting at a desk with a civilian. The civilian looked at me kindly and gently asked me my name in Yiddish.

"Mendel Levey." Hearing my accent, he looked at me sharply, then glanced at the lieutenant out of the corner of his eye. "Age?"

"*Fünf und dreisig.*"

"*Rumanisch?*"

I nodded.

"Bucharest?"

I nodded again. The British lieutenant was bored, and after a careless look at me stared at the ember on the end of his cigarette. With a wink the civilian motioned me out the door.

Outside, Label grabbed me and pulled me into the dark. I could almost feel his grin as he spoke in English. "OK?"

"OK." I felt excited and alive. "Is it finished?"

"Yah."

25 ✳ *The Detention Camp*

The first night on Cyprus, the crew members who had gotten through were placed in an empty Niessen hut. Having eluded detection, we could now rest and sleep in peace.

Morning was cheerful. In the bright, warm sunlight, the reddish-yellow clay soil contrasted sharply with the deep blue sky. At a faucet outside our huts we stripped to our pants, soaped our bodies, head, and feet, and washed away the caked dirt with fresh, cold water. Brettschneider, Rotter, Gutmann, George, Sholom, Miguel, Romero, and I had made it this far. Moka had disappeared. I felt the loss. He had been an anchor for me, for all the outsiders. There was no word of what had happened to him. Made his own escape? Picked out by the British?

About fifty yards from us the small tin huts began. They marched in soldierly lines up a hill and down across the hard yellow soil as far as our eyes could see. Thirty yards the other way was the thirty-foot-high barbed-wire fence. Twenty feet outside this fence was a similar fence. At seventy-five-yard intervals were forty-foot-high watchtowers manned by British soldiers. The fence looked a comfort in spite of our being inside; it was our protection from the British. Now we could rest a bit. Even in this place, the sunny day and the countryside seemed attractive. Of course, we crew members could afford an optimistic perspective; the Hagana would get us out of the camp as soon as possible.

I felt satisfaction that my responsibility for getting the people safely to Cyprus—as far as could reasonably be expected—had been discharged and relief that we had survived our confrontation with a minimum of injuries to passengers and crew. Despite our mishaps and the efforts of our opponents, I felt that we had won a small victory by getting as far as we had. I was proud that the crew to a man had faced the obstacles with courage and with a sensibility for the passengers.

Now there was no need to worry about the steering gear breaking down, the leaky condenser, stormy weather, minefields, or finding fuel oil. The *Paducah-Geula* lay tied to the dock in Haifa, alongside the *Exodus*, the *Arlosoroff*, the *Northland* all the ships that had brought people to Palestine or, like us, only this far, to Cyprus.

There was a subtle change in the feelings among the men. Being together on the ship had strengthened our morale and given us mutual support. Now I wondered what would happen to us as we were dispersed through the camp and coped with the bad housing and bad food. The stress of internment would replace the freedom of the ship.

But for now, I lay back, clean and rested, the cement floor hard under the thin blanket. Satisfying a fresh, healthy hunger was my only immediate need. I surveyed my roommates. Miguel looked over and gave me that sly smile. Sholom was telling George of his experience passing through the British search. Antonio Chirri, an Italian, was a new addition to our ranks. He had been second mate on the *Northland*, which was captured an hour after us off Haifa. Now he and Romero were arguing in Spanish. I had noticed that Romero was limping this morning, the result of an old leg injury.

I called over, "What happened to Heavy?" There was silence, and worry creased their faces.

Rotter gave a low warning whistle from where he sat looking out the door. We waited silently and tense. A moment later he spoke, "Some people just walked past."

George said, "We'd better watch our English. If strangers come around, we'd better speak Yiddish."

Ram, the Hagana escort from the *Northland*, walked in with a stranger. I didn't know whether the new man was English or not. Sandy-haired, thick-set, with a tough but pleasant young face, he might have been of any nationality.

"This is Yossef Ravid," said Ram. "We call him Ossie."

Ossie's English was good, though it carried traces of the same Palestinian accent as Ram's. "Glad to know you men," he said.

Ram explained, "He brought a ship in last week, came from Italy."

"Pack up your blankets and stuff," Ossie told us. "This place isn't safe. The British can see you from the watchtowers. And they know this place is supposed to be empty.

"Two at a time at 150-yard intervals," Ossie commanded. "Bring your equipment."

Waiting till the first pair was well away, Antonio and I started. Keeping our distance, we followed Ram and Ossie up the path between rows of little tin huts. People watched us from the huts. They were uniformly haggard, but their bright eyes studied us shrewdly before turning away noncommittally. We walked past the huts into a field where rows of tents were set up. Ossie waved an arm, indicating a tent.

By twos we filtered into the tent and sat on our blankets on the earth, until the small tent was packed. "Here is the situation," Ossie said. "This is Camp 70, a new camp, still but a quarter full. It is to be completely separate from the other camps. Since no people will leave this camp on the monthly quota of seven hundred and fifty for a year and a half to two years, we must get all of you into the other camps. At any time, whenever the opportunity comes up, be ready to leave at a moment's notice. Always keep in contact with the other men so someone around the tent knows where you are. And now, food."

We ate in the children's mess. Diminutive waiters and waitresses looked up at us with big eyes and shy smiles. Cereal, a big chunk of hard bread, and a tin cup of coffee constituted breakfast. It took the edge off our hunger but did not fill the hole deep inside.

Ossie brought a pack of Cyprian Greek cigarettes for each man. They had no taste, but they satisfied our need.

After breakfast we went to a huge pile of straw and lugged armfuls of it to put under our blankets to cushion the hard, rocky ground.

Leonard Rotter brought Jeanette, a pretty young woman whom he had been courting aboard the ship, by our tent. She gave us all a smile, and the two of them promenaded off on a sightseeing tour of the camp. Leonard first met Jeanette when he was on the gangway directing the refugees aboard the *Paducah*. The more conversation he had with her, the more smitten he became. On the fifth day of the voyage, he had asked her to marry him. She had accepted.

Label and his gang had already set themselves up as the camp police. Ossie, who had apparently taken over for the missing Moka, had recruited the gang as potential Hagana members and given them this responsibility. It was amazing to see the wolfish crew of young men organizing milk and food for the kids. Marta, Pepi, and the young girls worked in the kitchens of the various groups. We learned early that the people were not just an amorphous mass; they had grouped themselves by their various religious and political beliefs, with their own mess halls and adjacent huts or tents.

Early in the afternoon the remaining passengers of the *Geula* started to enter the camp. Until late into the night we crewmen exchanged stories about how each had gotten through the British control. As far as anyone knew, the chief engineer, Gooen, Bailey Nieder, and Keller were still hidden on the ship in one of the tanks. The last man to see her reported the ship was listing severely, apparently still taking water where the destroyer had rammed her. We worried about whether those hidden aboard were safe and whether they would manage to slip ashore safely.

After breakfast the next morning Rotter came running up, breathless. "Heavy's in the camp!" he exclaimed. "He's standing near the gate we came through."

Buiza reacted immediately, "Trap! Stay away from him." Some of the younger men wanted to get Heavy and bring him to our tents, but Sholom, George, and I agreed with Miguel.

Instead, Phil Bock was sent in search of Hannah, the English-speaking nurse. When he came back with her, we outlined the situation. Eyes sharp, she nodded quickly and left.

"Come and get your knapsacks," Ben Berg called out. Ben had been the chief mate on the *Northland* and spoke very good Hebrew. It was said he had spent several years living on a Moshav farm in Palestine. However, he was an American, had been raised in New York, and had worked a number of years as a sailor in the U.S. merchant marine.

"Where are they?" Al Brownstein asked.

"The Limies just brought the baggage they took from us on the dock at Haifa. But what a mess!"

The belongings of the people were spread out over the ground in rucksacks and bundles tied up in sheets. Pieces of clothing hung out of the tops. Here and there stray pots, photographs, and books lay on the ground where the British soldiers had dumped them.

Around the belongings stood guards from Label's gang. They formed a thin line that prevented the gathering people from getting at their baggage.

Ossie came up, stared at the scene, and commented grimly, "The British do it every time. It seems to be a conscious policy."

"What?" I asked.

"What they don't loot, they mix up, so that the belongings of a person are scattered through five or six rucksacks."

"Why do they do it?"

"Either brutal carelessness, or just to hurt the people even more. Watch," he said.

The news of the arrival of the baggage had gone through the camp, and the people were gathering quickly. Soon a solid mass pushed in toward Label's guards.

Standing on a little platform he had rigged up, Label took charge. Catching a rucksack thrown to him, he opened it and pulled out an old, crumpled shirt. Holding it high, he looked around for the owner. A man shouted excitedly, waved his hand, and pushed wildly through the mass to the platform.

Next Label held up a black coat. A man close by grabbed it and started backing away. But another man pushed his way to the coat, looked closely at it, shouted, and tried to pull it away. The first man struck him angrily on the head, and they grappled fiercely. People pulled them apart.

"That's what happens," Ossie said. "It will take the rest of the day for a person to find his belongings. People who have only a photograph, a ring, left of their families, their former lives, lose it when the British search their baggage. I'm getting out of here."

I looked at the madly anxious people and the pitiful garments and personal belongings held up as though at an auction, and I followed Ossie away.

Eyes sparkling, Hannah returned to our tent and told her story with bursts of laughter. "Heavy is a decoy. They questioned him last night, asked him why he was going to Palestine. He said, 'Why not? Everybody's going to Palestine.' They wanted to know if he was captain of the ship. He said no. They didn't get anything out of him. So they put him in the camp. He says the soldier in the watchtower is watching him very closely to see who talks to him."

"Is he feeling all right?" I asked.

"He's wonderful. Really enjoying it."

We arranged for Hannah to take Heavy to a different section of the camp and feed him.

Ossie and two strangers came into the tent. One of the new men was very short, scarcely five feet tall, with an unusually muscular body. He was wearing the usual khaki shorts and khaki shirt. Itzik, as he was called, had beautiful teeth. He came from Central Europe and spoke good German and Yiddish, but his Hebrew was poor. Kushi, the other new man, was medium-size and had a chest like a barrel.

"We'll switch four men from this camp to Camp 65 immediately. You're going to become a work party returning to 65 after putting up tents in this camp," Ossie explained. "Here are your new names." Mine was Karmine Rachi. Reluctantly, I surrendered my old name, Mendel Levey.

Four of us—Sholom, George, Miguel, and I—followed Ossie and his two comrades to another tent. There we found the four men whose names we were assuming and whose places we were taking in the work party. They slapped us on the back and greeted us with "*Shalom.*" We made a general exchange of clothes, a pair of pants from one man, a coat from another, so that each of us was wearing clothes that fit fairly well. We also had the khaki shorts and khaki shirts that seemed to be standard dress of the men in their camp. "They were given out by the Joint Distribution Committee," Ossie explained, "donated by the Palestinians." So I looked curiously at my khakis, my first Palestinian-made clothing. As we walked out of the tent, I wondered what would happen to the real Karmine Rachi and the other men whose places we were taking.

Ossie shook hands. "I'll be through later," he said.

Walking toward the big gate in the barbed-wire fence, Itzik held on to my arm to encourage me. "The British officer will call out your name," he told us. "Just say, 'Yah.' A lot of the yah-yah-yah. Act like they think you are supposed to act. You'll get through fine."

Two British soldiers peered through the barbed wire. "What do you want?" one demanded.

Itzik stepped forward as our spokesman. "How you do, Tommy? We working party. Go back where we come from, Camp 65." My mouth almost dropped open in surprise. Itzik, the serious, dignified Hagana soldier, was transformed. He wore a dull, stupid look and silly grin. "Hello, Tommy?" he babbled. "You like me. Me like you. Open gate. Me going home."

One British soldier told the other, "Get the sergeant." The sergeant came out of a little wooden guardhouse, a sheet of paper in his hands. He spoke to Itzik. "You the work party?"

"Yah, yah. We work here. Work finish. Go home."

"What camp you from?" the soldier asked.

"Sixty-five."

"All right, open the gate," the sergeant said to the soldiers.

As the gate opened, a truck backed up to it, its tailgate facing us. The sergeant called out the names from his list. One by one we answered "Yah" and climbed onto the truck. When he called out Sholom's new name, the answer was, "Here." It was clear and unmistakably English. I froze. Sholom was stunned by his mistake. But the sergeant didn't notice and motioned Sholom into the truck. As the truck pulled out onto a road, a soldier with a rifle stood on the tailgate.

It was a ten-minute drive to the other camp, which stretched for miles over the rocky red soil. When the truck pulled up to the gate, a sergeant checked the list the driver handed him against one he had in his guardhouse. "OK," he called out, and motioned us through the open gate.

Once inside, I sighed, glad to have passed another bad spot. Itzik was his sober, dignified self again. As he led us up a path between the huts, one of the men said bitterly, "Join the Hagana and screw the Limies."

We were taken to what was apparently a headquarters hut of the Hagana. We were given clothes and sent to an empty Niessen hut. "This is where all the sailors will be. We just moved some kids out to make room," Itzik explained. "I'll show you where you will eat."

Our mess hall was filled with English-speaking Jews, some natives of England but most German Jews who had escaped to England just before the war. They shared their slim rations with the four of us.

By noon of the next day all the sailors except Heavy were in Camp 65. Issued cots and blankets, mess kits, knives and forks and spoons, we settled down to wait for our release.

We found that biting flies made sleep during the day impossible. We also were tormented by the smell of the latrines, which ringed the camp and ran in lanes through its center. Whatever the direction of the wind, it bore the stench.

But the real trouble started the first night; Brettschneider complained of a pain in his stomach, and he spent the night in the latrine. He was only the first. Soon Dave, George, Rotter, and the rest came down with diarrhea. There were stomach pains, aching arms and legs, headaches, nights without sleep, hours spent on the wooden seats of the latrine.

Now we saw the truth: Cyprus was not going to be a restful layover after the labors of the voyage. Our worst travails were just beginning.

26 * New Friends Behind Barbed Wire

We settled down to our new lives hungry and tired, living just as the rest of the people of the camps lived. The British furnished each of us daily with about 1,800 calories of food, mostly in the form of potatoes. The camps had a population of twenty-three thousand people, housed in small tin huts and former army tents, full when three people were in them. The streets were red clay compacted by the pressure of thousands of feet. The inhabitants were Jews from Romania, Hungary, Poland, Germany, France, England, Belgium, Holland, Greece, Spain, Morocco, and Algeria. Around this city were the high double fences of barbed wire. One was never out of sight of the fences or the watchtowers and the wary soldiers looking down.

We were becoming increasingly isolated from one another. In the big hut, on cot alongside cot, men lay sick and weak, their heads covered with blankets to keep the flies away. Dave hadn't slept a full night for a week; day and night he made the trek to the latrine. The men's faces looked gray, and all had become much thinner.

Sholom saved his cigarettes to trade for food. Though he was always hungry, he took the punishment quietly. But some of the men were starting to turn on one another.

Ossie brought back news from Camp 70. "It is running smooth there now. The people have elected their camp committee. They are as well off as they can be here."

Ossie had become our surrogate Moka. They seemed to have come out of the same cocoon of Palestine.

"How is Heavy?" I asked Ossie.

His face lit up. "Fine. The British kept him under surveillance, so Heavy got a pencil and some paper. He'd walk around the camp, stop, and write notes. The British got worried and pulled him out for questioning. 'Are you a journalist?' they asked him. 'Certainly, and I'm going to give you the works,' Heavy said."

"What will happen to him?" I asked.

"He has declared that he is an American citizen and has demanded that he be deported. The British don't want to deport him. They don't want the publicity in the States while they're trying to borrow money there."

"Will they keep him here?"

"We'll carry on the fight in support of his deportation from the outside. But first we want to get the rest of you free."

Then a shock. "I'm saying good-bye," Ossie said.

"Good-bye?"

"Yes. I just got orders to report to Palestine."

"How will you get out?"

"The same way you will. Each month there is a quota of 750 people who the British release to enter Palestine legally. Some of the people slated for release surrender their certificates to sailors like you, because they know that if the sailors and Hagana escorts don't get out, no more refugees can be brought here. So one of the people will surrender his certificate, and I'll go out on it."

"When are you leaving?"

"This afternoon."

"How long do you think we'll be here?"

"You'll leave on next month's quota."

He started to leave, but stopped and turned back. "Some news for you. Your friend Moka's OK. We have just had news from Palestine."

"What happened?"

"He escaped from the prison ship. The seawater was not too cold, and he estimated he could survive an eight-hour swim to the coast. As soon as it was dark, he asked some immigrants to distract the soldiers. He took off his shoes, trousers and shirt, tied them around his neck, and swam in the direction of the lights on the top of Mount Carmel. When he made it to the beach, he evaded British patrols and finally walked to a kibbutz."

I said good-bye to Ossie.

"I'll be waiting for you in Palestine," he said. "I'll take you to my kibbutz."

His departure created an empty space in the lives of all of us.

That night, as I was eating the thin stew in the English-speaking mess, the chubby-faced man on my right nudged me sharply with his elbow. "Don't talk English. A British soldier is standing in the door."

I kept my eyes on my plate and my face turned away from the door. I relaxed when the man said, "He's gone."

"Do they come into the camp often?" I asked him.

"Only those who have some special job, such as checking leaks in the water pipes and the stoves when they are broken. But they use these men when they want information about what is going on inside the camp."

"My name is Pat," I said, offering him my hand.

"I'm Haim." We shook hands. "What are you doing tonight?" he asked.

"Nothing, as usual."

"Do you have enough to read?"

"Nothing."

"We have a library in English, the only one in the camp. Come with me after supper."

Haim's hut stood on a dirty lane surrounded by similar little huts. He introduced me to Yankel, a lank-jawed teenager. Two cots, a table made from a box, and a kerosene lamp were the furniture. Haim indicated a cot and invited me to sit down.

"Have you been here long?" I asked.

"Nine months," Yankel said.

"Nine months of this! When do you leave?" Haim looked at Yankel and grimaced.

"We were supposed to leave last month," Haim said, "but we gave our certificates to the mothers."

"Mothers?"

"Yes, we have five hundred babies born here a month. There is a very high death rate among them."

"What causes it?"

"Malnutrition and bad diet, mostly."

"And your certificates?"

"The Jewish Agency has gotten the British to agree to allow a thousand mothers and babies to enter Palestine. But the British demanded that certificates be surrendered by other people."

"And if a woman is pregnant, the British won't let her leave, even if it's time for her to go," Yankel said.

"Why?" I asked.

"They're afraid she'll have a child between Cyprus and Palestine and make the total a thousand and one."

"How did you get here?"

"On a wooden sailing ship with a small engine. She was big enough to carry six hundred people."

"Was it bad?"

"We left France in the winter. Made about five knots. Eight times we started through the Straits of Messina between Sicily and Italy. When we would get to the southern part of the straits, the winds would blow us back."

"And there was one big space inside the ship, four high the bunks were," Yankel added.

"Where are you from, Haim?"

"Poland. Warsaw."

"And Yankel?"

"Berlin."

"Where were you during the war?"

Yankel got up from his bunk and turned the kerosene flame a bit higher. The gloom was deep in the corners of the hut. Haim's round, boyish face was quiet, his eyes bright.

"I was in England, on a farm, preparing for Palestine," Yankel said.

"I was in Europe," Haim said briefly. Yankel watched him with an anxious expression.

"Let's visit Martin," Haim suggested. "He's in charge of our library."

Martin's hut was the same as Haim's and Yankel's, except that it had only one cot. The space of the other cot was taken by shelves made of wooden boxes filled with books. The books were a fine selection of classics, novels, scientific studies on agriculture, mathematics.

"How did you get them in?" I asked.

"The work of many people," Haim said. "They were brought in with the people or sent in by friends. And they leave them for the new prisoners." There was a respect for the books, almost a love.

The tin door of the hut opened, and a young man came in. He had a thin, sensitive face with a smudge of unshaven whiskers on jaws and chin. His eyes were deep, luminous pools with purplish circles. Untidy black hair was thrown back from his forehead.

"Martin, meet the skipper of the *Geula*," Haim said.

Martin smiled and shook hands. "Glad to know you." His speech had a British accent.

Selecting two books, I sat on Martin's bunk. "What do you do with yourselves?" I asked.

"What we can," Martin said. "I work in the tinsmith shop. We make kerosene lamps, cups, and stuff. But I'm getting tired of it."

"Haim's in charge of accepting the food from the British," Yankel supplied. "And I'm taking my Hagana training."

"Yankel's the soldier," Haim said. Yankel flashed a bashful, boyish grin.

"How old are you, Yankel?" I asked.

"Seventeen."

"Do you have any folks?"

"My sister is in the camp. She takes care of the babies in the nursery. I have a brother in England."

"No other folks?"

"No. My mother and father were in Germany."

"Do most of the people do some work like you fellows do?"

"No. There's nothing for them to do, and the people are in such bad shape they don't have any energy. They just lie around," Martin said.

"Is there much sickness?" I asked.

Martin laughed, a brief, hard sound. "I've been sick for months now. See the sores?" Martin showed his arms, covered with sores, rotten and open. "They won't heal."

"The sickness of the camp," Haim said quietly, "comes because this is another *lager*. People lived through the camps of Europe with the hope of reaching Palestine. But now they are so close, and they are so long here, this is finishing many people. When they leave Cyprus, they'll be of no use to themselves or anybody."

"Hunger, cold, sickness, hate," Martin summed up, "the destruction of more years of their lives. Time, which is the most precious possession they have, drips away in the miserable days here."

The sound of an angry man's voice carried clearly in the quiet night. My three companions smiled grimly. The voice was swearing in a strange language.

"He always swears in Uzbek when he's drunk," Haim said. "He was in Uzbekistan during the war."

"Where does he get liquor here?" I asked.

"The canteen has Cyprus wine and cognac," Martin said.

"Do the people have money?"

"Some is sent to them by relatives. Then there is barter. We have shoe-makers, tailors, also our black market."

"Who are the people marching up and down singing all the time? Your Hagana trainees?" I asked Yankel.

"No! Betarim! Another political group, revisionists."

"And the Irgun?"

"They engage in military, terrorist-type activities."

"What is their appeal to the people?" I asked.

"Revenge. People seeking some hard philosophy. Something that gives firmness. Some of the youth who suffered so, and who saw their op-pressors well organized, armed, marching, see the solution of the Jews in doing the same."

"But doesn't the Hagana march, train in arms, too?" I asked.

Martin spoke with nervous excitement. "The Hagana has its own pro-gram. I'll show you later."

Yankel excused himself. "I have to get up at five in the morning."

Haim laughed. "The future general!"

"How do you follow what goes on in Palestine so closely?" I asked.

"There are people coming and going between here and Palestine all the time," Martin said. "And we get all the papers from Palestine."

"Any in English?" I asked.

"The *Palestine Post* is about the only one in English," Martin said.

"Where can I find it?"

"In the children's library. Haven't you been there yet?"

"No. I haven't heard about it."

"Tomorrow," Haim said, "I'll show you."

Saying goodnight, I picked my way down the dark streets to my hut. It was ten o'clock, the latest I had been up since I arrived in the camp eight days earlier. Eight days—it seemed as if we had been on Cyprus for a year.

Lying on my cot, I could feel the cold. The lantern on the floor, in the aisle between the cots, flickered. Rolling the two blankets closely around me, I could feel the weakness of my body, the sick feeling in my stomach. Eight days! How many more?

27 ∗ Training for Palestine

The new day lacked promise. We lay on our cots, tired, reluctant even to start the day by washing our faces. After a breakfast of tough cereal and bad coffee, the whole day stretched before us. It was impossible to read or sit in the hut: the flies drove us crazy. And outside, the wind picked up about nine o'clock and blew all day, carrying the hard particles of red clay that filled our noses, our eyes, our mouths. Every day we were getting touchier; we found it harder to live with one another. And from this person and that we heard the same story: the rains were soon to arrive, and then the camp would be hell itself.

We had varying success in washing our clothes. The British turned the water on for two hours during the day. This was shower time, time for filling our tin cans with water to wash our faces and to drink, and time for washing clothes. Since we lacked cans big enough to wash our clothes, we held them under a faucet to get them wet, then rubbed them with soap and rinsed them. But this only partially cleaned them. We had to find a better way.

Label had a solution that everyone envied: his girlfriend, Pepi, who had a bucket, washed his clothes for him. While we envied him his clean clothes, we were curious about the girl. She was attractive, about eighteen years old, and came from Poland. In 1939, after escaping to Russian-occupied Poland, she went deep into the Urals, where she worked in a factory. When the war was over, she returned to Poland but could find no trace of her family. Wanting to get away from the scenes where she had lived with her loved ones, she took the road to Palestine. About five-foot-three and slim, she had straight black hair and long black eyelashes. Her face had a wistfulness about it. Label now was her family; she washed his clothes, hunted up a needle and thread when he tore a hole in his shirt, accompanied him around the camp. Label protected her and helped her find shelter and food. Their relationship was born out of the need to replace their lost families. This was not unusual among the young people in the camp who had similar histories.

The rest of us had to find other solutions to the wash problem. I found a deep tin can, an old biscuit tin, that I could borrow from my friends, two tiny orphan girls. I found them one morning when I was wandering around with the sickness in my body and, worse, the growing pessimism and sourness in my head. The two small scholars were studying Hebrew in their tiny hut. They looked at me with the sober expression universal among the children in the camp.

"*Boker tov,*" I greeted them—"good morning" in Hebrew. I didn't know whether it was my accent, or whether they recognized me as one of the sailors, but bright smiles lit up the two sober faces. It was like sunshine. Each morning now I made it a point to get up early and get the two bright smiles with a "*boker tov.*"

In their hut I saw the tin, which was fine for washing clothes. They were very pleased to let me borrow it. Around their hut were the huts of other orphans—one thousand orphans in their own village. But there was no demoralization. The children, ranging in age from six to twelve, were winning a struggle that began in the camps of Germany and Poland. Six million people were gassed, burned, murdered. In the midst of this horror, many of these children were born to mothers who were soon to die. In those camps the child who laughed aloud died for it; the tense, huddled ones who were silent escaped. They came to Cyprus, still quiet, sober as no children should be, unable to read, to write.

The organization of the orphans' education was undertaken by all groups, religious and labor: Mapai, Hashomer, Achduth Avoda, Aguda, Betar. The children studied eight to ten hours a day—Hebrew, arithmetic, writing, reading, history. In their groups of ten to fifteen, clustered around a table in the larger of the tin huts, they were the happiest they had been in all of their short lives.

Seeking one of the textbooks for beginner's Hebrew in the office of the orphan's village, I heard a crisp English voice behind me say, "Good morning." I did not turn around, but walked into the back of the office and through a door into a storeroom where the children's books and writing materials were kept. I knew without turning who belonged to the voice: the British major. The young girl in charge of the office had just finished telling me about the major. "He's a fine gentleman. He comes into the office every day to see if he can give any help to the children." Because of this human quality, I learned, he was the only British officer whom the people welcomed.

Safe in a corner, idly picking out a book, I turned to observe the major. Well over six feet, he had a ruddy face and the swaggering great mustache of the Eighth Army of General Montgomery. He wore khaki shorts and shirt and a blue beret. His eyes were keen as he looked to see where I had gone, but he didn't see me in the corner.

"And how is everything this morning?" he asked the girl.

"Fine, Major," she answered.

A small boy ran in breathless and spoke to the girl in Yiddish. She answered him calmly. The major looked the boy over, then reached out and seized his arm. "The child is dirty. Look at his arm. Come, my boy," the major said briskly, leading him outdoors.

Taking advantage of the major's departure, I walked out, nodding at the girl, who smiled in return. The major was leading the boy toward a big stone tub where some children had stored water for washing clothes. Curious, I followed. The major dipped the resisting boy's arm into the water, took out his handkerchief, and rubbed the arm. Coming closer, I could see it was an ink spot on the arm. As the major rubbed it, marks emerged from under the ink stain. Then I saw them—the tattooed numbers of Auschwitz. The child was staring into the major's face in fear.

When the major saw the tattooed numbers, his mouth dropped open. In a frenzy the boy twisted his small body loose and ran. The major called in frustration after him, "Come back, you little devil. I won't hurt you."

Later Haim took me to the library. "It belongs to the children, so you have to be very quiet." In a large Niessen hut, about twenty long tables were surrounded by the small scholars, boys and girls. They worked in teams of two—two little boys, two little girls. Perhaps it was policy to pair them off, but they stuck like glue to each other. A very mature silence reigned. In a hushed voice I asked where the English-language paper was. At the sound of my voice a little girl raised outraged eyebrows. Abashed, I gave her an embarrassed smile. Haim grinned and motioned me to a long wooden shelf filled with magazines and newspapers, all of them in Hebrew. Digging through them, Haim came up with a *Palestine Post*.

I found the occupants of the hut more interesting than the newspaper. Watching the children's faces as they silently and carefully formed Hebrew words in the books before them, I felt some of the sourness leaving me. At the far end of the library was a piano. From the overhead beams kerosene lanterns were hanging. I promised myself to return here and help pass the long nights with a book.

Outside, Haim explained the origins of the children. "They come on the Youth *Aliyah*."

"*Aliyah*? What's the meaning of the word? I hear it often in the camp."

"*Aliyah* is a Hebrew word meaning 'immigration.' It also has biblical associations meaning 'to come up to the promised land.' There is *Aliyah Aleph*, legal immigration, and *Aliyah Beth*, illegal immigration. *Aleph* and *Beth* are the first and second letters of the Hebrew alphabet."

"And the Youth *Aliyah*?" I asked.

"The immigration of the children, mainly the orphans."

"How's your Hebrew, Haim?"

"Bad. I find it very difficult."

We were almost knocked down by a man running in a panic. Chasing him were five more men. The running man's face was bleeding as though he had been in a fight.

"Holy smoke! What's that?"

"A squatter," Haim said. "The rains will be coming soon, and then the camp becomes a hell of mud. The rains pour into the tents, washing them away. So people in the tents are trying to find huts."

"But what's a squatter?"

"The camp committee set aside some big huts—ones that had been used by the people who left for Palestine on the last quota—for the mothers of the newborn babies. That way they don't have to make the long walks to the children's huts. But other families moved in from the tents and occupied these huts."

"That's a hell of a thing to do."

"That's nothing, considering the condition some of the people are in. Haven't you seen the barbed wire around some of the tents and huts?"

"Yes." Once, in the dark of night, I had stumbled into the barbed wire around a hut. One needed to know little to decipher what it meant: for many people who had years of the horror of life in the camps, where the familiar faces of the people around became associated with the *lager*, the overriding desire was to be alone. So here on Cyprus men or women would go foraging in search of lengths of barbed wire, which they twined around the outside of their tent or hut. They left only a small entranceway clear. Then, when they were inside, they reached out and closed the wire barrier, braiding it across the entrance, thus keeping the whole outside world away from their tiny refuge.

"Can't they get the squatters out?"

"The camp committee requested volunteers from the different political and religious groups to drive the people out of the mothers' huts. But these police belonged to the same organizations as the squatters, and they refused to move their people out."

"So who were the five men in pursuit?"

"I suppose those five belong to a different organization than the man they were beating up."

"What happens now?"

"Starting tomorrow morning the Joint Distribution Committee is going to stop all its supplementary food rations to the whole camp till the people leave the mothers' huts."

"No other way?"

"No other way."

In our hut some of the men had seen the "police" beating up the squatter. Sholom was burning mad. "What the hell kind of a thing is that, five guys beating up on one man!" he exclaimed.

Dave's sickness was getting worse, so I walked with him to the first aid hut. He found it difficult to walk. Awaiting Dave's turn, we sat on the short wooden bench in the hut. A boy of about eighteen with open, rotting sores on his arms sat ahead of us. His face, thin and gaunt, gave off a faint yellowish light. Dave spoke to him in Yiddish.

"Yellow jaundice," he explained to me.

The best the doctor could give Dave was a little powder for his diarrhea.

"The doctor is from Lodz. He says the British don't provide enough medicine for the camps. All he has is sent in by the Joint Distribution Committee," Dave explained.

Yankel paid us a visit in our hut. Sitting on my cot, he looked down the row of men, their faces covered with blankets to protect them from the flies. "Would you like to visit our training camp?"

"The Hagana training?" I asked.

"Yes. We have a six-week training course for the young men and women."

"Sure!"

Yankel led the way through the lanes between the huts, the wind blowing clouds of the hard, red dirt around us. To breathe I cupped my hand to my nose, and I made slits of my eyes in order to see.

Neat rows of small, two-man tents were flapping in the wind. On a flagpole the Jewish flag, the blue Star of David on a white field, whipped around in the red dust.

"This is it?" I asked. Yankel nodded and led me over to a larger tent, its side flaps rolled up to let light in on closely packed mattresses on the ground. A Hagana instructor demonstrated a hold and swiftly threw his partner, a stocky girl, over his hip onto the mattress. The other girls did the same with their partners.

"Wrestling!" I exclaimed.

"No, judo," Yankel said.

We moved to a flat stretch of land where a long line of boys and young men stood, brandishing five-foot-long wooden staves. Their instructor was Itzik, the Hagana man who with Ossie had brought us from Camp 70.

"What are the staves for?"

"The Arabs are experts in using them for street fighting. So the Jews have to learn, too," Yankel explained.

One hand gripping the other arm, the staff held in the fist, the boys lined up, then commenced walking slowly ahead in a continuous line, the staffs sweeping viciously back and forth. "To clear a street," Yankel said.

"How come the girls in the camp are so big?" I asked. All of our crew had commented on the size of the girls. Though not tall, they had big busts and heavy arms and legs. Sholom said they were a new race of Amazons, come to finish off all the men and be done with them.

"Two reasons," Yankel said. "Only the strongest survived the camps and the ordeal of war. And then they were swollen by a diet of starches. Potatoes were their chief diet for years."

Watching the girls wrestle, Yankel smiled wryly, "See that hold they are doing now? We learned that from the Germans. Their soldiers used it to rape women. The Palmach, our commandos, devised a counterattack."

"What will happen between the Jews and Arabs?" I asked.

"There are thousands of Bedouins in the great southern desert of Palestine, the Negev. They are nomads, and they raise goats."

"And you expect raids from them?"

"With peace some adjustments could be made, but today when the Mufti starts trouble, and the British try to keep the Palestine pot boiling between Jew and Arab . . . well, we must have powder and guns and keep them ready."

"Itzik can tell you more about the Arabs. He has been in Palestine for fifteen years. He led the famous trip to Masada."

"What was that?"

"It was the last great fortress of the Jews in the war against the Romans in the first century. It took the Romans two years to level it. Itzik led a small party of the Palmach on a march to Masada with light rations and only the water they had in their canteens. They averaged sixty miles a day for five days."

"Some stuff!"

On the way back to our hut I asked Yankel about Haim. "Why were you worried when I asked him where he was during the war?"

"Haim is one of the most unusual persons here, and this is a camp of unusual people," Yankel said. "To get out of the Warsaw Ghetto he climbed through the sewers, then bribed Poles standing guard at the sewer exits. Crossing from Poland into Germany, he survived by stealing farmers' animals, eating them raw when necessary. Three times he was captured and placed in concentration camps and was scheduled for the gas chamber. Twice he escaped, only to be caught again. Finally, when the British troops liberated his camp, he claimed to be a captured Palestinian soldier, and they repatriated him to England. This was the only way the British would release a Jew out of Germany.

"He then learned that his brother, who had left Poland in 1939 to go to Palestine, had joined the British army to fight the Nazis and was killed in the invasion of Sicily. There is much more, but it's bad for him to tell the story, because he lives it all over again."

"Survival of the fittest?" I asked.

"Sometimes the fittest didn't survive," Yankel said.

"Some of the crew have been coming into the hut with the stories of the death camps, but I don't like to listen to them."

"Why?"

"I don't quite know. I know they're true, but there seems a shutting off, like some censor in my head who cuts in, to stop the story. When the story's over, it's like some horrible fairy tale."

"Yes," Yankel said quietly.

Walking into our hut, I saw George lying on a cot, concentrating on a book, absentmindedly swiping at the flies.

"Did they notify you yet, George?"

He looked up in surprise. "Of what?"

"The wrestling match."

"What?"

"The Hagana girl wrestling champ of the camp has challenged the sailors to put their champ forward for a match."

"What's that got to do with me?"

"You're our champ."

George looked alarmed, but also interested. "I'm no wrestler."

"It's not wrestling, it's judo. And you should see the size of the girl!"

Larry Kohlberg looked up from his bunk. "I heard she broke the arm of the boy she wrestled three days ago."

George sat up. "You're fooling?"

"Yes."

"Oh!" He fell back on his cot, relieved.

Grinning wryly, one of the Shou-shous entered the hut. "Well, you fellows will have to move into tents," he said.

We were concerned. "Why?"

"A thousand more orphans are coming over from Camp 70. We have better facilities for them here."

"The British agreed?"

"Reluctantly, after a lot of pressure from Palestine."

"Well, if it's for the kids," one of the men said. "But it sounds to me like the tents are really bad when the rain starts."

28 ✳ *A Party*

The cold awakened me. Twisting, I pulled the blanket closer. It was early morning, and a gloomy half-light threatened a new day. David Blake's head was completely covered by his blanket, except for a fold where his nose protruded. There was a stillness in the air, unusual in its heaviness. I gradually realized that it had to be later than I thought. The sun was already up. There was a creaking of bunks as sleeping men shifted, seeking warmth. Suddenly the hut was filled with the strong yellow light of the sun. And just as quickly the queer yellow light was gone. The gloom rushed in colder and more threatening.

From far off, somewhere in the direction of the mountains, came a dull clap of thunder. "This is it!" someone yelled. I asked myself, "What? The end of the world?" Like an echo another voice repeated, "What? Armageddon?"

Then the thunder was like an artillery barrage, growing louder, coming closer. A short rush of wind pushed quickly through the hut, whistled in the cracks, shook the blankets on the men. Then there was rain. A few big drops rang out like shot on the tin roof, then they gained in numbers till the hut was filled with drumming. So . . . the rains were here.

I buried my head in the blankets. It was as if some horrible host had descended on us with all his strength and was bent on driving us out of the cold and misery of the hut and into the whipping cold rain and mud.

The rain and the cold that accompanied it made life miserable for those of us in the tin huts, but it washed away the world of the people in the tents. I saw a bent man, dripping with the rain, his coat off, long sleeves rolled gingerly to the elbows, carry some battered pots out of a tent; a woman, bandanna around her head, passed some blankets to him. The rain coursing down the hill had made a stream eight feet across and a foot deep, and it ran straight through the couple's tent. The tent, straining and wet, fell over before the buffeting wind, the tent pegs pulling out of the soaked soil.

Today was Saturday, the Sabbath, and this was the Aguda section of the tent camp. These devout people were working frantically, using stones as hammers to drive the tent pegs deeper into the red mud, gathering rocks to pile on top of the pegs and around the corners of the tents. Two young girls, tears mixed with rain on their cheeks, ineffectually tried to prop up their collapsing tent.

A young Hagana man came to us and directed us to the spare tents and poles. "Take your pick. When the rain lets up, pitch your tents. The kids are due from Camp 70 first thing tomorrow morning."

One of the men growled, "I'm not leaving the hut. What do they think I am? I have some rights." He walked off in a huff.

Miguel Buiza looked thin, and his normally straight body was hunched over. "All right if I share a tent with you?" I asked.

He agreed with a nod and a smile. Ours was a curious relationship. He was a former Admiral of the Spanish Republican Navy, older than I, yet I was above him in our makeshift line of command. He never seemed to resent it, but I felt awkward. Romero helped us carry our tent to the Aguda section. Ossie had suggested that we would be safest deep among the religious people if the British searched the camp for us. "Though I doubt they'll attempt it. It will be a major maneuver, the movement of troops into the camp, the search, and the withdrawal. They'll need more than their guns—at least a half dozen of their light tanks."

We found our tent held four cots, which enabled Antonio and Romero to come in with Miguel and me. Romero was an experienced tent camper. "Much experience," he explained. "French detention camps."

Antonio surveyed the channels the rain had made down the hill. Picking out a spot of ground that was the least rocky, and where the rain did not drain through, we set up the tent. Instead of using pegs for the rope supports, we tied the tent ropes to big rocks of white chalk.

Our cots set up, a mirror hung from the center pole, a kerosene lamp sitting on a box, our mess kit, which was also the basin for washing our faces, alongside our cots, our blankets rolled up at the feet of our cots— and our new home was complete.

Romero slapped his hand against the center pole. "*La vida es un sueño.*" Life is a dream. A grim voice added, "Or maybe a *pesadilla*, a nightmare."

The kids from Camp 70 began to arrive early in the morning, their welcoming committee the orphans from the kid's village. The contrast between the new children and the children who had been longer on Cyprus struck me at once. The children from our ship were unkempt and still wore their enormous Romanian caps and wrinkled clothes that were too large. The children of the camp had a year of some care, wore neat, tan-colored Palestinian clothes, were freshly washed, and had neatly cut hair. They looked different from our children, who, like young wolves, wandered around the camp, seeking out with childish curiosity the wonders of this new world.

Sholom found two sailor-admiring children whom he had befriended during our passage from Bulgaria. They followed him around like a miniature crew awaiting orders, staring up at him in wondering admiration. Sholom addressed them alternately in English and Brownsville Yiddish, and they seemed to understand everything he said, nodding with wide-open young eyes. There was a vitality in Sholom that the kids felt. He set an example of strength that they could follow. The concentration camps of the Germans were past, but the kids were still living the life of the *lager* behind barbed wire. The children needed courage to achieve their hope of a new life in Palestine.

Dave Kellner found among the boys one who had made a beautiful little carving on a piece of the chalk he had dug from the ground. On one side he had carved a Cyprus tent, and on the other he had carved the *Paducah-Geula*, our ship of two names, two lives. The carving of the ship was very good; her two rakish stacks and her sharp bow were all there. Seeing our admiration, he gave it to Dave, who got along very well with the children.

In general the children expressed concern for our sailors. One of the boys advised Eli Bergman to shave off his scraggly beard "for hygienic reasons." The youngster had been in camps in Europe and knew the value of keeping clean.

Quickly absorbing the new arrivals, the children helped them set up their cots and wash their clothes. The slim stores of clothes available for the new children were issued. They wore their neat khaki shorts and new shirts like banners, but still they went barefoot, for there were no new shoes. Wild football games sprang up in the streets between the tin huts of the children's village, and calloused feet were banged in the exuberance of this exciting new sport.

Hannah, Haia, and the doctor from our ship came over with the new children. They brought Peter, the little orphan Hannah had taken under her wing. Temporary sleeping and living quarters were rigged up in a first aid hut for them. All the sailors visited and paid their respects, each of us giving advice and opinions on Camp 65 versus Camp 70 and on the established life here. Now that we had become citizens of Camp 65, it was strange how quickly our standards had changed.

While the nurses and doctor were organizing their quarters, I took Peter out for a walk. His legs were very thin, and he had trouble handling them. He looked at me with his perfectly round eyes without brows, neither accepting nor rejecting me. Since it was Saturday afternoon and the regular Sabbath football game was going on, we walked toward the field. Finding a place on the sidelines, we watched. As usual, the game was a very slow one; the players all suffered from malnutrition and tired quickly. The audience alternately cheered a good play and baited a bad one in Yiddish, Romanian, German, Polish, French, and other languages.

Peter caught the excitement of the people around us. He clapped his hands and tried to yell, but he could not. Nor could he laugh; he grimaced as he tried, but no sound came out. I watched him soberly. He couldn't laugh, but he would learn. The children learned to live again.

When I returned Peter to Hannah, she grabbed him up, whispered softly to him, and rocked him affectionately. "He'll have to learn to laugh," I said.

"In Eretz," Hannah said softly.

"Come over to our tent tonight," I said to Hannah and Haia.

"A party?" Hannah asked.

"Sure!"

Hannah spoke excitedly to Haia, who clapped her hands and nodded.

When I told Antonio and Miguel that the nurses were coming over, Antonio slapped his fist into his palm. "We must have wine. What kind of a party is it without wine?" Rummaging through his meager possessions, he came up with a pair of khaki pants the Hagana had issued to him. "A man had his eye on them in the second tent from here, the shoemaker. I'll sell them and get some money to buy wine."

Miguel had an extra shirt. He looked at it doubtfully. "Not much wine for this shirt, but some." Together Antonio and Miguel went off on their mission. Feeling guilty, I looked through my clothes for something to sell. No value in a khaki shirt with several holes in it, or a pair of khaki shorts that were already in rags after the first wash. There were the pants and shirt I had on, the woolen jacket that had belonged to Ossie that he gave me against the cold of the nights. Ah, the sandals the Hagana issued to me! The very thing! At Sholom's tent they didn't know of anyone interested in buying a pair of sandals. Wishing to invite Haim and Yankel to the party, I went to their hut. Perhaps they knew someone who wanted sandals. They did—the man who swore in Uzbek. And the sandals fitted him. I collected four shillings—a dollar's worth of wine. Leaving a shilling deposit in the canteen on the precious bottles, I got three quarts of Cypriot wine, made by the Greeks on the island.

After a supper of soup with a potato like an island in it, I picked up Hannah and Haia at their hut. Peter was sleeping, and the doctor, on duty in the hut, couldn't come.

Our tent was immaculate. Bunks were neatly made up, and the hard clay floor had been swept clean of rocks and loose soil. Our few clothes were hung up, and our books stacked in a corner. Antonio, Miguel, and Romero stood up and gallantly invited the ladies in. Haim and Yankel hadn't arrived yet. Once the ladies had been seated, Antonio leaped up and poured generous portions of the red wine into shining clean mess cups. Romero ran next door to the tent of the two young girls and borrowed their two tin cups.

Yankel and Haim brought a salami, a rare treat. With talk of our experiences and life in the camp, seasoned with a slice of salami washed down with the strong wine, the tent was for the first time a happy place.

The strong wine and the excitement of a social gathering put a glow in the thin, pale faces. Yankel felt the wine fast, or perhaps it was the need for joy. He yelled to Antonio, "A dance!" Antonio leaped to the center of the tent and in the two-by-four-foot space performed a vigorous dance. The audience was spellbound. Antonio's dancing might not have won a great prize, but it was carried out with such energy and joy that it left me exhilarated and feeling a bond to other humans.

All of a sudden I remembered Antonio was not a Spaniard, he was an Italian. I asked him, "Where did you learn to dance like this?"

"Spain."

I felt the depth of the short answer. The Spaniards and Italians were men who had experienced the worst of the last two decades: the depression years, then the Civil War in Spain and the rise of the Fascists in Italy. The big war. And now this confused peace. The war had not nicely cleared away the problems that made the war. Franco was still in Spain. The Jews had nowhere to go. And the Spaniards had the same problem: no home to return to, no new place to go. The search of the Jews was a mirror of their needs. It was not just a job, a casual employment, for them to be sailor and engineer and hired helper on the emigré ships.

Hannah sang a song in Yiddish, a sad song with words, some of which I could recognize, of home and mother and green woods. A certain quiet settled over us after Hannah's song. Feeling this, she spoke to Haia. "Haia will sing a cheerful song, a Russian song."

Her hands on her hips, eyes wide and coquettish, Haia rocked back and forth as she sang. Even though we did not understand the words, her singing cheered everyone. Afterward, she explained the song: "It's about a very thin girl who couldn't find a husband. Everyone courted her, but no one would marry her till she put on more weight."

Antonio urged Romero to sing, and reluctantly he did. His voice was hoarse, but the song, a flamenco, seized one by the throat. There was a curious concord between Romero's Spanish song and Hannah's Yiddish song.

Haim was wild with excitement. Bubbling over, he grabbed Miguel, the solemn Don, by the waist and swung him around in a waltz. Antonio and Romero raised their eyebrows in surprise, but Don Miguel, his face split from ear to ear in a grin, waltzed with abandon.

Finally, our wine and salami were finished, and we were tired from singing and dancing. Our party ended. Hannah and Haia knew their way home, and they left. Yankel, who had to be up at dawn, had left earlier.

I walked Haim home. The strong, sweet Cypriot wine had affected him; he was exhilarated and wished to keep the party going.

The stench from the latrines was strong on the night air as we walked through the dark camp. The stars gave sufficient light for us to see our way through the winding streets between the tents.

29 ＊ The Pageant of the Imprisoned

The sailors, with a few exceptions, trudged in a demonstration before the Joint Distribution Committee's office in the camp to demand more blankets. It was a typically American way to pursue one's needs. But even as we walked back to our tents, we realized what we had done, and our aggrieved militancy began to change into dismay and guilt. Our demonstration was bad enough; even worse, some of the sailors had gotten drunk on Cypriot wine and held a mock union meeting to air their gripes. Their wild behavior had frightened the young women and children. The Americans had entered onto this battlefield late, and it would take time to get a perspective on how to behave in the fight.

Why had we displayed this self-serving behavior? For one thing, the unity of the ship—forged in different circumstances, directed toward a different goal—seemed to be slipping away. Our friend and adviser Ossie was gone. Moka on the ship and Ossie in the camp had given moral leadership and discipline to the men. The contact between the Hagana and the crew had dwindled. The Hagana was busy with a thousand pressing tasks: maintaining order, bringing in food and medicine, keeping up morale, turning the "wild kids" and others into cadres, preparing them to become citizens of Palestine. Chastened, we resolved to keep our problems subordinated to the general welfare in this sprawling camp of sorrows.

Our feelings of contrition were reinforced that night. A senior Hagana man, older, his bearded face severe, called a meeting of our group. He chastised us: "That was a stupid job, marching together in front of the Joint's hut. If the British were looking for you at that moment, they could have photographed the bunch of you, and you would be kept in here for months.

"Apart from the stupidity, there was something worse—demanding special conditions and benefits because you're Americans. It's only accidental that you are Americans. If your families had stayed in Poland, in Romania, in Hungary, in Germany, you would have come on the ship not as sailors but as passengers . . . if you were alive.

"If you're cold, everyone is cold. The same goes for hunger. You forget the most important thing: you're not on a tour as guests of the Hagana, but prisoners of the British."

Jumping off the table, he ended his speech, "Tomorrow morning at ten o'clock, you will get an extra blanket. Come to the Hagana hut." And picking up his lantern, he walked out.

Later, seeing people moving across the bridge to the west, apparently to attend some function, I fell in with them. The bridge, which spanned a Cypriot road and connected Camp 65 to Camp 66, had been named "the Bridge of Tears," after a bridge in the Warsaw Ghetto that cut off access to the free world. As I crossed the barbed-wire-lined bridge, I could see the lights of the town of Larnaca, thirty-six miles away, a string of jewels shining under the dark outline of the mountains. There people were living without barbed wire; there they could walk in any direction, could laugh and talk aloud without fear of being overheard by soldiers. The barbed wire had a deadly effect on me. In the beginning it had been protection, but now it had become something else; a fear was growing out of the wire, a fear that we would never get outside of that fence. At the start of our imprisonment we had been fresh with life and triumphant. I had been contemptuous of the wire; on a dark night, with skill and care, I could have slipped under it. Then, boldly, I could have found a way off the island. Now the confidence was dying, giving way to a fear that the wire was stronger than we were. I couldn't conceive that people on the other side of the barrier would aid us. Outside there was an alien way of living, where there was work and laughter, but here we were rotting and dying. What did people who did not suffer as we did care about us?

Following the mass of people, I discovered they were bound for the big mess hall in Camp 66. This was the camp I had heard about. The people in this camp, mainly Romanian Jews, had put up a tremendous resistance to the British boarding parties, and there were casualties on both sides. But then, when they were captured at last and imprisoned here on Cyprus, there was a small group who behaved as badly to their own people, robbing and fighting. The ruthless struggle for life, begun under the scrupulously scientific management of the jailers of the *lager*, continued here of its own momentum and carried the camp to the brink of anarchy.

But a counterforce arose. Men with knowledge of the law drew up a code, judges were appointed, a police force was recruited. Then the struggle between order and disorder commenced—with families and friends at one another's throats. And order won. I was told, "Some day the epic of Camp 66 will be told to the world."

Today, even amid the suffering and sickness, even though their lives eroded during the dismal routine of this new imprisonment, the people of Camp 66 had won their battle against the poison of Nazism: they had learned to live with each other, in this world.

I followed the crowd into the mess hall tent. There was a festive air. Yankel, acting as doorman, saw me and, grabbing me by the arm, pushed me to the front of the crowd. A stage had been constructed of boards placed across oil drums. A battery of kerosene lamps furnished more light than I had seen after sunset since we entered the camp. The audience, sitting on tables and the floor or standing against the walls, was buzzing with anticipation.

Gabriel, one of the English Jews, climbed onto the stage and raised his hands for silence. In Hebrew he announced the program, leaving me as confounded as ever.

Using my meager Yiddish, I asked a young man alongside me what was going to happen. In his answer I could make out the words "Chinese" and "bird."

Something soft bumped against my legs. I looked down and saw one of the kids who had just arrived from Camp 70. His clothes were unmistakable, and he still had to get his hair cut. A small, curious puppy, he had worked himself to the front to find out what went on in this new world, Camp 66.

In the corner of the stage a curtain was shaking with what looked to me like some child's merriment. Then the performance commenced. A strange creature tripped onto the stage and leaped about in weird robes and garments of white and green. The haughty face of some ancient and proud race was painted on the cherubic cheeks. "Chinese . . . Chinese"—the girl's eyes were painted exaggeratedly Asian! Making a circle, she stopped and looked toward the curtain, her eyes dancing. A swaggering young king, the points of his crown topped with red "rubies," walked across the stage and collapsed onto his throne, a chair bedecked with gold paper.

Looking down at my small shipmate, I could see he had taken flight far into fairyland. The adult face of the child refugee had magically disappeared. In its place was a small boy's pop-eyed, open-mouthed wonder in the land of "once upon a time."

The king's discomfort on his throne was the center of all eyes. It was eased by a feathered young girl who twirled onto the stage, flapping her arms. "Bird . . . bird!" Nightingale! This was "The Chinese Nightingale," by Hans Christian Andersen.

The costumes must have taken months of collective toil by all the artisans of the camp. So did the manufacture of a crown from the discarded tin cans of the camp. And the "rubies"? Lord knows where they came from. Perhaps Elijah gave them to his children?

The pirouettes of scantily clad danseuses, the flitting of the nightingale, the threatening, swaggering king, the dialogue in Hebrew—all was magic this night on Cyprus, and the conjurers were the orphan actors and a fairy tale. Through the drama of the nightingale who won freedom with her song and dance, each little actor and actress in the most splendid of garments took flight from this cold night and the rough boards of the stage.

Looking around at the faces of the audience, I could see their wonder and joy. The boy at my knee was rigid with amazement. His small head never turned from the stage. His starved imagination, which, goodness knows, had been peopled by horrors, opened to a new world of color and fantasy. But it was not only the children: the faces of the adults were also transformed. Their eyes shone.

The play ended. The nightingale and the proud king joined in as the audience sang the "Hatikvah."

30 * Rotting Away on Cyprus

The day in the tent began with
Antonio folding the flap back, letting the sun stream across the hard-packed
red earth, across Miguel Buiza's blanketed form. Sitting up on the edge of
his cot, one leg resting on the other, Romero wound a white cloth around
the old injury on his leg. During the war he had been wounded while fighting with the French Resistance, the Maquis, in the Pyrenees. When I raised
my head, he softly welcomed me to the new day. "*Buenos dias.*"

My tent mates were a source of strength. Although Antonio was Italian, I kept thinking of him as a Spaniard. Perhaps it was because of the way
he sang the "*Colores de Primavera*," the "Colors of Spring," in Spanish
with such uplifting grace. Romero was a bit of an entertainer, too: a vigorous dance by him carried one through a day of misery. Miguel remained
apart, with a reserve that made it hard for him to open up to us. It must
have been compounded by his aristocratic birth and his training as a naval
officer. Long ago he had rejected these old barriers, but he found it difficult to be one of us.

There was beauty in the Spaniards' and the Italian's relations with each
other. After a bad night, Romero would awaken sullen, as if he were still
living with the night's dreams. The dreams that persisted through the day
were bad, creatures that were not controlled by barbed wire. Miguel and
Antonio sensed rather than saw when Romero was in this mood and
showed an unobtrusive concern for him. In his moodiness, he didn't even
notice. They helped him to make up his bunk, casually offered a precious
cigarette, invited him to walk around the borders of the camp. Slowly,
Romero found his way back as the day moved along. Then, on another day,
it was Antonio or Miguel who was afflicted, and the others who cared
for him.

The previous night, the Spaniards had been deep in gloom. The camp
was swept by news of the large vote de Gaulle had received in France. The
Spaniards were uncertain what the election meant. They feared there

could be camps for the Spanish Republicans again. They discussed the possibilities of staying in Palestine.

Antonio went to the two tents across from us to greet his charges. One was a beautiful young girl who lived with another young woman. The girl had black hair, pale cheeks, and fine skin, and she was a magnet for all our eyes when we first moved to this section of the camp. She seemed a young Diana stalking the camp, her youthful beauty piercing the sourness and the gloom.

But when we got to know her, we discovered a strange gleam in her eyes. We learned that she had been in Auschwitz, actually in the line for the extermination chamber. Guards pushed her mother, just ahead of her, in to die—and then an Allied bombing raid disrupted the grisly work, and the girl was spared. When the Russian army approached and the guards fled, the girl was freed. But each day here in Cyprus she wrote letters, from her mother to herself, pleading her love, having her mother tell her all the details of the life that had been led by the family, of which our poor Diana alone survived.

Antonio had two other protégées, both sixteen-year-old girls from Paris. His French was not fluent, but he could talk with them. In their roundup of French Jews, the Germans had assigned these two girls to a brothel for German officers, and they had contracted syphilis. Their lives had been saved by the American army. Now they were getting treatment from the medical supplies of the Joint Distribution Committee. Often they were bright and animated, as if they had no past, but I could sense in them a certain tension in the presence of men. My tent mates and I all visited them, but it was only Antonio whom they trusted. When their tent pegs came loose in the rain, they called for him. When their little kerosene stove didn't work, they called for Antonio. He had completely won their trust, and he was at their beck and call.

As the day began, I dipped my tin soup bowl into the tin of fresh water at the side of the tent and washed my face. The rains had settled the dust, and my hair was no longer thick and dry with matted clay dust. Breakfast was a black, bitter brew called coffee and a piece of bread. Lunch would be no better: some potatoes and rotten meat. The camp would fall quiet in the early afternoon. The plague of hunger required a rest so the body could draw all the energy it could from the meager meal.

Some days I would watch a boat sail back and forth on the sea below us. From its size, shape, and lack of sail, it seemed to be a small fisherman. The sea lay quiet and blue, and there was only this small boat, riding with some of the freedom of birds and fish. In the afternoon the sun speckled the sea with gold, and the boat dipped itself in the golden water, ripples trailing behind it. When I stood on the bridge between Camp 66 and Camp 65, the barbed wire of the fence was below the boat on the sea. But when I took a step down, the barbed wire rose and imprisoned the boat. I found I could no longer look but had to turn my head so the boat could keep its freedom.

Many afternoons I would read. My mind seemed to have taken on some of the hunger of my body. I had been fortunate to find two books in English, Aristotle's *Politics* and an edition of *English Philosophers from Bacon to Mill.* And I had found a good spot to read when the rains stopped for an hour, a place where there were no flies: an open-air amphitheater built by the orphans for their plays during the summer months. The stage was a foot off the ground, and the roof was made of palm leaves. The wind rustling through the palm leaves was the only sound, and it brought a certain calm. Reading was of greater importance to me now than it had ever been before, for it was a way to shut out the horror of the camp, the creeping sourness of a weakening body and a mind that tended to wild pictures and panic.

One afternoon, a small boy—he must have been about three—toddled down the damp clay path to the amphitheater. He must have wandered away from a tent about a hundred yards away; the mother or the older child taking care of him must have been sleeping. He sat down on a patch of clay and started molding something. Rolling over on my back, I could see a watchtower about fifty yards away. The soldier posted there moved around restlessly, now looking into the camp, now out to sea. I thought of what Yankel had said about the British soldiers: "They are worse off here than we are. Their food is a little better, but they have no place to go when they leave camp. I heard the Greeks of the island won't have anything to do with the British. They are as hostile to them as the Jews of the camps are."

I turned on my stomach to see what the child was doing. He was making what seemed to be a little village—houses, streets, rough little tent-like mounds. Around it he was building something. It was a curious, irregular, thin mound encompassing the entire village. Then it hit me—the barbed wire! He had never lived outside of barbed wire, and he could not conceive of people living without it.

Walking back through the camp, I sighted the familiar figure of Yankel. He came up to me with a grin. "If you're not busy, as you probably aren't," he said, "come with me. I have something to show you."

He led me into Camp 67, to a long Niessen hut. As we went inside, I was shaken by the sight: an exhibition of sculpture, painting, weaving, and carving, all neatly arrayed on both sides and down the center of the hut. First there was a beautiful six-foot-square model of a kibbutz, the collective farm of Palestine. In the center was the white water tower surrounded by a platform with armor plate and slit peepholes as a watchtower against attack. The tiny neat rows of houses with gardens around them, even a machinery garage with a tractor standing in front of it, were complete to the smallest detail. Joyfully, Yankel pushed the tractor back and forth to show how the wheels turned. Around the walls were pencil sketches of life in the camp: a Hassidic group dancing to the full moon, their shadows wild and distorted; a football game; people in a tent with rain pouring outside, their faces fearful; a girl with the exaggerated proportions of the starch diet, big busts, immense swollen arms and legs and bottom. The artist, whomever she or he may have been, had kept a sense of humor.

In the center of the hut was a full-size figure of a man with a fist held high, sculptured out of white chalk. "The sculptor dug a big rock of chalk out of the ground," Yankel said, his face a study in pride.

"What does he represent?" I asked.

"The heroism of the Warsaw Ghetto struggle. We call it Warsawgrad," Yankel said.

Young boys and girls in neat blue shorts, white shirts, and blue ties stood by their creations. "Hashomer Hatzair," he explained, "is their organization. They are Laborites, and their morale is very good."

A young girl stood by a big book on a table. "The guest book, the Golden Book of Cyprus," she said. "Would you write something?"

After leafing through the book, I picked up the pen and wrote, "May the new Jewish Nation of Palestine win its State and free its people." I signed my real name and inscribed beneath it, "Skipper of the *Geula*." Never had I been prouder. It was an American sailor's small claim to posterity.

Walking home, I saw Sholom sitting on his cot, the flap of his tent tied back. Seeing me, he grinned. He had lost his solid, healthy look; he was thinner, and a yellowish tinge had spread over his face. But he maintained his composure and his quiet, save when something aroused him. Then he was a fighter. Sholom seemed to suffer more from hunger than any of us, but he didn't complain, saving his daily ration of cigarettes to trade for an extra piece of bread.

"How's it going, Sholom?" I asked.

"All right! Do you think we'll be here much longer?"

"Who the devil knows? I hope not! How're the other boys?"

"Good. Dave is better. Blake's been preparing for some kibbutz he's going to. Rotter and Eli are still alive, but not kicking much. Wurm is with Greer and Syd."

I had become aware that even our own crew members were isolated from each other.

Continuing down the street between the tents, I thought of the problems of our crew. It was as if they were in a maze. The little streets all ended up at the high barbed-wire fence. There was hunger and sickness inside us, and sickness and demoralization of the people around us. As Americans, the crew had experienced nothing like this. They saw themselves rotting and could find no escape. Eventually we would get out, but it was practically impossible to conceive of when or how. And we had entered the camp in fairly good physical shape. How, then, must the refugees have felt? After their wartime experiences and the long and dangerous journey to Palestine, how would it feel to be put aboard a prison ship and taken to imprisonment for two years on Cyprus? Yet we could sense within them a steel core of persistence, a determination that they would gain their freedom.

I thought of the stories of my grandfather, who had spent a year and a half in Libby Prison, outside of Richmond, during the Civil War. When I was very young, my mother had told me of how he had returned to their Missouri farm. There had been a look on his face that had not been there when he joined the First Kentucky Cavalry, a sad, wasted look, as if he had seen something horrible he could never forget. He didn't live long. He lay down quietly and died, leaving his wife with six children and a piece of land newly carved from the wilderness.

Would we carry this same look when we finally left Cyprus?

31 * The Crew Is Honored

"How do you explain the murder of six million Jews by the fascists?" I asked Avraham. He looked at me with his hard, blunt face, his bared arm marked with the blue tattoos of Auschwitz. He shifted uncomfortably on his cot, his sandaled feet resting on the damp clay ground.

"They died because the Book promised that many Jews would die in this period. They would be destroyed because they were not religious enough." Avraham, a twenty-three-year-old diamond cutter from Antwerp, belonged to the Aguda, an orthodox religious group.

"But, Avraham, don't you see the meaning of what you're saying? That it could happen all over again. Then you'd say it happened because the Bible said so."

Avraham didn't argue; he wished only to forget. I remembered my mother's words during the depth of the Depression: "This suffering has been brought on by the evil in people, by all the people forgetting their religion." She would accept no theory that traced depressions to economic problems. So too with Avraham.

That night I asked Haim why six million Jews had died. "Not only Jews were killed!" he replied. "Hundreds of thousands of Poles and millions of Russians were killed by the Nazis. They created the myth of the guilt of the Jew, the inferiority of the Pole and the Russian, so that the German troops might have the reasons to justify the slaughter. Highly organized by the German state with all its finances, press, organization, and police, and with the special forces of the S.A. and S.S. troops, the slaughter was a source of loot, the first the fascists gained, loot easily garnered in the cities and villages of Germany—the houses and lands and personal possessions of the Jews. Once people began to loot, refused to think of the consequences, then the fascists had won a great victory. They could go on to bigger and better looting—of whole countries and continents."

"But why didn't your people fight?"

192

"They did fight. As some died singing, so others died fighting. You know of the Warsaw Ghetto?"

"Only that there was a great battle there."

"There was a bitter struggle among the people as to whether they should fight or not. German troops surrounded the ghetto, starved the Jews. With death facing them, many Jews wished to surrender and end their misery with quick death. But others, mainly the youth, wished to take as many fascists as they could with them when they died. People from all organizations and religious groups joined these stalwarts. They fought, arming themselves from the German patrols who came inside the ghetto on extermination missions. The fighters hid in sewers and in the rubble of blasted buildings. They sent parties at night through the German lines out into the country to bring back food. As they got more arms, they fought pitched battles with heavily armed German troops. The stories of the Warsaw Ghetto are known by a few survivors; the world has yet to hear them. In Eretz, on the kibbutz I am joining, is one of the survivors. When you get to Eretz, you must hear his stories."

From a distance in the night a metallic banging sounded clearly. "Trucks?" I asked.

"No." Haim smiled grimly. "British light tanks."

"And do the people still fight?"

"Yes."

"But why, with the rains and the misery, don't they do something here on Cyprus? Why not a big strike? Have it organized so that Palestine and people all over the world will support it. Anything is better than rotting away."

Haim sat up on his cot and gripped his knees with his folded arms. "On May 1 a small group hung banners they had made secretly on the barbed wire. The slogans were, 'End Cyprus camps,' 'Down with the British,' 'For free immigration to Palestine.' There also was a hunger strike for about five days. Many people suffered. Some died; others have been sick ever since. Now many feel that a fight brings defeat.

"Four months ago the camp football team played the British soldiers' team and won. As there was no bridge between the camps then, the barbed-wire gates were opened. British tanks were lined up between the two gates, and the people walked between the tanks to get to Camp 66, where the football field is located. For some reason a British soldier shut the gate, cutting the children in two groups, one group in each camp. The children who were left behind got panicky and started yelling; then they started throwing stones at the British soldiers. The soldiers got panicky and fired a rifle burst over the kids' heads."

I had never seen women like the women on Cyprus; not only were they misshapen because of their diet, but they lived like no women I had ever seen. They wore poor, ragged clothes and had none of the feminine accouterments of women in the outside world, like cosmetics and a pretty dress. Their complexions were sallow and sickly. Many went barefoot, and poor soap and hard water took the luster from their hair, which hung limp from the rain or stringy from the continually blowing red dust. They lacked energy; they did not have sufficient strength for washing and cooking. Many had very bad teeth or came out of the *lager* with no teeth. Self-conscious, they engaged in none of the flirtatious play that life had taught men to expect. The very young girls still had color and animation, but at the age when most women would flower, the camps' women were haggard, old, and tired.

A sailor conceives of a woman, her dress, cheeks, eyes, and hair, in colors. Yet that was exactly what was lacking in the camps' women. Even the most ambitious of the Casanovas among our crew beat a lonely retreat to their tents and sought companionship among the other sailors or male friends they had made among the people.

As the time for the regular Saturday football game approached, clouds still hung heavy and low over the camp. Antonio, Miguel, and I left Romero on his cot with a pain in his back that had nagged him for two days. Picking our way up the rocky, muddy path, we skirted the barbed wire that separated Camp 66 from Camp 67. Originally, as the camps grew from 65 to 66, the fence was removed, but the barbed wire was left on the ground. Now the people used it to hang their wash out to dry.

All the small fry were heading up the hill to the football field. The kids were animated and thrilled with the promise of the game. Since the game lasted much too long for them to stand, some of the older men brought little stools they had made from sticks.

The teams lined up in makeshift uniforms, in sweatshirts, undershirts, khaki shorts, underpants with buttons sewn on to strengthen them so that conventions might be observed. The captain of the Camp 67 team was a man in his thirties, his head shaved bald in the Russian sports fashion. The whole camp knew his story. He and his two best friends had played with the Prague Sokol team before the war. The war separated them. His two friends escaped to Palestine, but he was imprisoned in a *lager*. Now he was on his way to Palestine. His friends, rumor had it, were the best players on the first team of the Maccabees, the best Palestinian soccer team. "The Russian," as we called him because of his bald head, was the outstanding player of the camp teams. We all wondered how he would compare with his two friends when he finally got to Palestine.

In fact, the Maccabees, who had toured Europe and the United States, had been in the neighborhood of our camp. For three weeks they had played the Greek teams on Cyprus. They hoped to play before the people in the camps, but the British had refused them permission.

As the game got under way, we saw the Russian's wondrous skills. With great nimbleness, he feinted, whirled, weaved between opponents, passed, found openings in the defense.

But now some of the spectators turned away from the game and looked down the hill. Following their gaze, we saw nearly a dozen black-coated men coming toward us. Today was the Sabbath, and from their dress these were Orthodox Jews. When they came closer, I could tell they were rabbis. An edge of uneasiness ran through the audience. What did it mean?

The rabbis marched to the edge of the football field and stood, faces grimly turned toward the players. Then it was clear—the rabbis were demonstrating against playing soccer on the Sabbath. If the players were aware of them, they did not show it. The game continued.

There was a huddled discussion among the rabbis, and they marched in a tight group onto the field. The players continued playing, carefully avoiding the black-garbed figures, but anger and frustration showed on the faces of each side. Tension ran through the spectators as the game took on an unexpected drama.

The ball rolled slowly past one of the rabbis. Fiercely, he ran over, grabbed hold of it, and hugged it to his chest, his body rigid and accusatory. A young player marched up, grabbed the rabbi stoutly by the beard, and tugged. The man tottered forward. His companions swarmed over the player, and the athletes came to his aid. Spectators poured onto the field. Yankel and a party of young Hagana men separated the football players and the rabbis, but the game did not resume. The rabbis, football players, and spectators walked home, hotly arguing.

Later, I asked one of the Shou-shous about the aftermath of the struggle. He answered, lightly, "The Masquerod, the camp committee, took up the issue. This committee is composed of delegates from all political and religious groups in the camp. No penalties on either side, save one, and a warning was issued to both sides. The Sabbath football game can be continued, and the rabbis are not to disrupt it. But the player who grabbed the rabbi by the beard cannot play for four Sabbaths."

On my way back through the camp I saw a small fire where a young girl huddled for warmth. She looked at me keenly as I passed her. She was one of the young Hagana guards who maintained the watch throughout the camp every night to see that there was no stealing among the people and that the British did not enter the camp.

Yankel arrived with an invitation. "You are all invited to a party. It is for the sailors and for the young people who have completed their Hagana training."

The party was in the children's library. The tables had been put end to end to create a long banquet hall. We were a little late, and the Hagana youth, with shining faces and clean white blouses, blue ties on the boys, blue neckerchiefs on the girls, sat impatient for the program to commence.

The sailors sat at special places reserved for them. Itzik, the muscular young man who had helped smuggle me from Camp 70, sat on my right and explained as the program went along. A young Palestinian opened the party with an address in Hebrew. I recognized him as the girls' judo instructor. Then a young man with an accordion played a folk song. "The accordionist was one of those Polish Jews saved by the Russians in '39," Itzik whispered. "He was in the Red Army during the war, and most of the songs he learned are Russian."

I recognized the song as "Meadowland."

There were several skits in Yiddish that I couldn't follow—something about the jammed conditions on the refugee ships, at which they poked fun. Itzik was laughing too hard to translate.

A tiny girl with black hair and big shining eyes, wearing blue shorts and white blouse, stood up nervously and recited a piece. I recognized the words, "Captain . . . Captain." Itzik looked at me, his eyes shining warmly. "It's for you, the captain of the refugee ship."

A dryness grabbed my throat, and I could feel the sweat on my face. I was moved by the child's recitation; it had that universal flavor of children's love and admiration of the sea and sailors, plus the special meaning the ship had for these children. But my chief emotion was fear: I was afraid I would have to make a speech. I would have sailed three ships between Scylla and Charybdis rather than make one speech.

The little girl forgot some of the lines. In her nervousness, she faltered, stopped. A cheer and a wave of hand-clapping applauded her. She smiled timidly and sat down.

The chairman announced the next part of the program. Four girls in sailor suits moved into a cleared space between the tables. To the music of the accordion they danced sailor's dances.

Next was a recitation by a young Polish Jew. We all knew him well and called him "Sailor." He was with the Russian navy in the Black Sea during the war, and his muscular arms were covered with tattoos. Itzik was very moved by what the boy said. "It is the poem by Mayakovski, 'I Am a Citizen of the World,'" Itzik explained. "I will get the words in English for you."

Refreshments were a tiny sip of the Cyprus wine, served in the enormous tin cups of the camp. The red wine scarcely covered the bottom of the cup. "When you get to Eretz, we will feed you better. And have something to drink, too," Itzik said.

The tables were pushed back to the wall, and to the music of the lone accordion the hora was danced. Arms linked to form a circle, and the movement began, feet kicking in one direction, a stamp, and feet kicking in the other direction. The circle moved swiftly around. Young people formed a smaller circle inside the larger one, and it moved in the opposite direction. Sweat poured off young faces. The hora was easy to learn, and the sailors joined in, George hooting and chanting with the rest—in English! Sholom was sweating and laughing and dancing. Miguel leaned against a tent pole and watched with a smile. Antonio joined the dance, as did Romero, despite his sore leg.

The dance quickly tired us older ones, and we dropped out to suck fresh air into our heaving lungs. Despite our exhaustion, we found the energetic collective movement of the simple hora profoundly satisfying.

The Spaniards and I left the party. Far out in the darkness, as we picked our way over the muddy ground, the sour smell of the latrines in our nostrils, we could hear the laughter of the young.

32 ✳ Bound for Palestine— and a New Jail

Cyprus had plowed us so deep into its red earth, with its sickness and hunger and demoralized people, that when the news came we found it hard to believe.

A Hagana representative gathered a group of us in one of the huts and told us, "The British still control immigration quotas to Palestine. Legally they can still do this under the League of Nations Mandate and their White Paper. This month the Jewish Agency chartered a Greek ship to send our quota of immigrants from Cyprus to Palestine. Since the Hagana wants to get the crews off the island, we have asked for volunteers to surrender their places to the sailors."

There was shocked silence. A surge of emotions swept among us. Finally, someone shouted, "That's great! What do we do?"

"The seamen of the *Paducah* and *Northland* have to get ready, starting now. We'll give you each the name of the person who gave up his place for you. Memorize it. The British may question you. Then you'll get khakis. All your new clothes will come from Palestine. In case you are picked up in Haifa later, you can say you're a Palestinian. Pass the word among the men and meet in this hut at eight tonight, after it's dark."

The news swept among the seamen like a whirlwind, bringing animation, new energy, and joy to their faces and bodies.

Later, curious, I asked about the man who had given up his place for me.

"Carmine Roth," the Hagana representative said, looking at his list. "Would you like to meet him?"

"Yes, I would."

"Wait here till we've finished, and I'll ask Haim to take you to his tent."

Haim leading, we navigated through a tight little village of tents and stopped before one whose flap was tied back. It was a gloomy day, and I could scarcely see inside. Bending and following Haim inside, I saw a man stretched out on a cot. He turned as we entered. When Haim spoke to him, he sat up wearily. His hair was curly, thick, and matted with the dust that persisted despite the rains.

The man offered his hand, and I shook it. "Carmine Roth." Haim was amused to introduce each of us to the other.

"Is he all alone?" I asked.

"Three other men share the tent with him. But he has no relatives in the world."

"How does he feel about letting me take his place?"

After Haim translated, Roth answered slowly, carefully picking his words. They dropped from his lips wearily. Haim explained, "He said, 'If no sailors leave, then no new people can be brought this close to Eretz.' He will give his place so that more people can be brought."

The man's eyes were tired and his face gray. He lay back on his cot.

Fifty people had surrendered their certificates to the crew of the *Paducah* and to some Italian sailors who had been in a distant part of the camp.

The night before leaving I made a round of my new friends—Haim, Yankel, Martin, Itzik, the nurses Hannah and Haia, and Peter—and bade them goodbye. There was hunger in their eyes at the thought of reaching Eretz, but they all had cheerful farewells and exacted a promise that some day I would visit them when they were established in the new land.

Haim made me promise to visit his friend's kibbutz and to tell him that he was coming soon.

The morning was cold and dark, but for once it was not a struggle to wake up: today we would leave Cyprus! The long-suspended voyage would resume, and this time we would reach our final port: Palestine, Eretz, "the Land" of the people.

With our little bundles—extra shirt, pants, toothbrush, and razor— we gathered before the gate of Camp 67 with the others who were to leave. We were told that food would be available on the ship that was to take us to Palestine. We were glad it would not be a British prison ship, but a Greek ship chartered by the Jewish Agency and crewed by Greek sailors.

A convoy—the same Ford trucks that brought us to the camp—lined up on the road outside the barbed-wire fence. British soldiers again formed a gauntlet, and we walked through it as our names were called by a sergeant. He stumbled over the pronunciations, but no one failed to answer his call.

Several hours passed before my name was called—"Carmine Roth." I passed the sergeant and climbed into a truck. Finally, all the people were loaded, the trucks roared into life, and we moved down the road. The trucks stopped before some long huts, and we were told to get out. Again we passed in single file through the search huts, though this time there was no strip search. The sergeants merely patted down our bodies and looked through our small bundles. In the last hut, a British major sat alongside an interpreter from the Jewish Agency. There we each received a small red card with our name on it; this was the precious "certificate" that allowed us into Palestine.

We boarded the trucks, and our convoy started off. Looking back, we could see the disappearing barbed wire and tents and tin huts. Ahead, the road wound through the barren, rocky countryside. The sun climbed higher, and the day had a cheerfulness we had not known in two months. Two months: they had gone harder than any two years of my life.

About five miles from our camp we passed through a neat military village of wooden houses. Men in vaguely familiar khaki forage caps stared at us curiously. Then I realized with a shock: this was the German prisoner-of-war camp we had heard about. Here there was no barbed wire, only neat houses. We had heard that the British even allowed the German prisoners to go into town on leave. The Germans looked at us with hostility. Here and there right arms snapped up in the Hitler salute. And the survivors of their hatred were still prisoners! What madness it was to try to understand who was fighting on which side in the war!

The road sloped down toward the sea, and we could see the top of what looked like a church spire. Skirting the edge of the town, the trucks got snarled in the traffic of the harbor of Famagusta. MPs, yelling and snarling, cleared a lane for us. Each truck backed up to the gangway of the ship, discharged its people, and pulled away. On the dock we formed a long line, all 750 of us, and passed before a British colonel flanked by two sergeants. They silently examined our certificates and waved us onto the ship's gangway.

Aboard, we still couldn't express our relief, for there might have been some Criminal Investigation Department civilians among the Greek sailors. We found a bunk in the cabins, dropped our bundles to establish possession, and went back on deck to see what was happening.

The people were filing up the gangway, older ones helped by the younger. There was animation in even the oldest, who looked at this ancient, rusty ship as if it was some shining trans-Atlantic liner. The name on the bow and stern was *Aegean Star*.

When all the people were aboard, the lines were let go. The colonel and his two sergeants climbed into a jeep. Soon we were out past the harbor and at sea again. I slapped George fiercely on the back. We had made it!

Dov, a young Hagana member, a Palestinian who had completed a tour of duty on Cyprus, was in charge of this voyage. He informed us that the captain had agreed to give the people two hot meals on the voyage to Haifa, but now refused to provide any. This was no surprise to the old sailors among us, for the Greek shipowners were notorious on all seas for their rotten food and their rusty old ships that carried more insurance than cargo. Finally, after Dov signed a statement that he would pay for the food in Haifa, the captain agreed to furnish tea and one sandwich per person.

To us, the dingy cabins were luxurious suites. As far as we could tell, there were no C.I.D. men aboard. We felt free for the first time since we had been captured.

We were warned, however, that we were far from free. "When we arrive in Haifa, a British convoy will pick us up and take us to Athlit Prison," Dov said. "Athlit has better food than Cyprus, because the Jewish Agency sends fresh food in daily, but the British mingle freely with the people, and you will be constantly under surveillance. After two months in Athlit you go through a very stiff interrogation before you are freed."

"Any chance of escape?" Sholom asked.

"The Hagana did a job on Athlit about six months ago. The British had some key Hagana personnel. One night, a strong Hagana party dug the barbed-wire posts out of the ground, entered the camp, bound and gagged the British and Arab sentries, opened the cells of the men they were looking for, and made their escape. Since then, the British have doubled their sentries and reinforced the barbed-wire fences. If they get us inside Athlit, there's little chance of escape. The only hope is between the time the ship arrives in Haifa and the time we arrive in Athlit. Be on your toes, and take any opportunity you can to escape."

It was sunset before the call for the cup of tea and sandwich. Sholom was placed in charge of serving the meal—lukewarm tea, a thin piece of ham on a single slice of soggy bread. The orthodox refused to eat the ham, throwing it over the side instead.

Standing on deck, I watched Cyprus disappear beyond the wind-tossed sea, the purple rain clouds as dark against the sunset as the island itself. Ahead of us in the southeast the gloom of night had already descended. I could hear Sholom urging the people to grab the cup of tea and bread and move on, so that all would have their bit of food.

The ship was rolling comfortably, and our speed had decreased. On the poop, George found a taffrail log, and from the striking bells on the bridge we checked the speed. It had decreased to six knots.

I found Leonard and Eli below in the passageway looking down at the great steel arms of the engines moving up and down. There was the smell of hot oil, and we could catch a glimpse of an oiler rhythmically squirting oil onto the bearings. A fireman brought a little tray with tiny cups of coffee for the engineers. It brought back memories of coffee time on the *Paducah*, of how in the early part of the voyage we could open the refrigerator in the mess room and find cold meats and butter and make a thick sandwich and wash it down with fresh, hot coffee. That seemed a long time ago!

I returned to the deck, passing a few people wandering restlessly up and down the passageways. Most of the passengers had turned in. Only a few stood inside the passageway enjoying the warmth of the hot air pouring out of the engine room. On deck there was a cold mist that condensed on the steel structure of the ship, moistening the decks. The cold drove me below again where I could watch the great revolving arms of the engines. The turning shaft, at least a foot in diameter, comforted me, assuring me we were moving toward our goal.

A young oiler, his sweat rag around his neck, his skin pale and glistening, looked up at me. He smiled and raised his hand in salute. I waved back. He climbed the iron ladder up to the engine room grating, came over, looked into my face, and asked in German, "*Sprechen Deutsch?*"

"*Bissen*," I answered. "A little."

He seemed to relax. "Fascism no good!" I nodded. "My country, Greece, have fascism now. No good. Must be careful, policeman on ship, watch all sailors." He continued grimly, "Can talk with Jew. Jew suffer most. But Greek suffer now much as during war." I was moved.

The oiler motioned me to stay where I was and disappeared into the engine room. He brought back one of the tiny cups of coffee and offered it to me with a smile. I took it and sipped it. It was delicious—coffee that was really coffee.

He looked at me apologetically. "No more."

"Fine, thanks." With a short wave of his hand he returned to work, leaving me with a warmth greater than that of the fire-heated air gushing out around me.

Reluctantly I returned to my bunk and climbed in. The first day outside the barbed wire had ended. Tomorrow meant either escape and freedom, or imprisonment again.

33 * Escape

Lying in the dark cabin, still but half awake, I sensed a change in the movement of the ship. The slight, rhythmic rocking of the bunk had stopped; the engines must have been slowed. Through the open porthole, I saw only the dark sea and a starless sky. I had a compulsion to keep my finger on the movement of the ship to be alert for an opportunity to escape. Pulling on my pants and shirt, slipping on my shoes, I opened the door quietly so as not to awaken the three men in the room.

From the deck I could see the lights of Haifa at least fifteen miles away. Sholom came warily around the corner of a lifeboat, saw me, grinned, and stopped beside me.

"What's up?" I asked.

"Slowed down so they don't get into Haifa before daylight, I think."

"Wish the Hagana had a launch to pick us up here. We could slip into the water nice and quiet."

"Yeah, but too far to swim."

Even at the slow speed we were making, the lights of Haifa grew in size and distinctness. The bulk of Mount Carmel could be made out against the faint light creeping into the eastern sky.

With the dawn came two British destroyers. They approached slowly, gray ships on gray water, and took their positions, one on each side, watching to see that nobody tried to swim to the Promised Land. All must enter it in the correct manner—through a jail.

The approaches to Haifa were filled with anchored ships. With the increasing light we could make out flags of many nations. Dov, who had joined Sholom and me, explained, "It's the orange shipping season. That's why there are so many ships. And it's good for us. There'll be a lot of activity in the harbor—it may aid an escape."

Sholom jammed his elbow into my side in his excitement. "There she is!" I looked and saw the two stacks, the rakish bow—the *Paducah*, the last in a line of refugee ships tied along the breakwater of Haifa.

Alongside the *Paducah* was a bigger ship with two very tall smokestacks shooting straight up into the sky. It was the *Exodus*. We recognized her from the photographs we had seen in the French newspapers. The old ships lined up alongside the breakwater were empty. Some of their people had filtered into Palestine, some were still held on Cyprus. The ships were bedraggled, battered monuments to a struggle still continuing.

Once inside the breakwater of Haifa, we studied the details of the docks. An American Export Line ship, the *Excalibur*, was discharging cargo; a British ship, red rust marks painting her side, was tied up astern of the American ship. A small fleet of trim British navy launches, their sailors watching to ensure no one dropped off the ship to swim ashore, convoyed us through the harbor. The destroyers steamed back to sea.

A clear space on the dock toward which we were slowly moving was apparently where our ship would dock. We could see khaki-colored buses lined up. "Army buses?" I asked.

"No. Jewish buses. But the British will have an armed escort. If they get you into the buses, it's almost impossible to get away."

Heaving lines were thrown ashore to the dock crew; heavier lines were made fast to the heaving lines and pulled to the dock by Arab longshore-men. The longshoremen and other Arabs on the dock looked at us curiously; there was no demonstration of hostility. Alert Jewish longshoremen scrutinized the new immigrants.

"If the Hagana has some plan for us, we have no knowledge of it," Dov whispered to me. "Keep next to me, no matter what happens."

British soldiers lined the dock alongside the buses; sandwiched between were armored cars.

I had never seen such dangerous looking vehicles as those armored cars, four-wheeled with extra-heavy tires. I could see three machine guns mounted within the cars, their snouts poking out through slits in the armor. A driver and a policeman were in place on each side of each armored car, and a soldier sat in an open hatchway on top, a machine gun mounted in front of him. Soldiers with Sten guns were mounted on motorcycles; other soldiers lined up to watch the ship tie up. Several jeeps filled with heavily armed personnel were parked where the gangway was being prepared to be put ashore. Dov looked grim. There was a wiry nervousness in his body as he sharply scanned the whole dock area.

"Anything doing?" I asked hopefully.

"Can't see anything," he whispered.

The old ship was heaved in and hit the dock with a dull thump. Lines were drawn tight and the gangway was lowered. British soldiers poured aboard the ship and started our people down the gangway. On the dock Jewish nurses in uniforms gave each person a sandwich and a big glass of milk. I was right behind Dov as he went down the gangway.

Sholom was twenty feet ahead of me. A British soldier directed him to one of the sixty-passenger buses. Sholom threw fast phrases at the soldier, who moved over, grabbed him by the arm, and forced him toward the bus. Then an officer called to the soldier. Sholom opened the bus door and stepped up. As the soldier turned away, Sholom stepped back from the bus and slammed the door with a bang. The soldier, hearing the door close as he walked away, must have thought Sholom had gone inside. A nurse passed with an empty tray, and Sholom grabbed the tray. She looked at him in astonishment, but he was already walking through the line of British soldiers. Luck, boldness, and great timing. The last I saw of Sholom he was climbing into a Jewish ambulance.

British soldiers were separating the column, one person to the left, the next to the right. I felt that the last chance to escape was gone. Here we were in a strange town, with no money, among allies who didn't know us, and all around us were armed soldiers ready to shoot.

In the bus a wave of nausea swept over me. In my weakened condition, the excitement and anticipation had been too much. I dropped my head between my knees until the illness eased.

The convoy started off, armored cars sandwiched between the buses. We swept out of the harbor area and on to a road skirting the sea. Eli and Rotter were the only other Americans in my bus. As I watched through the back window, the soldier on the armored car hatch looked into the bus, his hands on his machine gun. For an Englishman, he had peculiar features— high cheekbones and a prominent jaw. His soldier's cap, shoved forward, seemed too small for his head.

Turning to look at the back of the bus driver's head, I saw his neck muscles go taut. His head jerked up and he turned back toward us, "*Achtung . . . achtung,*" he whispered fiercely.

Alerted, I slipped out of my seat and, bending low, moved up the aisle toward the driver. Peering through the windshield I could see a jam of buses, armored cars, and motorcycles. One bus had crashed into the rear of the next ahead, and our driver skirted the jam slowly.

Seeing a clear spot to the right, he jammed the accelerator and drove up on the sidewalk. Opening the bus door, he shouted, "*Geh veck! Geh veck!*" Scram.

Without thinking, I jumped to the sidewalk. Eli and Rotter were right behind me. An Arab in flowing robes looked at us curiously, his dark eyes noncommittal.

To our left on the corner some soldiers had parked their motorcycles and begun to set up a roadblock. Turning to the right, we walked quickly but didn't run. A three-story apartment building was on our left. A gap between two buildings revealed a lane running away from the street. I turned into the lane.

Ahead of me I could see a waist-high, vine-covered fence. I was barely aware that Eli and Rotter were no longer with me. I leaped the fence and ducked into the back of a garage, took off my jacket, and threw it into some high grass. Two men were working on a car's engine. They straightened up to look at me briefly, then bent over and continued their work. I walked to the street that led back onto the main road where the buses were jammed.

Behind me I heard shouting, and despite myself I turned to look. An Arab was waving his fist at me. By then, the British soldiers and police had a cordon around the buses. A soldier motioned me away as I stared into the tangle of buses, motorcycles, armored cars, and all kinds of people. Slowly, I headed back toward the city. A hundred yards ahead of me I saw Dave Greer calmly walking in the same direction.

Quickening my pace, but careful not to seem to be in a hurry, I slowly overtook Dave.

Together, we turned to the right at the next corner and headed up a residential street where the names on the placards of each house were in Arabic. We were in the Arab quarter of Haifa. At the next corner we turned to the left, where small butcher and tailor shops lined the street. All the signs were still in Arabic.

A bent man coming down the street with a bundle of newspapers appeared to be Jewish; we saw that his newspapers were printed in Hebrew. At last, we hoped, someone who could give us help.

Dave spoke to him in Yiddish. The man looked at us suspiciously, then started arguing. Dave, who was getting angry, spoke again, but the man walked away from us.

"What happened?" I asked, surprised.

"I asked the bastard where the nearest synagogue was. He wanted to know why I wanted a synagogue. I told him that we had to get off the street, and that when one Jew asks another for a synagogue, you should tell him, not argue. He was suspicious of us."

On pins and needles, I saw a watchmaker's shop with a sign in English and Hebrew. We ducked inside. The watchmaker, one eye distorted through the thick magnifying lense, looked up at us.

I got right to the point. "Do you speak English?" I asked.

"Yes."

"We've just escaped from the British. We were brought over from Cyprus this morning. We've got to get off the street fast. Will you help us?"

Without a word he took off his eyepiece, put down the watch in his hand, then with both eyes studied us thoroughly. Motioning us to follow, he got up and walked out of the shop.

We hurried down the street to the corner. At the doorway of the third house he stopped and went inside, climbed up two flights of stairs, opened a door, and entered. Holding the door open, he motioned us to follow, then shut it carefully. A man smoking a cigarette looked up from his desk. When our guide spoke to him, the man at the desk asked if we knew Yiddish. Dave told our story. The thin-faced man patted Dave's shoulder gently, then asked me my name.

"Pat . . . Pat." He shook his head. "Funny name for a Jew."

The man, who headed the local Jewish community council, made a phone call. Hanging up the receiver, he smiled at us. "Good, good." He spoke again and Dave translated: "The Hagana will pick us up in a few minutes."

Through the venetian blinds of the window we could see cars passing, the usual street traffic. Across the street was an open lot where children were playing. The angle was sharp, but I could see partly into the windows of a shoe store and a clothing store. We were back in the real world again.

The watchmaker shook our hands and left. Our host asked if we were hungry. We were. He went out, shutting the door. Dave and I looked at each other soundlessly, and then I walked over and pounded him on the back. We had made it! But the thought popped into my head: What of the rest? How many escaped? Any casualties? What of those who couldn't get away? Would our escape affect them, cause them more difficulties?

The door opened, and our host brought a little tray with coffee, cake, and sandwiches. Setting it on the table, he motioned us to start eating. The sandwiches—tasty bread with some delicious meat that tasted like lamb— were welcome, and the coffee was nectar.

There was a knock on the door, and before we could open it, Dov rushed in, his face split by an enormous grin. He shook hands as if we hadn't seen each other in a long time.

"How did you get away?" I asked. A silly question; he was officially in charge of the convoy and had a legitimate entrance back into Palestine.

"Any of our gang get away besides us?" I asked.

"No reports yet—you two are the only ones so far. We've alerted the Hagana to search the streets for any others. Come with me!"

Parked in front of the building was a large automobile. The driver, a young man, started the car. We sped through the streets and drew up in front of an imposing hotel.

"Histadruth Hotel," explained Dov.

We were shown to our quarters. Dave and I would share a room. It had three full-length windows, ceiling to floor, shaded with venetian blinds. There was a little sun-porch over the street. We had our own shower and bath and reading lamps by our twin beds. It was like being moved from hell to the gates of heaven in one jump.

Knocks on the door. George Goldman was there with Jackson from the *Northland*! More handshakes and back-thumping. Jackson shared his tale of escape. He had stepped out of a bus and walked over to a garage, where Larry Kohlberg joined him. When they tried to communicate with the garage owner, he yelled for them to beat it. They walked past the cop on the corner and down the road. A motorcycle stopped, the rider wearing the goggles and khaki of a British soldier. It was a Hagana man who had been following the convoy. He told Jackson to get on the motorcycle seat and instructed Larry to keep walking until he returned for him. As they started off, however, two British soldiers on motorcycles shot past; they rounded up Larry and some of the other men on the road.

"Rest a bit, then we'll get you a new outfit," Dov told us.

When we were alone in the room, Dave looked at me, sighed, stretched his arms over his head, and lazily looked out the window. "Trying to lure me off guard," I thought. "Well, I'm wise to you." I had my shoes and pants off before he turned around and was in the shower before his pants were off.

Hot water, sizzling. I soaped myself, washed it off, soaped myself again. It was with reluctance that I stepped out and dried myself. The soap and hot water not only cleansed the dirt from my pores but washed the aches from my muscles.

Golden sunlight poured through the window slats. The room was now quiet, and we experienced the peace of being free.

Another knock on the door. I opened it, and there stood Sholom.

After wild handshakes, he told us of his escape. "I hid on the floor of the ambulance under a blanket and rode right out through the gates. A soldier looked inside but didn't see me. The driver dropped me off at a friend's house while he contacted the Hagana."

George's story was simple. "I jumped, walked back into town, and went into a store. A girl took one look at me. I hadn't said a word, but she motioned me into a little room in the back. She asked in English if I'd just gotten away from the British. When I said yes, she laughed and told me to stay there till she got in touch with the Hagana. The Hagana guys picked me up and brought me here. They also had news of Dave Wurm and Eli Bergman. They were picked up by a Jewish truck driver headed for Tel Aviv. The British set up a roadblock, and their vehicle was the first one stopped. They were taken to the Zichron Yaaqov police station and from there to Athlit in an armored personnel car."

We were told that we would be taken, three at a time, to get new clothes. George, Sholom, and I were taken to a store on the main street of Haifa. With new underwear, a suit, shoes, suitcase, a set of khakis, toothbrush, paste, razor set, and combs, we were citizens again.

Feeling a new confidence, we walked out of the store and met our new guide and counselor, Avraham. Sholom quickly Americanized Avraham to "Avvie." He warned us, "You're not out of the woods yet. You still don't have I.D. cards."

"I.D. cards?" I asked.

"The city is full of British patrols; they may challenge you at any time. We have to make out some I.D. cards for you."

As soon as we were back in the hotel, a photographer came and took pictures of us, and an hour later we were each given a small brown card bearing our photograph and our new name. I was again Mendel Levey. Occupation: lathe operator. Nationality: Jew.

Supper was a feast—two big glasses of orange juice, soup, steak with potatoes and vegetables, coffee, and cake. Though we were very hungry, we had to stop in the middle of the meal; our stomachs had contracted so much that they could not hold more food. Our eyes were bigger than our stomachs.

Avvie informed us that we had credit at the hotel and that we would take our meals there. He issued us Palestinian money for recreation.

After supper Sholom, George, and I decided to see a movie, an old American picture.

In the quiet of the early evening we watched people promenading on the streets or returning from working late. The neat, clean stores were filled with goods. Modern apartment houses and business buildings lined the streets. After the dreary idleness of Cyprus, the bustle of a modern city was stimulating.

"The desk man in the hotel told me that houses are built extra strong because of the earthquakes," George confided.

"Earthquakes!" I exclaimed. Why not? We had faced every other catastrophe. "This country certainly has all the disasters one could imagine."

The clink of guns behind us startled me, and I turned around.

A six-man patrol of British soldiers, their rifles on their shoulders, approached. Acting unconcerned, we turned and brushed past them. They didn't stop, didn't even glance at us. An armored car, followed by soldiers on motorcycles, their Sten guns in their laps, raced down the street. We were uneasy; it would be serious if we were recaptured.

Outside the theater, waiting in line to buy tickets, we enjoyed watching the people, a varied group. Some were whiskered and wore beaver hats. Young women were giggling and flirtatious.

Suddenly a tremendous explosion sounded over our heads. A shower of small leaflets drifted down toward us. "Leaflet bombs." We had heard of them. Picking one up, we saw that the writing was in Hebrew. We couldn't read it, but we guessed that it was part of the campaign for an independent state. George shook himself to get the shock out of his body and grinned wryly. "They do everything in this country with a bang," he joked.

After the movie, the streets were still filled with people. Life seemed to teem here. Row after row of heavy, modern, private homes was being constructed. Stores were open and busy.

The clerk nodded grimly as we entered the lobby. "One of your men was injured tonight," he said quietly.

"What happened?"

"Beaten up by a British patrol. He's in Room 17."

Sholom opened the door softly. Jackson lay on the bed, a bandage around his head, one eye shining brightly at us. He waved an arm nonchalantly at us.

"What's the story?" asked Sholom.

"I was walking along the street when a British patrol stopped me and asked for my I.D. card. They saw 'Jew' on it and took me to a back alley, where they beat me with their gun-butts. I must have passed out. When I came to, they were gone and I was lying in the alley.

"You have to watch yourself around here," continued Jackson. "The clerk at the desk told me that the Irgun killed four civilian British workers from the oil refinery. The British CID stopped a bus with Jewish workers and let go with a Sten gun, killing two, wounding the others. Don't speak English where any soldiers or CID men in civies can hear you."

Nonetheless, as I lay on the soft bed in the dark, the windows open and cool night air flowing through the room, life seemed like a dream. Our first day in Palestine. Dave Greer, my roommate, was snoring gently. I squirmed to get the most pleasure out of the bed. We five were apparently the only ones who had made it.

34 * A Glimpse of the Promised Land

Sunlight poured through the room. I knew I was free—free of Cyprus, British custody, the camp smells, latrines, rotten food. Here in the Hagana hotel, in Haifa, in Palestine, my head was clear, working. I thought sadly of Haim and Yankel, Hannah and Peter, waking to another day in a detention camp.

Dave lay motionless except for the small movement of his chest as he breathed. His arm was thrown under his head, half under the pillow.

There was a feeling of finality that morning. For the first time I had slept in a land where the very earth was sacred to so many religions. As a sailor I had slept, either ashore or on my ship, in many different countries, but I had never sensed history in the air as in this country—Palestine, Israel, Arabia. So many peoples, with so much background of struggle, of rising new hopes for the future, a future of conflict as well as progress. I felt that I had been on a pilgrimage, seeking some rare values that existed in and yet beyond this land, with its various peoples.

I got up and luxuriated in the shower.

Avraham, our Hagana escort, had breakfast with us and outlined our immediate future. "The Hagana wants to show you some of the country. If you're willing, we could leave this afternoon. It'll be dangerous, but my advice is to go."

"Any reports on the boys who escaped?" asked George.

"As far as we know, thirteen people succeeded in escaping; nine who attempted to escape were caught. Syd escaped by staying aboard the *Aegean Star* and disembarking with the Hagana personnel who were handling the baggage. Among those picked up by the British were Bergman, Lipshutz, Bock, Wurm, and Brettschneider. Too early yet for any more news. We'll get a report during the day. No more men were picked up by us, so the British must have most of them. We may hear that some men escaped onto a truck, or were picked up by people along the road."

"What about those we never saw on Cyprus?"

"Those who hid in the boilers of the *Geula* were Baird, Nieder, Menachem Keller, and Gooen. On the *Northland*, Lebow and twelve others were able to hide in a water tank for twenty-six hours.

"After the British tied the ships up to the wharf in Haifa and left, the men came out and walked ashore. Those who wanted to return to the States have gone back; the others are scattered around Palestine."

"Are you a Palestinian?" Sholom asked Avvie.

"Yes," he replied, "a Sabra."

"What's a Sabra?" asked George.

"It's a Hebrew word meaning cactus, a native of Palestine," explained Avvie. "Hard on the outside, sweet on the inside."

"Where did you learn your English?" I asked.

"Here, as a boy. Then I volunteered for British submarine service during the war."

With our extra clothes packed in our suitcases, we waited in the lobby for Avvie to give us the go sign.

A taxi stopped in front of the hotel, and we all piled in and rode down to the bus terminal, where Avvie bought the tickets for the big "Eggert" bus. Since the man who outfitted us in the store had given us clothes identical in color and design, we felt as conspicuous as if we had been turned out in the same factory.

As the bus roared out of Haifa and down the coast road toward Tel Aviv, Mount Carmel rose behind us. Its brown flanks were speckled with white houses surrounded by green trees. We passed Athlit, the old Crusader fortress, and strained to look at the barbed-wire camp that had almost been our new home. We thought of our companions who were now jailed there.

We rode on, with the blue Mediterranean on our right, the tawny brown, rock-covered hills of Galilee on our left. Now and then we passed through a green oasis of orange trees, fenced by the cypress trees used to mark the boundaries of the kibbutzim, the collective farms of Palestine.

When we entered the outskirts of Tel Aviv, Avvie told us, "Twenty years ago this was all sand dunes." We gazed at a magnificent new city, with great boulevards, modern apartment houses, office buildings, parks with lanes winding around shade trees. Everywhere people flowed through the streets.

We were taken to a hotel on the Tel Aviv waterfront, where the sea stretched below our windows. Miles away on the horizon we could see two British destroyers patrolling. It was evening when we went into the streets to have supper. The signs on the stores and restaurants were all in Hebrew. We were viewing the development of a new state before our eyes. There was a feeling of pioneering in the streets. This was exhilarating after the primitive life on Cyprus.

Tonight the girls seemed beautiful, wearing colored dresses, a little rouge or lipstick. There was a brightness in their eyes, a sheen to their round cheeks, and beauty in their walk.

The next morning we packed our bags and set off for Jerusalem.

Excitement rose as we entered the ancient city that had left its mark on world history. As we pulled into the bus terminal, we were aghast at the number of soldiers on the street. All branches of the British forces were represented in the six-man patrols. Armored cars ran rapidly up and down the streets. Security had been increased because of growing tensions arising from the United Nations debate on the partition of Palestine.

Our bus passed one fortified zone after another, guarded by soldiers. Getting out of the bus, we walked up a narrow street to an ancient gate and crossed a dry moat into the Citadel, the old fortress of Mount Zion.

Standing on the walls of the Citadel, Avvie pointed out excavations within the walls. "Roman baths, the Tower of David—each conqueror added something to the architecture. See this?" He pointed out a white block of stone, six feet high, eight feet long, six feet thick. "It is one of the original stones from Solomon's Temple. The Bible described his temple as 'white as snow,' because of the salts in the rock. This block was removed in some early period from its original position to bolster up this wall."

From the southern wall of the Old City we could see in amazing detail the Mountains of Moab, thirty miles away, on the far side of the Dead Sea. To my left was the Mount of Olives and Gethsemane. Down in the valley was the Pool of Siloam and the Tomb of Absalom. Somewhere among those ancient walls just behind me was Golgotha.

Names out of Sunday school reminded me of my boyhood in a small town. The words of Leviticus in the Bible came to my mind: "And if thy brother be waxen poor, and fallen in decay with thee, then thou shalt relieve him; yea though he be a stranger."

After supper in the hotel, George asked, "How about some night life?"

"Better stay off the streets tonight. The U.N. is voting on partition," Avvie said. "The Mufti may have some of his gangs out."

We all turned in early, to beds comfortable and secure. I lay quietly a long time but could not sleep.

Here in Palestine was the key to understanding this experience that had moved me so. Neither seeing the people nor living with them on Cyprus fully explained the great passion and endurance they had shown to get to Palestine. Thus far it had been like trying to see a mountain when your head was forced down and all you could see was the grain of sand an inch from your eyes.

The silence over Jerusalem penetrated the room. The future seemed to be here now, foreboding, charged with danger. It was unthinkable that Moka and Gingi, Avraham and the others could be driven off this land they loved so; that thousands of people to whom this land was life itself would be unable to reach their haven. Now I felt certain, because of their courage and commitment, that they would finally achieve the creation of a state, a place where they could feel safe, where their children would not be subjected to persecution leading to genocide.

World War II had uncovered for our generation the terrible ethnic fears and hates festering in the world. We had seen what horrors resulted and what indeed could happen to other peoples if these hatreds were allowed to erupt again.

In the morning we were awakened with the news that the United Nations had approved the partition dividing Palestine between the Jews and the Arabs. We heard that on Cyprus the reaction had been tremendous. They had been mad with joy; they would be able to start coming over to Palestine on May 15, the date the British had promised to leave. A new stage had been set. The drama would change now.

From the entrance of the hotel we could see masses of people surging through the streets. Young and old, thin, pale boys in black jackets and brown, strong people from the kibbutzim, welcomed the news with joy. A woman sitting on the stairs of the hotel held in one hand a photograph of Theodor Herzl, the founder of Zionism. In her other hand she held a flag, the blue Star of David on a white field. A crowd of children came riding down the street, the greenish armor plate of a British police car in view behind them.

Avvie arrived to bring us our final news: "And now you go home."

On the ride to Haifa a vision of all the events of the last eight months flashed through my mind; the Azores, Lisbon, Bayonne, Varna, and always the sea around us, the sea . . . our ally. In Haifa harbor lay the *Paducah*, a dead ship, its cabins empty, its engines silent. A wave of homesickness swept over me.

Before dawn the next morning a car whisked us through the silent streets past the spot where we had escaped, past the edge of town, out along the road paralleling the shore. It turned down a side road and stopped only when its wheels were almost in the surf. A small rowboat, a man standing by, was pulled up on the sand. As soon as we got out of the car, he slid the boat into the water. Avvie and I helped, and in no time the boat was waterborne. The silent man grabbed the oars. Avvie shook our hands good-bye. "*Shalom*" was his last word.

A few minutes rowing and we came to a good-sized fishing boat. As I climbed over the rail, a hand reached out and helped me aboard. I watched as the little boom swung out and the block was hooked onto two metal eyes in the bow and stern of the rowboat. It was hoisted up and nested on the deck. The diesel engine chugged, and we headed out into the open sea.

I left Palestine as I first reached it, in the night. Past the fishing boat's stern the bubbling wake was phosphorescent. The outline of Mount Carmel could be felt rather than seen, rising in the dark like a conscience.

Epilogue

After the crew of the *Paducah* was freed most of the men returned to the United States, though a few remained to live in Israel. We were dispersed and for the most part lost contact with each other. In 1987 I was surprised to read a small notice in a local newspaper that the American veterans of the Aliyah Beth of the 1940s were having a reunion in Israel. I joined them.

Men from the ten American ships that transported refugees converged to meet old shipmates and relive one of their most memorable experiences. To our gratification the largest contingent was from the *Paducah*. Together we toured Israel from the Lebanese border to the Dead Sea. Some bowed, some prayed at the Wailing Wall. We felt the wonder of Jerusalem and the awe of Golgotha and Masada. To me there remained a mythical quality to the country.

Now, after forty years, we heard what had happened to our ship and our shipmates.

After the establishment of Israel in May 1948 the *Paducah* was put in minimum shape for a sea-test to see if she was worth repairing. The plan was to make her one of the first cargo ships of the new Zim Steamship Line. However, the hull plates had been so badly damaged by the ramming that the ship was brought back to the dock and tied up. Later she was sold to the Italians for scrap.

The *Northland*, our sister ship, became the first warship of the Israeli Navy. In May 1948 she was renamed the *Elath* by Premier David Ben-Gurion. In 1959 she became the barracks ship *Matzpen*.

As for the people:

Moka Limon had a distinguished career, first as Israeli Chief of Naval Operations, then, from 1950 to 1954, as Commander-in-Chief of the Israeli Navy. In 1969 he masterminded the escape of the Israeli missile boats from Cherbourg, France. Later he was special envoy for Europe of the Israeli Ministry of Defense. After leaving the Defense Ministry he served on the

216

boards of directors of such companies as Zim Navigation and Israel General Bank.

Louis Ball and Reuben Shiff joined a Hashomer Hatzair kibbutz. They enlisted in a Palmach brigade in the Israeli Army and were both killed in the Negev taking a strong point from the invading Egyptian army in 1948.

David Blake also fought in Israel's War of Independence. He lost a leg in a Jordanian minefield. He lives on Kibbutz Tel-Yosef.

Syd Abrams settled in Seattle, Washington, and became western states governmental affairs manager for the California Wine Institute.

Eli Bergman is executive director of Americans for Energy Independence, a policy association in Washington, D.C.

Phil Bock worked for the U.S. Postal Service and is now retired.

Lewis Brettschneider is a senior executive of the Army Corps of Engineers in Germany.

Al Brownstein is an executive of the Social Security Administration in Chicago.

Miguel Buiza returned to Oran, North Africa, and later moved to Marseilles, France. He died in June 1963 at a hospice for Spanish Republicans in Hyères, France. He never was able to return to Spain.

Peter Gilbert operated an electronics business in New York. He is deceased.

Walter "Heavy" Greaves joined the fledgling Israeli Merchant Marine as bosun and trained a generation of Israeli merchant sailors. He later returned to the United States, where he died.

Dave Greer opened an art gallery in New York City. He is dead.

Dave Gutmann is professor of education and psychiatry at Northwestern University. An authority on aging, he has published widely on the subject.

Arnold Kite was head of security for a transportation company in Chicago.

Menachem Keller returned to his kibbutz, Kfar Giladi.

Larry Kohlberg became a professor at Harvard University. He developed a new field of study, the psychology of moral development, and attained a worldwide reputation. He is deceased.

Ben Kulbersh returned to Kibbutz Hatzor, where he taught school.

Bailey Nieder was an executive in a brewing and steel manufacturing company in Seattle and is now retired.

Leonard Rotter is a partner in a civil engineering firm in Los Angeles County.

Paul Shulman, who first interviewed me for the captain's position in New York and was a graduate of the U.S. Naval Academy at Annapolis, became the first commander of the Israeli Navy.

Sholom Solowitz, who had aircraft mechanic training, helped repair planes being ferried from the United States and Canada for the air force of the new state of Israel during its War of Independence. Then he returned to the United States and established his own business.

Haim Weinshelbaum returned to his kibbutz, Tel-Yosef.

David Wurm worked in retail sales and is retired in Nevada.

I stayed ashore and worked in the composing room of several newspapers for a number of years. Later I returned to sea and captained oil exploration ships, including the *Glomar III*, which made the first major oil find for the British in the North Sea.

I have no knowledge of what happened to the other crew members.

In 1963 Eli Bergman, who was working for a U.S. company in Iran, vacationed in Cyprus and visited the site of Xylotymbou, our detention camp. He could find no sign of the camp. There were no barbed-wire fences, guard towers, or huts, only the wind blowing across the barren red soil. But the memories shall not blow away.

Appendix
Paducah *Crew List*

NAME	NATIONALITY	POSITION	AGE
1. Rudolph Patzert	USA	Captain	35
2. Evan Morgan	USA	Chief Mate	39
3. David Greer	USA	2d Mate	35
4. Paul Christie	USA	3d Mate	22
5. Martin Gooen	USA	Radio Operator	21
6. Sholom Solowitz	USA	Bosun	26
7. Elihu Bergman	USA	A.B. Seaman	19
8. Sydney A. Abrams	USA	A.B. Seaman	20
9. Ernest Lipshutz	USA	Oiler	23
10. David Blake	USA	A.B. Seaman	27
11. Eugene "George" Goldman	USA	A.B. Seaman	25
12. Walter "Heavy" Greaves	USA	A.B. Seaman	29
13. Reuben Shiff	Canada	O.S. Seaman	21
14. Albert Brownstein	USA	O.S. Seaman	22
15. John Sandin	USA	O.S. Seaman	20
16. Pierre P. Baird	USA	Chief Engineer	25
17. Charles Fariello	USA	1st Engineer	44
18. Alton Henderson	USA	2d Engineer	23
19. Richard MacGarva	USA	3d Engineer	20
20. Philip Bock	USA	Oiler	25
21. Peter Gilbert	USA	Oiler	22
22. Ben Ami Sussman	USA	Oiler	25
23. Leonard Rotter	USA	Fireman	23
24. Bailey Nieder	USA	Fireman	25
25. Arnold Kite	USA	Wiper	18
26. Daniel Lombard	USA	Wiper	17

27.	Lewis Brettschneider	USA	Fireman	25
28.	Lawrence Kohlberg	USA	Jr. Engineer	19
29.	David Shass	USA	Chief Steward	47
30.	Ralph Schindler	USA	Messman	37
31.	David Kellner	Romania	Seaman	36
32.	Moshe Kallner	USA	Messman	36
33.	David Wurm	USA	Messman	25
34.	Louis Ball	USA	Messman	25
35.	David Gutmann	USA	Messman	25

In Bayonne, France, Al Henderson (2d Engineer), Richard MacGarva (3d Engineer), Paul Christie (3d Mate), Ben Ami Sussman, and Ralph Schindler left the ship. They terminated their contracts and returned to the United States. Morgan was transferred to the *Northland* as captain. The following persons joined the crew in France:

	NAME	NATIONALITY	POSITION	AGE
36.	Hans Holtzer (Haim Weinshelbaum)	Born in Austria	Hagana Escort	—
37.	John Rosenfeld (Moka Limon)	Born in Russia	Hagana Commander	23
38.	Francisco Romero	Spain	Chief Cook	60
39.	Miguel Buiza	Spain	Chief Mate	49
40.	Ben Kulbersh	USA	2d Radio Operator	24
41.	Menachem Keller	Germany	Hagana Radio Chief	—

This is a comprehensive list of all individuals who served aboard the SS *Paducah* and is based on a list prepared in Bayonne by Syd Abrams, who served as purser in addition to his other jobs, and by Eli Bergman.

Most of the Hagana (Mossad) representatives who came aboard or had responsibilities for the ship used assumed names. When true names were made known, they are used.

Index

221

ABOUT THE AUTHOR

Rudolph W. Patzert began his merchant marine career in 1928, at the age of seventeen. During World War II he sailed in the North Atlantic, the Caribbean, and the Mediterranean, receiving combat ribbons in all three theaters. His first command was the SS *Paul Hamilton Hayne*, a liberty ship.

Now retired, Captain Patzert and his wife, Terry, reside in Encinitas, California.